Mira Rothenberg

Children with Emerald Eyes

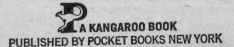

A KANGAROO BOOK
PUBLISHED BY POCKET BOOKS NEW YORK

Distributed in Canada by PaperJacks Ltd., a Licensee
of the trademarks of Simon & Schuster, a division of
Gulf+Western Corporation.

Chapter One was first published in *Harper's* Magazine
in 1960 under the title "The Rebirth of Jonny."

 POCKET BOOKS, a Simon & Schuster division of
GULF & WESTERN CORPORATION
1230 Avenue of the Americas, New York, N.Y. 10020
In Canada distributed by PaperJacks Ltd.,
330 Steelcase Road, Markham, Ontario.

Published by arrangement with The Dial Press
Library of Congress Catalog Card Number: 77-24458

ISBN: 0-671-81966-6

First Pocket Books Printing August, 1978

Trademarks registered in the United States and other countries.

PRINTED IN CANADA

ONCE WE WOULD HAVE CONDEMNED THEM —OR WORSHIPPED THEM!

Once these extraordinary children would have been burned as witches. Or revered as gods.

Today we recognize them as ill and deeply troubled. Yet, as this shattering and truly remarkable book makes clear, we have much to learn from them about our needs, our souls, and our own humanity.

To my son Kivie
Who I love most

ACKNOWLEDGMENTS

It took many, many years to live and write this book, and the people instrumental in creating it are too numerous to list fully. I wish to thank them all.

I particularly want to thank:

The children. All the children that I've worked with. And their parents.

My very old and very special friend, Peter H. Buckley, who believed in me, cajoled me, threatened me, dared me, inspired me, nagged me, and bribed me with a set of Ashanti weights to resume writing again—this book that I had given up on. He helped me do it—my private editor. He edited it with great sensitivity and devotion.

My very new and very special friend, Richard Marek, who in spite of my misgivings about it, found the manuscript to be worthwhile, fell in love with the kids and their stories, and even thought me nice. He also helped me do it —my public editor. He edited the book lovingly, painstakingly and perceptively, and set in motion its publication.

The late Dr. Kurt Goldstein, who taught me and loved me so comfortingly. The late Dr. Joost A. Meerloo, who in his great generosity gave me, among other gifts, the greatest gift of all—time—a full week of his so quickly ebbing life, during which he read and commented on my manuscript and convinced me to publish it. And Lucy Meerloo, my kind friend.

Tev Goldsman, to whom I was married, with whom I shared part of my life, the creation and running of Blueberry and the work with some of the kids—Jonny, Peter, Anthony.

And Susan Wood, who was like a sister to me, who

encouraged and supported my work, who gave me my first publicity, which helped start Blueberry, and who among other things so generously shared with me her parents —Ethel and Bill Greenburg. And Ethel and Bill Greenburg, who were like parents to me—Ethel, who stood behind me and supported me in every one of my "crazy" ideas and ventures and who made Blueberry possible.

And Homer Page, for whom I wrote Jonny. And Marion Sanders. And John M. Allen, for whom I wrote Chaim. And my good friend, Dr. H. Gumprecht. And Dr. A. Siegman. And Nasir Pirani, who helped me face my pain for Danny, and having faced it, be able to finish writing the story, which had lain untouched and unfinished for ten years.

And Jim Silberman, Chris Lehmann-Haupt, and Ed Doctorow.

And Raya Friedman, Michael Korman and Zizie.

And all my friends at The Dial Press.

And Janie Shaheen and Nettie Warres for diligently typing the zillion versions of each story.

And Lenore Loeffler. And Hansfried Kellner.

And all the children at Blueberry, and the staff.

And the Board of Directors of Blueberry.

And my son Kivie, who suffered through it all and was often shortchanged because of it. I also thank him for giving the book its title.

MR
May 1977

CONTENTS

PREFACE

The Case of Mira

by

Joost A. M. Meerloo, M.D.

Why a preface when Mira's reports speak for themselves? I am afraid that is a remnant of our scientific compulsion to explain and our delusion to interpret every riddle we experience. But explaining means flattening things out, making them more superficial, while Mira's work concerns going to the depths of all communicative possibilities between human beings.

That is her gift, that is her daily work. She is no student of communication; she reaches her goal by just being there with her youngsters. Just being there and suffering their impact, having endless empathy with their craziness. Her method is doing nothing, *wu wei*, the way Lao Tse pleaded things had to be done. Observing is applied, just letting these children live in their rage together with somebody who does not counteract. And suddenly their rage has no sense any more, defense is not needed, and sanity survives.

No, I could not describe exactly this way of acting-out therapy for which Mira and her staff developed endless patience, tolerance, and endurance.

I have myself witnessed the results. Mira's anecdotal

form of writing speaks for itself; the reader is dragged into the process itself, without any theoretical conductor. That is the great importance of the book.

Joost A. M. Meerloo, M.D.
Former Associate Professor,
N.Y. State University
Former Lecturer in Social Psychology,
New School for Social Research

THE DP KIDS:

An Introduction

A professor came into my classroom at Columbia University—I think his name was Hopkins—and said to our instructor, "I was told you have somebody who speaks some eastern European languages." I died: Nobody, I thought to myself, as I tried to disappear into the wall.

He looked around and said, "Nobody. Wrong class, I guess," and walked out.

Relieved, I got out of the wall, and went back to my work. The relief was short-lived. Hopkins came back a few minutes later. "Right class," he said. "Come out, we need you. Who is it?" I did not exist. "Look," he continued, "there is a group of kids. Eleven, twelve, thirteen year olds from Europe. Most were born in a camp —and were thrown out by the mothers to save their lives from the Nazis. They were picked up by peasants, nuns, whoever would have them. Now they are here. They were found and brought back, some by relatives, some by agencies, some by natural parents. They are wild, they are raw, they are in pain. They are wretched and they don't know this language. They don't trust a

1

soul and they need someone who can speak to them. There are thirty-two of them. There is a Babel of languages; they don't understand anyone. They don't understand each other. Some speak Polish, some Russian, some German, some Czech, some Yiddish. Someone's got to translate," he said in desperation. "They are to become Americanized in the Yeshiva. But no one has been able to get into that classroom and stay there long enough to talk to them."

Hm, hum, I knew it—not me, I thought. I had left Poland under slightly similar circumstances. I knew their pain, their terror, their sorrow, and their rage. Not me. I am not going through that all over again—.

I kept my mouth shut.

"So," the professor continued, "who is it? Who is going to help these kids?"

My roommate from International House looked at me. "Drop dead," I whispered. But the professor, who was on the lookout, noticed the interplay.

"Okay," he said to me, "what's your name?"

I told him.

"Yep, that's you. I thought I'd find you," he said victoriously.

What a fool, I thought, he is being a "humanitarian." Doesn't he know it's been out of fashion for a while?

"So when are you going?" he said.

"I am not," I said.

He was shocked. "But they are your people. Don't you want to help?"

"No," I said. "The scars are too deep."

"Whose?" he asked.

"Mine and theirs," I answered. "I want to forget. Theirs will become mine. I don't want it."

God, if you had seen the expression on his face! If it weren't so tragic, I would have died laughing. He was so nonplussed. How do you deal with something like what was on his face.

How do you deal with something like that, I thought, too, looking at his face. Do you turn back the clock and say, "No, there is no bitterness, no hate, no pain, no torture"? How do you make believe? The professor understood none of what I was feeling.

I was so young; he was so old. Yet I was so old and he was so young.

How do you run in the sunshine and say, Yes, I love. How do you touch the wheat and say, Yes, I am good. How do you smile to the earth and say, Yes, I want. How do you feel the breeze and say, I'll help. Gently, tenderly, and warmly.

All those dead. Dead, dead, dead. If you walk with death, you become death. I thought I had left it all behind. I'd tried.

And now these kids would bring it back to me.

"No," I said. "No, no, no." He left. The students in my class just stared at me. Next day he came again. He had thought about it and tried to understand. But couldn't.

He tried again. I still said no. He came again the next day, helpless and bewildered. "One of the kids was very sick, but wouldn't trust a doctor," he said. I went.

I heard Professor Eisenberg say to his assistant, "Columbia is crazy to send her. She's the same size as the kids, and most likely not much older. What the hell can she do? I can't let them loose on her——."

But to me he said politely, "Here is your room," and he pointed to a door. "Inside are the kids. I'll get you anything you need. You can set up your own program, whatever you want——I'll support you if it works.

"If you need me, I'm in my office down the hall. Just come and get me, or yell——."

And the expression on his face was "Oh, Christ!"

Did you ever hear the ocean grumble before it is about to roar?

Did you ever hear the lion growl before it closes in on its kill?

Did you ever hear the wind howl before it breaks down a tree?

Did you ever see a man kill, when the terror and rage in his face changes into pleasure, and derangement takes over——omnipotence?

3

I walked into the classroom and surveyed the situation. Battlefield.

Thirty-two hungry, angry, raging, and wounded children. Just waiting for something to focus their rage on.

Hitler? But Hitler was dead. Their parents? They were too afraid. Me? Yes. Amerika. Me.

Children. They weren't really children. I saw thirty-two faces of old men and women on bodies of children. And the bodies were twisted, contorted, like limbs of a tree not given a chance to grow naturally. Children distorted, not by ravages of time, but by ravages of hate. By inhumanity perpetrated by one man against his brothers.

What is childhood for these children? The faces were masks, but not of the Greek tragedies, put on them by the "Super race."

Kill, Kill, Kill was the sound in the air. We measured each other.

I told them my name in Yiddish. I told them the languages I speak.

"Are you a goya?" one asked.

"No, I speak Yiddish," I answered.

"So what?" he said. And then from every side I was attacked with words. Questions, questions, questions. They answered them all themselves.

Professor Hopkins was right. A Babel. He was a good man. But because he was so kind, he did not fathom the depth of their tragedy. You have to hate to understand it.

One girl with venom in her eyes asked her question in French.

I had forgotten my French—a kid interpreted. She wanted to know why I was here! Another attacked in Czech. Was I American? Then another, in Russian, pleaded to be allowed to go back to his peasant "parents."

Another showed me a knife hidden in his sleeve and said in Polish that it was for the goyim if they came to get him.

4

Another asked me in German how come I was alive? Who or what did I sell to stay so—?

Day after day I came and listened to them spend their venom on me. Day after day I watched their hopelessness take over. Day after day I heard tales spat at me. Worse than the sickest imagination could produce. Day after day I heard them say—We want to go back to our own country. We want to go back.

Oh how well I knew that litany; how well I knew that feeling! My country. Our country. My country.

But never did I see them cry.

I was to teach them. I was to teach them to be American. I was to teach them to be grateful that they were here. I was to teach them the language.

They did not want to be American. They wanted to be what they were. They did not want to be grateful, for they did not want to be saved from their own country, from where they belonged. They did not need to know the language—they had their own. They'd rather be dead in their own country than alive here. Professor Hopkins didn't understand this, and Dr. Eisenberg didn't. But I did and that made it only the more brutal for me and for them.

If you take a wild horse from the mountains, feed him and take care of him, the horse may love you, but he will never be grateful to you. In his veins forever there sings a song of his mountains, of his fields, and of his freedom. And in his blood, forever, sings the hope of a return to it.

I was to teach them history, reading, writing, arithmetic. I was to civilize them, to make them acceptable to Amerika. It was a bitter, cruel joke. They learned nothing. Then one day, during a lull in their hate, I told them about the American Indians. The Indians whose country this was and who became refugees in their own country, who were dispossessed from their own country. And I found a book of poetry about the Indians by the Indians. They wrote about the land they loved, the animals they lived with. Their strength, their love, their hate, and their pride. And their freedom.

5

It struck a chord in the kids. America. The Indians must have felt about America just what they felt about their own countries.

And we all became Indians. We moved all the furniture out of the classroom, and we built teepees, and painted water on the floor. We built canoes and animals out of papier-mâché, large, 7-foot-tall animals. As that is how large their rage was.

And poor Dr. Eisenberg, who was a timid soul, though brave, said, "Leave her alone," to the president of something-or-other, "they understand each other." And the president of something-or-other shook his head and said, "Okay, if you say so, but this is not education."

And slowly the kids began to unwind. We lived in the teepees. We ate in the teepees. They did not want to go home. And every day I'd tell them stories, each more wondrous than the last, about the Indians. I'd make the stories up, stories of kindness and love and giving, of pride, bravery, devotion, love of freedom and of the animals. Of such fierceness and awe and respect for nature that the kids got caught up in it. God, I thought, if ever my imagination ran dry, I'd lose these kids and they'd lose their new-found world. And if ever the Indians caught me, they'd scalp me for lying. My only excuse was that I could never really do an injustice to the Indians, no matter how nice or fierce I depicted them. That relieved my conscience.

The children listened. God, how they listened! They drank it all in. How starved they were for pride and dignity, for love and kindness and devotion. They were so thirsty.

But at the beginning they did not dare to really be the Indians. They became their animals. And we put on a play about these animals, only for ourselves. We were the animals: tigers, lions, wolves—only the fiercest, only the angriest. But we were free. Forever looking for our prey. Forever killing and avenging.

Then we put on another play for ourselves. But we also invited Dr. Eisenberg.

And again we were animals, but some of us were

gentler animals and we did not just kill. Oh, we were still lions and tigers and hyenas and wolves, but we were also eagles. Proud, proud eagles, soaring over the mountaintops. And horses, free, fierce, sensitive Indian horses that were friends of the Indians. And we were deer. Swift, gentle, beautiful deer. And we were buffaloes, and Rachel was even a kitten. A kitten she "found in the garbage can," the way she herself was found. Each child was an animal of his choice—an Indian animal. And each made up and recited his own poem—the spirit of his animal.

Joseph even put his knife aside for the while, for he had nowhere to strap it. As a mountain horse he was almost naked except for his paint. And Dr. Eisenberg looked a bit shy and a bit uncomfortable hearing all the rage and fierceness, love, kindness, and poetry coming out of the mouths of these children. He asked, "And who is Mira—is she the keeper of all these animals?" And one kid said, "Oh no, she is the fiercest animal of us all. She is the lioness." And another child said, "Yes, but she is also the sun and the earth where these animals live." And Dr. Eisenberg left, because he cried. And then he came back with ice cream and said to me, "The president [of 'something-or-other'] was wrong. This is education." And the kids and I were proud. And we stuffed ourselves sick with ice cream.

And then we truly became Indians. Proud, strong, fierce, good Indians. And we put on a play about them and we invited the whole school. And the children in their broken English made beautiful poetry about the Indians they were. It was so beautiful, so pure, so gentle, so strong. And they meted out justice so fairly.

Soon after the play, Joseph died. All I had left was his knife. He was an expatriate who could never make it. He had lived in the woods or on garbage, by the skin of his teeth, and survived. But freedom was too much. Too much for this little child. The diagnosis of his death was undetermined, because one does not die of freedom in the medical books. Just as one does not die of happiness. But one does.

7

The rest of us, as Indians, learned Indian crafts. We learned how to weave and to make pottery. We read Indian stories and Indian poetry. We wrote Indian stories and Indian poetry. We studied Indian history and folklore and each compared them with his own.

I still remember a storm. The thunder was deafening and the lightning blinding. The rain poured in sheets. The children, all their Indian bravery notwithstanding, were terrified. There was a Bible on my table, as there was in every Yeshiva classroom. The children warned me not to touch it, the superstition being that if by some chance it fell to the floor, God would strike me, and possibly them, dead. The means of my execution would be the thunder. My desire to show the children the fallacy of the superstition got the better of me. So I shoved the Bible "accidentally" to the floor. There was dead silence in the room. The children disappeared into their teepees, hardly breathing, waiting for the on-coming doom. The only sound in the room was the thunder. I waited. They did not come out. I began to hum a melody I liked, and busied myself with something or other. Slowly, but oh so so slowly, little faces, tear-stained faces, like flowers after a rain, began to appear in the entrances of the teepees. They stared at me singing and at the Bible on the floor. Then slowly, oh so slowly, they began to creep out. Suddenly I was surrounded by thirty-one little children, with thirty-one pairs of arms, and my face was soaked with their tears and their kisses. It was the first time any of them had kissed me.

Then we began to go outside. At first it was only single file, to come to school and to go home. Because there were "goyim" in the streets and "that won't be safe." Soon we discovered "tag." Of course it was an "Indian game" and we were all horses and Indians. Then we even ventured all the way on the subway to Inwood Park, because there were Indian caves there. And we followed the old Indian trails and spent time in the caves. Meanwhile they were learning. Math for measuring distances, geography and map-making for the caves, and so on.

Then one day I received a letter from the Foster Parents Plan about a French orphan. Instead of telling them the usual "Indian" story at the end of the day, I told them about the orphan. They were moved. They did a lot of talking and thinking among themselves. A lot of feeling. And then they came to me with a request: they would like to adopt this French orphan. I was stunned. It meant they'd gotten enough security to be able to give some in return. Dr. Eisenberg thought I had gone mad. But we pursued it. We wrote the Foster Parents Plan and explained the situation. The children said in their letters that they wanted to share with this child the love and the security they had found. That they wanted to share in this child's loneliness, so that she would not have to be so alone. That they wanted to comfort this child the way I comforted them. And that they knew now how to comfort her. They said they would raise the money somehow to support her. They would weave Indian rugs and sell them to make the $150 required per year. The Foster Parents Plan agreed.

So they wrote a letter to the orphan, who sent them an answer and her picture. Poor child, after that she got monthly thirty-one letters, thirty-one pictures, sometimes thirty-one packages, thirty-one life stories, and thirty-one different expressions of love. But she became a sister to them. She shared with them her story and all her woes. When she outgrew her shoes, she wrote them about it; when she had a toothache, she told them about it. When the orphanage mistress mistreated her, she told them about it; and when she got a beating she told them about it. And in exchange they told her their pains, the ones that they never were able to tell me about, and she understood, just as they understood hers. And in this interchange the healing continued, forever.

They paid their bills regularly. They made the money by putting on shows and selling the rugs they wove. At first we'd sell them standing in the street to whoever would have them. And the kids were hard bargainers, forever on the lookout for being cheated, abused, or mistreated. Then one day a nun stopped and bought a rug. The kids cheated her! She was doubly tainted. A "goya" and a "nun" made a "double goya."

She paid the exorbitant price of $10, one-fifteenth of the support for the French orphan. I felt badly and explained the situation to her. Next day fourteen nuns appeared and each bought a rug for $10 from the children. The children were aghast. They could not fathom it. What of their hatred for the goyim? What of their double hate for the Christian clergy? They would not be robbed of it. They refused the money. They said the rugs weren't worth it. But the nuns insisted. And the kids and the nuns became friends.

I was with these kids for two and a half years of my life. Besides learning to be, to love, to live, and not to forget to hate, they also learned their academic subjects. They were at their grade levels in everything, and often above.

When I was to leave, they went on strike—they had become American enough for that. They made signs and carried them for a whole week in the street, marching around and around the school block. "We want Mira to stay with us," one sign said. "Mira don't leave us," another one said, and so on and so on. They got the nuns to help them and so did Dr. Eisenberg.

I had to finish my work at Columbia; my work with the kids was finished. A few years later they were still supporting their foster child.

And so I went back to my work at Columbia University. For about three months I was like everyone else, proper, studious, enjoying the peace and quiet. Then a young man named Lawrence Greenberg joined our class. He was working at an institution for delinquent children, and trying to revolutionize the place. He was taking our course as a refresher since he was to write a book about the institution. I listened to him politely, curiously, and at times even eagerly. Two weeks later I was on a train with him on the way to the institution. What I saw there scared me: all these almost grown-up people. Criminals, crazy, and so many of them. It was not for me—if I were a man, maybe.

He kept on showing me the little ones. There were some. I was not impressed. "They need you," he kept on repeating. "They do." I would not be seduced.

A month or so later I signed the contract to work at Katy Kill Falls with the little ones.

I was there for a year. A year of my life unbearable and unforgettable. A "fancy lady" would come to Katy Kill on visiting days. She had a son there, one of the younger children. My only contact with him was that whenever he got frightened, whether of himself or of bigger boys, he would run into my classroom, yelling "Kay Rothenberg" for some reason or other, and hide behind me for protection. He was different from the other disturbed children there. I felt the difference but had no name for it. The "Lady," as we called her, began approaching me and telling me about a school that was being opened in New York. She said it was for schizophrenic children, for autistic ones like her son. It was Greek to me. I did not understand the terminology, but she did not mind my ignorance. "I feel you would be good in it. You would love it. Just try it, go for the interview, I'll set it up for you." She was on the board of directors.

I went. I met Peter,* and Katy Kill seemed heaven in comparison.

That fall I began to work there, with Danny, my first autistic child. The "Lady" was right. I did love it, and at times I was even good at it.

I've written these stories about these children because I loved them. And having loved them, I've learned somewhat to understand them; to have compassion for their pain, respect for their effort, and admiration for their courage.

And this I would like to share. Through loving them I have learned once again to see human beings in their dignity, without prejudgment of the good or of the bad.

Through loving them I have learned that in spite of the tragedy in the human condition, there is beauty,

* See "Peter" chapter.

there is hope, there is strength, and there is a tremendous energy to be utilized, no matter whether in the "good" or in the "bad."

This too I would like to share.

I have worked with disturbed children for over twenty years officially. I've known them, sought them out, and loved them most of my life—unofficially.

When I was a little girl in Poland, we had a town idiot. He mumbled instead of talking, made faces, laughed when he should have cried. He was thirteen years old. He had no parents, no home, no country. He lived by begging and by coercing people into giving him whatever he needed to survive. They gave it to him partly out of pity, mainly out of terror.

Once, as I was walking through a field and eating a piece of bread and butter, he appeared. In his demanding, seemingly pleading fashion, he babbled out his request and reached for my bread. I refused. Instead, I gave him only a bite out of my bread. I was ready to share it, not give it away; I was recognizing our equality and not really accepting his insanity. He was surprised. He took his bite out of my bread and spat it out at me, in fury. He walked away. A few minutes later he turned around and with a face no longer crazy, he came back, took a bite out of my bread, and in a voice as clear as a bell said, "Okay. Thank you."

The pact was made, the bridge was built. Forever. Whenever we met, we went off into the woods and shared a piece of bread, a pretty stone, a flower, a soul. With everyone else he remained crazy—until the Germans killed him.

Thus I knew that sanity and insanity are part of the same continuum. The difference is only in degree.

Through all these years I have been fascinated by the variety of fortresses these children build for themselves in order to protect themselves against the horrors they sense around them. In all these years I was determined to get to them within their fortresses. I wanted to know what kind of bridge to build in order to get across the moats they set up around their fortresses; and how to find the crack, the door through which to enter their fortresses. I wanted to help them to help themselves creep out of their terrifying fortresses.

Whenever any of us are hurt, we build our own fortress around the wound, and thus insulate ourselves against further pain. The strength of the walls depends upon the degree of the hurt. Some fortresses have walls that are so thin and so collapsible that they crumble very easily and we are out again. Some have walls that seem measureless in their thickness and in their indestructibility, and those can protect us well. Sometimes forever. These children live within such walls, some not so thin, often forever.

I would like to tell people about these children. About their walls and the child within the walls, why they have erected them, and how they have erected them, and how their fortresses serve them.

I would like most of all to tell people that these children, sane or insane, are part of the human continuum. The insane child is forced to take a path within his psyche, the sane child a path more familiar. And that is a difference not so much in kind as in degree. The insane child, just like the sane child, is frightened, hurts, rages, and cries. He too protects himself by rage, attack, or withdrawal. Only more so.

The sane child goes through all the stages of development one can see in the insane child. However, the insane child often stays arrested in a stage and uses it to a different end, while the sane child passes through it and grows.

The only worthwhile commodity any human being has is himself. "Himself" is made up of the fabric of his experience and heredity. It is this that has to be respected. The child, sick or healthy, is made up of that fabric. By recognizing and acknowledging the insane way, we affirm that the insane children exist, and that they are important.

I would like people to know that the seeming illogic of insanity is really very logical within the context of the individual insane child. Each individual insanity is,

13

given its author, a very reasonable and sensible creation, made to protect its author from what he is mortally afraid of.

Each child builds his own citadel. And, as each child is different from the other, so are the citadels, and so are the kinds of bridges one must build to get into the citadels. Each child defends himself against his terror in his own inimitable way. Yet all protect themselves against the same terror—destruction. Each child fights in his own inimitable way. Yet all fight for the same thing—survival.

It is a labyrinth they've built. It is a spiderweb they've woven. Once the thread is found, the opening discovered that will lead into the insanity, all the logic becomes clear and we understand it.

Once we understand it, the terror of it disappears, the magic is dispelled, and our superstitions pass.

I want to show the humanity of the insane. I want to show the common denominator of sanity and insanity in all kids. I want to show how we in our world contribute to these children's terrors and misconceptions of our world. I want to show how they have defended themselves against it, and how in our terror we have defended ourselves against them. I want to impart to people some of my fascination and awe at the incredibly ingenious ways these children find to defend themselves against the terrors and to obliquely seek what they so desperately want, just like any other child, the love and understanding that mean survival.

I want the reader to see the variety of these ways.

I want to tell him that sanity or insanity is neither bad nor good, but that they both exist. And both are an answer to a need to survive. It is what we do with them and about them that is good or bad. How we in our ignorance use them, abuse them, misuse them, and deny them. That insanity, no matter how it hurts society, hurts the child more.

I also want the reader not to sentimentalize insanity, as is the fashion of the day. Murder, crime against one-self or others, is harmful and wasteful. And it hurts.

14

What we must do is to help the individual actively; not condone and forgive, nor, inexcusably, ignore.

No insanity is incurable—it is just that we don't know how to cure some forms of it. No insanity is so frightening as to make it untouchable and hence incurable. If touched with understanding and compassion, it *becomes* curable.

As there are millions of souls, so are there millions of ways of reaching them, each different from the other. Out of each crevice the child can be seduced, teased out, tantalized into our world, so that it can live in it fully.

Each story in this book tells of a different edifice of insanity, and of a different way of reaching the child within. I want to show that these children are our children. And how sometimes, wittingly or more often unwittingly, we the adults have wrought destruction upon them, our children.

How fine the line is between sanity and insanity! How delicately treacherous it is in our children.

I want to dispel the fear of these crazy children—these children with their all-seeing emerald eyes. Once people see the reasons for their insanity, if not the cause of it, the fear will be gone.

But the children can be frightening.

Some are terribly bright, yet enclosed in their brightness. Others are very dull yet at the same time have unexplainable genius in a few areas—and that is hard to understand, so it, too, is frightening.

Some are so frightened, so attuned to their terror, that they often see and feel things before the average person does—a quality developed to avoid destruction —and that frightens us.

Some are so frightened and so hurt that they turn any help given to them into destruction and defend themselves against it. That frightens us and often angers us.

Some are so frightened and angered by their hurt that they hit out physically at us. And that frightens us.

Some are wordlessly aware of all that goes on around them, but do nothing with this knowledge, too frightened

15

to tell. But forever, by their very existence, they act out their terror. That, too, frightens us.

And last—I want the reader to see the kids and love them, whether sane or insane. Not because they are sick or not sick, but because they *are*.

JONNY'S STORY

He was one of the smallest baby boys ever to survive in the United States, weighing 1½ pounds at birth in 1950. Five and a half months in the womb, three and a half months in the incubator. Then, at 5 pounds, he was out in our world.

Jonny was not a beautiful baby, nor one easy to love. His hair was singed a bright orange from the heat of the incubator, his skin shriveled and burned chocolate brown. As time went on, he became no more human; he never cried, laughed, smiled, or cooed. He didn't learn to focus his eyes, nor hold his head up, and he could not bear any physical touch. When diapers were changed, he would stiffen up completely; if he was held, he would refuse his bottle. He slept irrregularly for just a few hours at a stretch under sedations which worked at times but more often didn't.

And then there was his head, which would roll in a circular motion or sway from side to side. As he became stronger, he began to use it against himself and others, batting it against the sides of the crib, against the walls of the house, against other people's heads, and against windows.

Jonny seemed to lack sensation, seemed not to feel pain. You could strike him—or he might punch himself black and blue—but he wouldn't cry out. If you tickled him, he didn't laugh; if you called his name, he didn't respond; if there was a sound in the room, he didn't hear it; and if you got within his range of vision, his ill-focused eyes didn't look at you but somewhere above or beyond you.

Until he was five, Jonny was either wheeled in a carriage or carried about. When he did walk, if one could call it that, he was like a drunkard, reeling for a few steps and then falling on all fours to the floor and crawling. His whole body seemed disjointed, as though each member were autonomous.

In addition, from the time he was nine months old until his eighth year, Jonny suffered croup attacks which landed him on the average of once or twice a year in a hospital in an oxygen tent.

And so Jonny existed but did not live, tenaciously holding on to life, yet not taking part in it beyond the minimum needed for survival.

Until he was two, Jonny's parents did nothing special about him. Give him time to "catch up," the pediatricians advised. But one day came the startling realization that instead of "catching up," he was "catching down." He was deaf and dumb. And so they began a pilgrimage which left them helpless, hopeless, and almost destitute. It took them all over the United States. Along the way, a well-known medical authority said that Jonny at two had a degenerate hearing nerve. Diagnosis: complete deafness.

Six months later the boy was flown to New York for a more refined scientific hearing test. Diagnosis: *almost* complete deafness.

He was given a hearing aid and handled as a deaf-mute. Several desperate attempts were made to enroll him in schools for deaf children. Usually he was turned down. When he was accepted, it was only to be expelled

18

after a short time because, "He doesn't fit" or, "Something else besides deafness is wrong with him."

In 1953 his parents took the child to a large medical center. Specialists there made an intensive search for the "something else." In pediatrics, X-rays were taken of Jonny's skull, legs, and body to find out whether a deformity prevented him from walking. His bones were perfect.

An unsuccessful attempt was made to take an encephalogram, the diagnostic test that measures the brain's electric impulses. In psychological tests, however, he was found to be very quick. A child psychiatrist told the parents that he believed there was no brain injury, but it was from him that they heard for the first time of the possibility of autism—a symptom of serious mental disturbance. Perhaps, they were told, the child was autistic, yet no one could suggest what to do about it since little was known about the illness.

Again the parents set out on a quest for schools for this strange small child with a hearing aid and a label of autism now attached to him. They combed the whole country and found twelve schools: some were too expensive; others said that "nothing can really be done for him since not enough is known about his mental illness."

So they tried chiropractors, private physicians, and clinics. Some diagnosed Jonny as spastic, others as mentally deficient. The suggestion they received most often was "Commit him and forget about him."

But the parents refused to give up. Their reasoning was based on the child's behavior. It seemed strange to them that this dumb, badly coordinated child who could not hold anything in his hand, nonetheless when he was three years old could use his fingers well enough to draw meaningful and artistically good pictures; that he knew the alphabet and could spell out his name with blocks; that he could manipulate complex puzzles and stand a dime up on its end.

When he was five, Jonny was taken to another large pediatric clinic. This time an encephalogram was taken. It revealed no brain injury; the skull and bone X-rays likewise showed no damage. Psychological tests again showed him to be very quick but overactive. A psychiatrist hinted that the child might not be totally deaf, but he could suggest nothing to do with him. Another doctor in an aside said: "He is mentally retarded, put him away." Still another, a young psychiatrist, suggested that they try me.

I remember that in 1956 I was approached by two different psychiatrists. Each asked me whether I would be interested in seeing and perhaps working with a deaf and dumb six-year-old boy who might be deeply disturbed emotionally.

In January 1957 Jonny's mother called me and I realized this was the same child. It had taken her many months to try once again for help because she was afraid of another "I don't know." I, too, "did not know." But I wanted to try because somewhere within me was the feeling, I *do* know.

Generally, I prefer not to hear any diagnoses until I have seen a child myself a few times with my own eyes, with feelings unprejudiced. I told this to Jonny's parents and so, with a minimum of information, the child and parents arrived.

It is hard to recall the past symptoms of a child when one is so absorbed in the present. But that first interview I think I will always remember.

I've never seen so strangely ugly a child. The parents led in a boy who looked to be about five or six years old. He didn't exactly walk but dragged himself in, his legs, feet, hands, and arms seeming to get in one another's way, making a most complex activity out of the simple process of walking. Every step seemed to require an effort almost beyond description. The boy couldn't look at you straight; his eyes were out of focus, and his head was constantly swaying either forward or backward or from side to side or pivoting on his neck like a bobbing balloon. He dropped to the floor in one big heap as though the essence of his being were disintegrating—a leg here, an arm there—as if gravity were too much for him and had too strong a claim on his body and its parts.

The child looked nowhere and made no sound. He seemed encapsulated from life and sound in his own private world, his own fantasy. The flabbiness of the muscles in his body and face caused him to look almost grotesque. Dark circles made his eyes cavernous. The "no expression" in his face, as if nothing, no one—not even himself—existed, was frightening.

Every now and then his arms would shoot up into the air, and then his hands would flap up and down like the broken wings of a bird that never knew or had forgotten by some terrible misfortune how to fly. From time to time he would form a fist with these hands and hit himself in the face.

In the utter silence of the room I could almost hear the child's need, his terror, and his unasked questions: "Will you love me? Will you know the truth? Will you see the lie?" I had the sensation of being very closely watched and measured by this child's whole being, even though his eyes did not look at me at all.

I looked at him hard and in that moment I felt that I *knew*. I put a record on the record player and let Jonny watch it spin. Supposedly he heard nothing. When he was completely absorbed in the record, I suddenly said in a calm, natural tone: "That's enough, Jonny. Turn off the record player." Jonny turned around with arms akimbo, faced me, and shook his head quite angrily, motioning a "no" before he was aware of what he was doing. Then, realizing that he had given his secret away, he put his hands over his ears as if to shut out any sound, and his face expressed a strange combination of terror and relief. He was to repeat this gesture many times over the years, at first unconsciously, then consciously; at times with anger, later with laughter, to symbolize what he was doing with his hearing and how he shut out the world when he didn't like what was going on there.

From that point on, the fact was established that Jonny could hear, that the lie, his secret, was out. It was clear, too, that the relationship between us was to be a real one, an honest one, that I loved him enough, understood him well enough to know him beyond his defenses, into his shell; that I would protect him not only against the outside but against himself. Somehow I also took away from him to some extent the magic that he had created, the terrible power to deceive and so "control" the world. He became instead a child who could be prevented from hurting himself and the world. He recognized that I was stronger than he and that I intended to use my power for his welfare and protection so he could become a child, helpless and weak, yet responsible.

After that first session I saw Jonny four and then six hours a week. The hearing aid was off and gradually he made more and more mistakes with his "non-hearing." At first he would hear only with me; then at home and later with strangers, especially when it was about something he wanted to have or do. Three years later Jonny heard quite openly and at times, it seemed, much more acutely than the average person.

Almost parallel with his trust in me, his walking began to improve. At first, after just a few steps, he would fall to the floor on his hands and knees but the performance began to be less desperate and helpless, more deliberate. For a while he would walk only in my house or to go upstairs to see my neighbors. However, the inevitable had to be faced, and so we went out into the street and from there to the park. He got there part walking, part dragged or carried by me. At the playground, after some terrors and tribulations, he discovered fun on the swings. And so for a while we made daily pilgrimages, with the swings as a goal. As soon as I felt him getting stronger, I refused to carry him when he fell and sometimes let him crawl for almost a block. This phase didn't last long, since it was neither profitable nor comfortable. Within a few months Jonny walked upright like any other boy his age.

After our relationship became a reality for Jonny, he dared to sleep longer. From four to six hours a night, the span increased to eight and eventually ten hours. I asked his mother to cut out his sleeping medication since I felt he could control it in a damaging way. After two or three months he slept without it, perhaps because he felt more confident now that he wouldn't disintegrate or disappear in his sleep. One afternoon at my house he fell into a deep sleep for about fifteen or twenty minutes. As he slept I noticed him making sucking motions with his mouth and reaching out his hands. I got a baby bottle, filled it with milk, and when he awoke I put the nipple in his mouth. He stayed at rest sucking on the bottle. As he sucked, I put his head on my lap and began to stroke it. For the first time he did not stiffen to reject the physical contact but consciously allowed himself to be touched. For several days I continued to give him the bottle and hold him while he sucked.

Not long afterward I was half lying on the floor while Jonny played with blocks nearby. Suddenly he crawled over to me, curled up against me in what I can best describe as an embryonic position, with his back against my stomach, and, in an instant, fell asleep. He slept this way for what seemed an eternity to me though it was actually only five or six minutes. Then he woke up, yawned comfortably, and for the first time on his own initiative began to touch my arms. I took him gently on my lap, kissed him, and cuddled him, and he seemed to enjoy it.

Although he never repeated this "embryonic behavior," he continued taking the bottle for some weeks. Then suddenly he gave it up. But from this time on, if I touched, fondled, or kissed him, he would accept it with a mixture of caution, fear, and curiosity but also with pleasure. Shortly afterward his mother said to me, "I finally have a child." She too could touch, kiss, and fondle him now. And as time went by, Jonny made physical contact with more people up to the point of actually wallowing in the arms of anybody who would have him. He was quite free about it but also discriminating. Only if he liked you would he hug and kiss you or climb up on your lap. Every now and then he did as

23

the blind do, touching the outlines of a new thing or a strange person as if to get better acquainted.

From the first, I was struck by Jonny's tremendous preoccupation with lights; the brighter the light, the greater his need to get close to it. He would crawl right under a lamp, stare directly into the bulbs, then his hands would flap in his winglike motion, his body would become firmer, and his face would be contorted as if in some superhuman effort. Later, when he was able to use his voice, he would at the same time let out a couple of yells which were a kind of cross between the sound of a sea gull and a sea lion. It seemed as if he wanted to climb into the lights, which called and claimed him in some special way. Without blinking he could look up at lights of blinding intensity; he could touch hot bulbs without burning himself or feeling pain.

When we went out, Jonny would drag me from one camera shop to another, spotting the lights long before I did. Then I bought him some flood lamps of his own. He would turn them on and off constantly (blowing innumerable fuses in the process), look into them, touch them, and carry them around. Suddenly this relationship to the bulbs changed. He began to feel their heat and scream when he touched them and squint when looking into them. The lights were beginning to have a different meaning for him. For a long time I was mystified by his behavior. Then I began to think of the warmth of the electrically lighted incubator. Perhaps to Jonny the lights were a symbol of warmth—possibly of life itself. As he became able to accept the more real warmth of his relationship with me, his family, and others, he began to give up the fake warmth of the "mother lamps." And so his bulbs went the way of most things. He broke them one by one.

However, as his fascination with lights began to have meaning to me, I felt it should be pursued further. I decided that the way to do this was to give him an incubator. I had a hunch that this might help him to move forward a bit further, but I also knew there was a real danger that it could push him backward. I discussed the risk with his parents and they made the decision. His father built a lifesize replica of Jonny's incubator and brought it to my house. In it we put a doll of the same size as Jonny when he was an incubator baby.

Next day the parents went to Mass, then brought Jonny to my door, and left him with me. The lights of the incubator were on as he walked into the room. He spotted it immediately and stopped short. His whole body began to tremble and his face turned green. Then came the decisive moment. He seemed to reel back but instead, within a split second, he turned and looked straight at me with his eyes completely in focus for the first time. On his face was a look of pain, anguish, and accusation that said, "How could you do it to me?" It took all my strength to remember that I had been brutal only for his good. Within a few minutes he seemed to have become a different child. No longer was his face blank. It expressed feelings. For the first time I saw Jonny integrated, intact emotionally and physically. I knew then that this part of the battle was won.

I went to the window and signaled to his anxiously waiting parents that all was well. Turning back to Jonny, I watched him stalking the incubator, like a creature both hunted and hunter. Then he investigated it as he was to do for many days. He played with the "baby," washed it, spanked it. And each day, his face revealed more feeling. The "dead wash," the bottomless detachment, was disappearing.

When he played with the incubator or the doll, Jonny also began to make more sounds—as if he were trying to communicate with or about it. This usually silent child became so audible that I stopped worrying about whether his vocal cords were defective or nonexistent. As I watched and listened, it became clear to me that among other things he wanted to escape responsibility for making or hearing his own voice, just as he had tried earlier to avoid the responsibility of hearing others. So I put a recorder next to the incubator and all the sounds he made were captured on tape. When I played the recording, his first reaction was shock, which he expressed physically by covering his ears with his hands. But Jonny was enthralled by all mechanical gadgets. After a while the fascination was too much for him and he began deliberately to record his own sounds and listen to them. Gradually his sounds became more varied, including, one day, "Mama."

The recorder became the means of telling Jonny things too painful for him to hear directly. It was in this fashion that he wept for the first time. This came about through his relationship with the puppy he was given when he overcame his earlier fear of dogs. After some weeks his pet fell ill. Fully aware of what was happening, Jonny brought his parents a medical book. Everything possible was done but the dog grew worse, was taken to the vet, and died. Jonny did not know this when next he came to see me. As I told him the puppy was dead, I could almost see him "turning off" his hearing to look at me blankly. However, I had taken the precaution of turning on the tape recorder. Later in the day I unexpectedly turned it on and Jonny, caught relaxed and unawares, heard of the death of his dog. Then, for the first time in the two years I had known him, he broke down and sobbed bitterly. After this it became possible for him to cry quite easily when he was hurt. And along with daring to cry, he began to dare to laugh, often heartily and with a mischievous sense of humor.

Three years after our first meeting, when Jonny was ten years old, he had gone a long way. He heard most of the time, walked well, jumped, ran, leaped, swam, rode a bicycle, painted, drew, put together hi-fi sets, used all kinds of power tools, and built. He cried when hurt, laughed when happy, loved, and evoked love in others. He had relationships with other children and adults, manipulated people consciously and with a deftness beyond his years, and was altogether a very bright youngster. Above all, he was alive.

But he still had a long way to go. He still did not talk, though he once said, "Go to hell," and "I can't." He was heard speaking in his sleep, was suspected of talking to the dog, and was seen talking to his panda.

ANTHONY

"Your move," he said. I moved.

"I got a king," he said, and he did.

Six months, three times a week, an hour at a time, sometimes one game, sometimes two, sometimes the game was carried over.

Across the table from each other we sat, over a checkerboard and, using checkers as ammunition, we carried on our fight. It was a battle of wills from the start. The stakes were high. Anthony's sanity.

Anthony came to me tired. Tired of a fight waged too long unsuccessfully. Tired of a love too painfully unfulfilled. Tired of a world so inconsistent—where good and bad are juggled by a magician so skillful as to make them interchangeable. Tired of his world, where the strong kill and survive, and the meek wait to be killed. Tired of not being able to be either.

Anthony came to me on the verge of a decision to give up the fight, to give up his right to belong to a world he could neither understand nor knew how to take part in. And so he was about to withdraw into a world of his own making where neither "reality" nor "sanity" have any place.

I did not know how long a time he had until he made this frightening decision. But I knew well that once he made it, it would be difficult, if not impossible, to reverse. Time was precious and was running out.

The fight in Anthony was still going on. The hopelessness about it spelled defeat. At times, he seemed to be a stagnant pool of water with no life to him, passively there, waiting to be dried away.

At other times, the helplessness and pain and fury at his impotence would well up so in him that he seemed ready to explode. He reminded me of a pirate ship with lights blazing, munitions exploding, all hands dead, the captain bleeding, heading straight for destruction. Against the jagged ocean rocks. To be ravaged. His pride and fear were great; he would not be caught alive, nor show his weakness.

Anthony was a child who was about to make his choice. Trusting no one, he refused all help: out of fear; out of shame; out of a wish to die.

And as I watched the child, a horrible suspicion slowly crept in. The ammunition on the side of his insanity was stronger than the ammunition on the side of his sanity. And so we played our checkers game with Anthony's sanity at stake. Directly, he could take nothing, as he was too afraid to ask, to get, or to receive. Directly, I could give him nothing, as I was too afraid that I might give too much or push too hard or want for him too fiercely; lest by my own ineptness, I'd force him into the decision I feared the most—suicide, of his sanity, of his self. I was forever hoping that somehow I could help him strengthen his munitions on the side of sanity.

Anthony had a great inner strength, but it was scattered by the internal struggle in which his wish to live fought with his wish to die, in which his wish to fight fought with his wish to give up. I had to encourage his wish to live, no matter how weak his will to fight was. And so it came down to my will against his will.

30

Our wills fought through the game of checkers. On the playing board, Anthony had to learn how to play by concentrating his strength and his will, and he had to learn how to really win and how to really lose, and still keep on playing.

The battlefield was life. The game was only checkers. When he eventually learned how to use his angers, his joys, his hates, and his loves, the energy to play, he learned automatically, a tiny bit, to love. While the game was going on, we hardly ever talked about anything that pained him. We circled his pain, touching it here and there, and then we ran from it by silent, mutual consent, except for a few times. While we played this awesome game of wills and gambled for his sanity, something was happening to Anthony which helped him choose to live.

When Anthony came to me he was ten and a half years old. He was accompanied by a controversial diagnosis: mental retardation, brain damage, childhood schizophrenia, autism, juvenile delinquency. The most immediate complaint was that Anthony was terribly physically violent against children, against adults, against anything he came in contact with. He consciously identified with Hitler, and was covered from head to toe with swastikas.

When he came to me, the authorities were ready to throw him out of school and send him to a state hospital.

Anthony could not read. His speech was slurred—incoherent. He communicated through his body, mainly through his fists. At times he was beautiful, at other times dull and listless; at times angular and disjointed, and at other times extremely well coordinated. He behaved like a delinquent, and was thus constantly involved with the police. At home, he engineered violent beatings from his father; at school, severe punishments; and in the street, constant warfare.

He had made many attempts at suicide. He lived in a jungle of terrors and his life was spent dodging them.

But when the terrors became too much for him he walked right into them.

"I got nothin' to say to you, an' I ain't listenin' to you neither," he said when he came to see me the first time.

"How about a game of checkers?" I said. "Want to try your luck?" I caught his eye glancing at the checker game.

"Okay," he smirked. "I'm gonna beat you," and he looked me up and down.

He was tall for ten and a half, I thought, and handsome and lanky and graceful.

I got the checkers out; he set them up. The game was strange, for at times winning the game meant losing the battle, and at other times, losing the game meant winning the battle. It depended so much on how it was done.

He won. "You see, I beat you," he said smugly.

"Because my opponent is not worth my while," I said sarcastically.

He paled. "I ain't stupid."

"That is exactly the point," I told him.

"Have a game?" Anthony asked.

"Okay," I said. "I've got a strong will. You've got a strong will. Let's make the fight worth each other."

Anthony's mouth began to tremble helplessly, but in his eyes I caught a smoldering of pride. I understood his strength; I recognized his strength.

We played. I won. Anthony threw the checkers off the board and left.

"Have a game?" I asked as he came in.

"Nope," he said.

"You are afraid," I said, and he got up to leave.

"You are a coward," I said. He turned on his heels to hit me; instead, he lined the checkers up. He played in a rage. He almost won, but lost.

He looked at me with a hate that was so impotent that instinctively my arms flew out to him to shield him, but I put them down to my sides and held them tight. He wanted no compassion and no pity. He needed dignity—a respect for the strength in his hate. He left.

"A game," he said, tight-lipped.

The child has guts, I thought. He came back for more.

"I take the blacks," he said.

I took the reds. We lined them up. As we lined up our checkers on the board, we made no bones about our fight, and that was good. I had said I wanted an opponent worth fighting, because I fight with all I have, and he had agreed to that and come back to fight with all he had.

"Wake up! I moved," he said.

"Okay." I moved.

"I jump," he said, determinedly, and he did. He beat me.

There was no joy in him, only the satisfaction of a job well done and of time well spent. He wiped the perspiration off his forehead and left.

"Your move," he said.

I moved.

"I've got a king," he said. He did.

"Okay."

"I jump. You like Hitler?" he asked. The swastikas on his arms and chest loomed bigger than ever.

Hard worked—for victory brought forth a relaxation and a greater honesty.

"Nope. Your move."

"I like him. He was strong and he could kill. Big boss."

"I beat you, Anthony! You don't like your school much?"

"My move. Hold on. Nope. I'm stupid. Didn't they tell you?"

"I didn't talk to 'them.' " I moved.

"Boy, wait till you do. I got a king."

I did talk with Anthony's teacher. She told me, "He just hasn't got it. You know how it is. Some do and some don't. No sense pushing him. He's retarded. I'll recommend a transfer to a special class. He's a juvenile delinquent and no brains to boot. He thinks he's Hitler. It's disgusting."

She whispered into the phone deliciously, "And you know what else? He's dirty."

"I see," I said, but I didn't.

"He plays with himself," the teacher went on. "You know, he touches his private parts. He's queer. A fairy. He always combs his hair and," she whispered even lower, "there is a little colored girl. He is always after her. You are wasting your time."

"Okay," Anthony said sullenly, "let's have a game."

"You better play well today," I said through clenched teeth.

"You mad?" he said, unemotionally stating a fact.

"I spoke to them," I said. "The school."

"Oh," he said, looking self-conscious.

"You sure did a good job on them. You convinced 'them' that you are stupid."

"I am, ain't I?" he demanded.

"Like hell you are. You are too darn smart."

"But the teacher says so. That hospital said so on the tests. My mother says so. My father says so. So I am stupid!"

"You left your grandma out."

"Okay, your move," he said, and then he asked me softly, "You don't believe I'm stupid?"

"Your move. Scared, yes. Stupid, no."

"I ain't scared of nobody," he shouted in a rage, and jumped my checkers three times and left, trailing his swastika-covered jacket on the floor behind him.

I called Anthony's mother. She said, "Maybe you're right. Maybe he's not stupid, but he hasn't got much brains. He's just trouble. Fight, fight, fight, that's all he knows. Police will take him away one day for good. Okay, Mira, I will try, but he's like his father. Never made nothin' out of himself. He can't even read." Anthony's mother paused. "You really don't think he's

34

dumb?" she asked gently. I could feel her welled-up pain and her hopeless hope in this one question. The air weighed heavy with tears uncried so long.

"I take reds. The game is on," he announced.
We started.
"Your move. My father, he is stupid."
I moved.
"He never made nothin' out of himself. I'll get you in a corner."
"Think so?"
"He cleans fish. I hate fish. I beat you."
"I beat you back."
"He beats me with a strap."
"I'm sorry. Got you. I'll ask him to stop beating you."
"Wait. I've got the red. Don't interfere with him and me." Then Anthony added quietly, "He won't listen to you."
"Maybe he will. I got a king. Your mind is not on the game."

Anthony's father listened. He came in to see me, tall, tired, and shy, handsome like his son. I saw the scar on his left hand.
"While scaling fish," he said. He smelled of fish. "I came here straight from work." He smiled apologetically, and sat down heavily. "I'm tired. I work a long day. I start at four in the morning and don't end till seven or eight in the evening. I clean and cut and scale the fish." He kept on talking.
There was a dignity about him. A picture sprang before me. I smelled the salt of ocean on this man. Proud and beautiful he stood there, the sun- and sweat-drenched body straining at the net. The sinews bursting with the effort and the job. Pulling in the day's catch. A good catch. The silver and the gray and the green of fish reflecting in his eyes and in his blue Mediterranean Sea. The good smell of fish was permeating his world.
His words were slipping through.
"I came from the old country when I was a child of seven. I had not time for school. I did the work I knew,

35

with fish. To them, now, I am dumb. I can't read well. I can't help the kids now with their homework. I don't know how to talk to them. Maybe if I had an education," he says with a futility that asks no answer, "but they will go to college."

"A game," Anthony said.

We played.

"He said he won't beat me any more. You must know God."

"No, but I got to know an interesting guy."

"Who?"

"Your father."

"You're nuts. He never made nothin' of himself. He just cleans fish."

"That isn't nothing! By the way, that is the closest he can get to the fish he loves." I told Anthony what I saw about this man that was his father.

He set the checkers up. "Another game," he said. His hands were trembling with the joy and pride about his father. "He can't even read," he raged.

"Yes, he can, but slowly. Is that why you don't want to learn to read?" I had hit a sore. He winced.

"Your move," he said.

"I moved," I told him, and he understood.

"I mean with the checkers," he said, furious at me, cursing me under his breath. "He hits, this great man of yours," Anthony continued.

"So what? You ask for it!"

"What do you mean?"

"Come off it, Anthony. For some reason you want to be beaten. You like to be beaten by him. You lie on the floor always in his path and scream and kick and roll, waiting until he beats you. Only when he beats you up, only then are you satisfied."

Anthony kicked the table leg with fury. "Goodbye," he said.

"Not until this game is finished," I said.

"Like hell I will," Anthony said, but he stayed. He wanted to hear more about his father. "I take your checker for not jumping," he added, and he did.

36

"You know, Anthony, your father beats you because he wants to get some affection out of you and some respect."

"Hm," he smirks. "That's one hell of a way to do it."

"And you know something else? He loves you very much," I added.

"I hate him. I don't care if he never loves me."

"That's why you lie there and provoke his beatings, I guess." I finally asked, "Why?"

Anthony ran away. He had heard what he had hoped to hear, that his father loved him.

"I'll take the reds. A fast game, then I leave," Anthony announced.

"How fast?" I asked.

"Five minutes."

"You travel ninety minutes to come here, and you'll travel ninety minutes back home just to spend five minutes with me. Must be a very important five minutes."

"I moved," he said. "Yesterday, a cop chased me for seven blocks. Then I lost him."

"A great diversion."

"I slashed some tires," he continued provocatively. "I broke six windows in the project," he added, plaintively, frightened by my lack of reaction.

"Why?" I asked.

"I don't know," he said importantly. "I get moods."

"Okay. You get fifty-five minutes to figure out why, and no hogwash either. I'm waiting."

"I leave," Anthony said. "I told you."

"You stay," I said. "I'm telling you."

He stayed, and after thirty minutes of pure hogwash, injured dignity, and frustration, he said, "I want to be sent away from home and from school. I am nobody there. Nobody loves me."

I told him what it is like in a reformatory, sparing him none of the gory details.

"That ain't like it is in the movies or on TV," Anthony said.

"You don't know nothin' about it, Anthony. I've worked at such a place." That finished that.

"Okay," Anthony said warily, "let's have a game." We started.

"You Jewish?"

"Yes."

"I'm Italian."

"I know."

"I can't read."

"Sorry."

"I'm not. Another king. I'm going to be like Hitler."

"He could read."

"Like hell he could." Suddenly, Anthony pushed the checkers off the board in anger and stood up. "I don't play no more today." He was losing.

"Just like Hitler," I said disparagingly. "You can't lose." I thought how beautiful he was. Sicilian. Arrogance to cover his fear and his defeat.

"What do you mean?" Arrogance turned into suspicion. "What you just said."

"I said you were like Hitler. As long as he won it was okay. As soon as he saw he was losing, he killed himself." Anthony searched my face. "He couldn't lose," I continued. "It's easy to be strong and stick by your convictions when everyone is with you. It takes real guts to face what you are and to stand by your convictions when everyone is against you."

"Just the same, I don't want to play."

"Sure. You want to quit because I'm winning."

"Who cares."

"You care, Anthony, but you haven't got the guts to use your head and fight it out and either win or lose gracefully."

"Today we have a short game," he told me.

"Are you going to win that fast?" I asked.

"Yep. I take reds. Mira, who else was like Hitler?"

"You mean who killed that many people?"

"No," he said in disgust. "Who was as strong a leader, a good general?"

"Lots," I answered. "Washington, Lincoln, Napoleon, Roosevelt." I went on and on, throwing names around. "God, they were fascinating." I got excited. "If only you could read, I'd give you books about them."

"Your move. You would?"

"I jump you. Yeah, I would. You're losing your checker. You didn't jump me."

"That's no fair!" His eyes were full of tears, but not only for the lost checker. "Your own books, you'd give me?"

"Who else's?"

"I jump two now. But I'm dumb!" he yelled in agony.

"That excuse is worn out," I said, looking detached.

"Why?"

"Because you are very smart, Anthony. I know it, and by now you know it too."

"I'm gonna win this game with seven and I'm gonna learn to read, I think."

"Your pleasure," I said calmly.

"A game?"

"A game."

"My father didn't beat me yet."

"I wouldn't bank on it much longer."

"Why not?"

"Because if a child of mine locked himself in the bathroom for hours, then held his head underwater until he lost his breath, I think I'd beat him too."

"You would?" A strange excitement entered Anthony's face. "You really would?" he asked intently.

"If the child did it as a steady diet as you do, I think I would. Why do it, Anthony? You might really get hurt. Your timing might be off, and you'd get dizzy and you could drown."

A haunting loneliness came into Anthony's face and silently he whispered, "He'll be sorry and he'll love me then."

"A game."

"You are late."

"I know. The train got stuck."

"Don't bother, Anthony. I know the story. You beat some kids up and the teacher kept you in. She also told me you can read now."

"Big mouth." The child flew into a rage. "She's got no business telling you about my readin'."

"Look, Anthony, the books are there on the table. Anytime you're ready, take one."

"Your move," he hissed.

"And by the way, Anthony, from now on your teacher signs your notebook every day so that you and I will know you're behaving."

"Says who?"

"Says I. Your move."

"I'm no baby!" He moved.

"Agreed. Sometimes, however, you behave like one, like today. You say you want to be promoted."

"You go first today. Go on!"

"Anthony, are you trying to get yourself thrown out of school?"

"Your move. Come off it. You know they won't throw me out of school. The teacher won't let them."

"I didn't know she is so taken with you."

"She'll get less money. You know. They get paid for each kid. She throws me out, she's poorer!" All the cards were in his hand. Anthony smiled triumphantly.

My explanation of how our public school system works disillusioned him and left him feeling less cocky.

"I'm first. Hold tight," Anthony yelled in great excitement. "I brought you somethin'!"

"Fish!" I yelled, delighted.

"No. Something from me, not from my father!" Anthony whipped out his report card. All his marks were passing.

"Much better than all failing," I said calmly. "I am very happy for you, Anthony," I said, wondering how much praise the child could take.

Then with a great flourish he opened his notebook and there I saw written: "Congratulations! We've made it. Not only is Anthony's conduct and his school work better, but he is real smart. He knows historical figures and current events better than anyone else! I must hand it to you." This was signed by his teacher.

Anthony's eyes searched my face. His face was red. His checker game was lousy. He couldn't win, he couldn't lose. He couldn't even play.

Anthony came in wearing his new sea cadets uniform, sheepishly twirling his cap in his hands. He looked very handsome.

"They got it for me. My father and my mother." He added almost inaudibly, "Do you like it?"

I was delighted. It took a great effort to get him to join the sea cadets, and it took even more to get him to stick it out.

Anthony played checkers magnificently. With every trick and cunning he possessed.

"I like Napoleon," he announced. "I'd rather be Napoleon now than Hitler. He faced the music when he lost."

"Okay, Napoleon. Which color do you want?"

"Red," he said.

We wondered why Napoleon had to be so powerful.

"He must have felt very small, somewhere," I said, "way down deep inside him."

"Stupid reason," Anthony said. "The only place he was small was in his size. I mean, he just never grew tall, that's all," he added.

And then I had to ask it. "Anthony, why do you soil your pants? Are you that small somewhere down deep in you?" I had hit below the belt, but I had to do it. It seemed strange to topple Anthony over after all the time I'd spent helping him to build up his strength.

Anthony looked at me bewildered, betrayed, his spirit crushed. He suddenly, like a wilted flower, folded up and began to weep, bitterly—for the first time since I knew him. My dog came over and began to lick his face. Anthony accepted this with gratitude.

Anthony was a child who lost his Eden too early, but never gave it up. And so the child remained suspended

41

between his heaven and his hell. Touching on both, having neither. He was in constant fear of falling to the earth, and on this earth of ours becoming mortal—weak and strong, giving and taking, and so, undramatically, eventually dying.

So at the portals of his babyhood he stood and longingly tried to catch glimpses of his long-lost paradise. But all he managed to catch hold of was the inability to control his bowels. And the fairy tale that infancy had not gone by but was still here, within his reach. In that dream lay his love, his shame, and his undoing.

The child was like a zombie. It took a week, two weeks, a month; I do not know. Exposed was his ugly secret, which he had hidden, hated, and treasured for so long.

He kept on coming to me as to one's executioner. His games were lifeless. He no longer cared whether he had won or lost. He moved much more slowly than he usually did, as if he were in a trance. And when he walked, he dragged his feet as if he were knee-deep in his own excrement and his excrement was dragging him down.

And there within the quicksand of his excrement, the octopus of his unfulfilled infancy was dragging at him with all its many arms of strong dependencies, of fears and needs and hurts. Within this seeming passivity the battle for Anthony's sanity was waged.

Then, one day, Anthony came in angry.

"A game," he growled.

"A game," I said, relieved.

"Blacks," he muttered, as he set his checkers up. "How did you know?" he asked. And then he answered, "They told you."

"Anthony, you aren't coming here just to play checkers. They told me and you told me."

"I?" he said, bewildered.

"Yes. The way you walked at times. The way you smelled at times. In many other ways."

Anthony glared at me.

"How long do you hold your bowels in?" I asked him.

"Few days, sometimes a week, sometimes longer," he said reluctantly.

"Doesn't your stomach hurt you?"

"Hmm, hmm, no," he answered, his face getting red.

"And then you lose it in your pants?"

"Yeah," he answered, squirming.

"A bit at a time?" I continued.

"I don't feel it when it happens." His lips were visibly trembling now.

"Anthony, I hate to rob you of your great secret uniqueness, but there are plenty of other kids like you. They do the same thing. And some come here."

"How old?" he whispered, out of breath.

"One is eleven," I told him. "One is thirteen, and one is over fourteen."

Anthony jumped up.

"Excuse me, may I use your," and then in a whisper he added, "bathroom?" It was the first time.

"My game."

We started.

"Who cleans your underpants?" I asked.

"Your move." Anthony ignored the question.

"It's dark outside," he said.

"You are playing poorly, Anthony. What gives?"

"It's dark," he said, "and it's morning," seemingly ignoring my words.

"It'll rain," I said. "It scares you?"

"Not me. It scares my grandma. Will it explode?" he asked.

"What do you mean?"

"The thunder. I don't like it." He added, "It can kill."

"Sometimes," I said, and then I explained about thunder and lightning.

"Everything can kill," he said, and then he added, "Sometimes, sometimes when it explodes like that inside," haltingly as if putting pieces of a puzzle together, "you fall apart into a thousand pieces. And then sometimes you may never find your pieces again and you're nothing."

"Your game. I'm going to leave soon," he said.
"What's the rush?"
"It's gonna storm. Besides, I was just followed."
"Anthony?" I looked at him incredulously.
"A man. I lost him. Did you read about that girl in Manhattan? He raped her, then he killed her."
Anthony went on to tell me all about it in detail.
"Anthony, she was only four and you're eleven. You've got more sense, I hope. You don't go alone with a stranger to the roof of a sixteen-story building for candy."
"But there was that boy up in the Bronx. And he was seven and he's dead now, too."
What could I answer?

My phone began to ring daily. I picked it up but nobody answered.
Then, one day, I followed a hunch and said, "Anthony, I'm here. You can talk to me," and the child answered shyly, "Okay, goodbye."

"I take the reds," he said. "You take the blacks." Then with a vengeance he added, "I hate the commies. They are bad."
"The what?" I asked, surprised.
"The reds, you know. I heard a commentator say that they're everywhere. Even in your own family."
"Who did you pick in yours? Your grandma?"
Anthony laughed, but seemed perplexed.
"Jack Kennedy's one commie," he said, "and tonight maybe they'll elect him President, and we'll all get killed. You know."
I could hardly believe what I was hearing. Anthony's face had that look of tautness about it which was always there when he panicked.
"Well, he's not like Ike, so he must be a commie," he answered my look of amazement.

We talked about the two-party system in the United States. We talked about democracy and freedom, and we talked about the elections. Anthony was entranced, absorbed and interested.

His fears seemed to wane. We turned on the television and listened to some last-minute political debates. Anthony seemed fascinated and became very much involved, without the need to kill or to be killed.

"My game," he said, and moved. "The commies," he stated, "the world is divided in two. The commies and us. Right?"

"Wrong," I said to him, and explained to him that other ways of thinking existed in the world. This made it harder for him. If his father wouldn't beat him, and thunder wouldn't kill him, and the man in the street wouldn't slay him or rape him, at least the commies would.

"But Castro in Cuba. He threw out the good government and put in his own bad government, and they're all commies."

I explained about the revolution in Cuba, and compared it to our own revolution.

"But Africa," Anthony insisted, "at least they are just plain commies."

I explained what was going on in Africa, again in terms of our own Revolutionary War with England. Anthony was exhausted.

"You mean there ain't no commies?" he said in disbelief, but with great relief.

Then I told Anthony about communism, about Russia and Poland and Hungary and China and other Communist countries. We settled down to one more game of checkers while we continued to discuss communism and democracy, and the effects which both have had on current history.

"My move."
"No, my move."

We went over the moves in the game. Anthony was right.

"Where is your African friend from?" Anthony asked.

"Kenya."

"Then he's a commie," he decided, moving his checker.

"No, he's just fighting for the freedom of his country," I added.

The Kenyan came in. Black as the night and just as awesome. The child stood up and they shook hands. With awe and admiration, Anthony tried to read the history of Africa in the man's face. Then Anthony relaxed. Suddenly an understanding existed between the two of them. The big man's fight for dignity, for the independence of his country, was like the little boy's fight for dignity and independence of his self.

"It isn't so different," Anthony decided.

The bogeyman, the commie, was dying a very slow death. Anthony was beginning to have a sense of history and an understanding of men's pride in their own country, and of his in his own country and in himself.

"I read in the paper today," Anthony started, as he moved his checker, chasing after mine, "that at the UN they will discuss Africa. Will you take me there? Please?"

Anthony's world was enlarging. The world was beginning to creep into the tight little island of his misconceptions and prejudices. Anthony was beginning to creep out of it.

"Let's change the colors of the checkers," Anthony said, jumping my two kings. "Black and red aren't okay any more. We should have a lot more."

Whenever I received something from another country, Anthony got something from it, too.

"It's almost like I travel there through this," he said

one day, pointing to the wrapper of a pack of Spanish cigarettes.

"Let's have a game of checkers," Anthony suggested, as if this was a new idea. There was something different about the child.

"Do you think I'll ever get to high school?" he suddenly asked.

"It's up to you," I said. "I don't see why not."

"And then I'd like to go to college," he added very quietly. "And then I'll travel and see a lot of places and a lot of history."

I felt proud. Anthony played his game calmly and with dignity. I knew he'd do it.

I hadn't seen Anthony for two months as I had been in the hospital with a relapse of a back injury.

"Let's have no game now," he said quietly and firmly. Anthony looked me over carefully. "You look pale," he said, "and thin. Tomorrow I'll bring some of my mother's cooking. She cooks well," he added. "It'll make you fatter."

I smiled, delighted that he looked so well. He worried me so much.

"I sent cards. You got them?"

"Yes. Thank you, Anthony. They were beautiful."

"Sorry I bothered you in the hospital. I had to call. I had to know that you were there."

"You mean alive?" I said.

"Yes," he said, blushing. And then with childish enthusiasm he insisted, "You know why you got it in the back, 'cause you sit on the floor."

I explained my car accident to him. Then Anthony said with determination and yet half-pleadingly, "No more checkers. Please, no more games. Let's just talk from now on. Okay?

"It was good and you know so much, and you explain so much to me, and things became okay. Then when you got sick it was as if it was dark all over and then the world stopped and everything stopped. And now," in his innocence he continued, "it's okay again and it's light again and the world will go on again"; then he added as an afterthought, "for me. So don't sit on the floor any more and don't get sick."

The beginning was ended. Anthony's trust was won. From this point on, we talked, we walked, we did many things together, but never again did we need to or want to play checkers.

I saw Anthony three times a week at my house. I constantly kept in touch with everyone in his family. The fine balance of his health and of our relationship was too precarious to risk allowing anyone to upset it. "After God came Mira," was often heard in Anthony's household. "I will tell Mira," "I will ask Mira," "I will talk to Mira." I was used as praise, as punishment, as law and order for the whole household. The other children would call me too, after Anthony began bringing them to me, one by one, whenever they got into trouble, but that was much later. I became a household name like Ajax.

Anthony improved, at school, on the street, at home, a little bit at a time. He continued to beat up kids, slash tires, continued to be involved with the police, continued to disappear from home, continued to hold his head underwater until he lost consciousness, continued to hold back his bowels, and failed some subjects in school, provoked his father, provoked, provoked—but less so.

His fears were surfacing, and he was able to tie them up with his experiences and tell me about both. He told me about his ruptured appendix at the age of six and how frightened he had been during his long hospital stay. He also told me about the circumcision which was performed at the same time, and the terror that came with it. And he told me how, as long as he could remember, his father had demanded to look at his son's penis every morning to make sure it was not too small. He told me how his mother hit him, mainly in the face. He told me how much he wished to be somebody, not just anybody, but somebody who "counted," a "man," a priest, a Marine, a policeman, a soldier. Above all, he

48

wished to be seen, to be noticed, to be recognized, to be known, and he told me how afraid he was that he would always be nobody like his father. He told me of his fear and of his fascination with fire, his fear of being trapped in it, "burned alive like a roast pig." He told of his excitement whenever he saw anything burning. He told me it was a thrill beyond description. He told me of his desire to run away from the fire while, at the same time, he felt compelled to run toward the fire. "A hypnotic pull," as he said. Anthony said fire also had the power to "freeze" him so that he could neither move toward nor away from it. He told me of his fear of closed places, of being trapped and buried alive. Then he told me that when he beat up kids it was because they made him feel trapped, and in order to free himself from this trap he had to beat them.

He tried to explain his terror of thunder and lightning —any kind of storm. To Anthony it was as if these explosions were bursting inside him, bursting him apart into a million pieces, pieces which no one could ever put together again unless he held on. (Except maybe now I could.)

He explained that he held on to his bowels because he was afraid that if he let them go he would explode, and that part of him would be flushed away. He explained how, when he finally moved his bowels, he was able to keep the movement because it would not be flushed out of his pants. He told me of his terror and his shame about it.

He told me how really terrified he was of his father's beatings, how he thought that someday his father would beat him so hard that he would kill him. Anthony told me that what frightened him even more was that his father would make him disappear, fall apart.

He told me how desperately he wanted his father to love him, to touch him, to smile at him, and he told of how he sometimes engineered the beatings because, in spite of his terror, they made him feel loved. Sometimes the beatings gave him the same excitement, the same pleasure, that fire gave him; but sometimes they gave him such inexplicable pain, seeing his father's disap-

49

pointment, seeing his father's rage, that he too became so enraged and went out to beat up the first person who spoke to him, no matter who it was, regardless of the age, size, or strength of his victim. He also told me how in hopeless rage he beat his fists against walls, on the floor, just as his father did to him. He told me how he wanted to be able to hit just like his father, be strong just like his father. Then he told how sometimes the beatings made him feel "all better" because they expiated all his sins of thought and of reality, and made him feel that he was good again.

He told me over and over how much he wanted to be loved by both his father and mother, and by his brothers and sisters, and everybody else, how tired he was of being the "bad boy"; but that he couldn't stop being bad, and he told me how impotent he felt if he wasn't the "bad boy."

And he told me many other things. We talked and we talked and we talked, and together we tried to find a way out of Anthony's infernal labyrinth. He continued to improve.

One summer, Anthony went to camp; a camp for bright, creative, and fairly well adjusted children. I was able to get him a scholarship. For the first time in his life, Anthony was recognized as somebody, somebody good and worthwhile. For the first time in his life, he traveled farther from home than my office in Brooklyn.

Going to camp was a tremendous jump for Anthony. It was very difficult for him to move from a world where he was considered retarded, incorrigible, bad, to a world where he was respected and liked.

Anthony's parents didn't make the jump any easier for him. The night before he left, his mother told him she wouldn't write to him all summer as a punishment for some minor sin, and as his father couldn't write, he never heard from either of them.

Anthony stuck it out through the whole summer and he even ended up with some friends. He was helped by being at camp, and this in turn helped me to teach him how to communicate with people other than with his fists. But on coming home again he returned to his old behavior, partly because he had not learned the new way well enough, partly because it was the only way to be in his home, on his street.

Anthony's gang had been getting into greater and greater trouble with the police, with the neighbors, and with each other. Anthony's school lost control over the children, and Anthony was playing hooky most of the time, only going to those classes that interested him, history and science.

His father, totally enraged by the lack of control over his son, began beating him mercilessly. I was afraid of murder. Either the son would provoke his father into killing him, or from utter frustration at his own impotence, the father would kill the child who to him was a replica of himself. He had already kicked Anthony in the ribs so repeatedly and with such force that he had broken them. He had bashed him against the floor; he had flung him against the walls; he had thrown him down the stairs. In his frustration, he tried to kick in the cast that covered Anthony's broken arm.

At the time, Anthony's mother was about to enter the hospital for surgery, and since there was no other choice, Anthony came to live with me and my husband. He arrived with his bundle of clothes for a few weeks and stayed with us almost a year.

No matter how terrible his home, no child ever really wants to leave it. Even if the love he so longs for does not exist, there is always a hope, there is always a dream, there is always a wish that things will be different the next time: that the next time the love will be there, if only he can be different, if only he can find and push the magic button. Anthony was very much attached to his mother, to his father, his brothers, and his two sisters. Leaving home was a mixed blessing for him. As much as he wanted to get away, he did not want to leave. The constant battle with his father defined the only relationship he knew with a man, and he was going to miss it in our house.

Though my husband and Anthony's father could

both become enraged, they were, beyond this trait, totally different. My husband was an extremely verbal, highly intellectual professional. No sooner was Anthony in our house than my husband set limits for the child. I too was very different from Anthony's rejecting, deprived, and depriving mother. We were also Jewish while Anthony was profoundly, dogmatically, Catholic. As much as he had accepted me as his strength, living with us was a very different story; for to him we were killers, Christ killers.

Anthony's school was near his home, which meant he had to travel at least three hours every day to and from school. He would have to be consistent with his homework, as both my husband and I would be on his neck. He would have to read not just what interested him but all that was assigned to him in school.

Though the change was difficult for him, it was the best thing that could have happened to Anthony. He was strong enough to accept the intensity of the new relationship with us, and he was well enough not to break under the new-found limits. He used all the love he found in me, in my husband, in the unborn child I was carrying then, and in Dobie, the dog, who shared his bed. And in turn, Anthony loved us.

I no longer saw him regularly three times a week. He was with me and my husband whenever he was not in school. He enjoyed the warmth of my love and I loved him very much. But to love Anthony seeing him three times a week, and to love Anthony seeing him all the time, were two different things. He provoked us all the time, he tested all the time, my husband more than me. It was endless! Anthony and his homework, Anthony and his Church, Anthony and his reading, Anthony and his Hitler. Anthony and his sullenness, Anthony not answering, not hearing, not talking. Anthony disappearing, playing hooky, not coming home. Anthony and his bowels . . . Anthony, Anthony, Anthony!

The suicidal acts were now gone. He was too busy taking care of my unborn child, "my cousin," as he called it. He watched me constantly.

"Don't do anything dangerous, Mira, so the baby wouldn't get hurt."

He wanted me to eat steak all the time so that "Mr. America," his other name for my child, would be strong. I sensed that Anthony wanted to be reborn himself with "Mr. America," for he wished that the baby would be born on his birthday, and his wish almost came true. My own son was born three days after Anthony's birthday.

We set up a schedule together. Anthony left the house for school at 7:00 A.M. If he did not behave or perform properly at school, his teacher would immediately tell me. He was supposed to be home at 5:00 P.M., and do his homework. This was always a painful process as Anthony could not read unless he liked the subject. Sometimes my husband, more often I, sat over him watching him stare at his book with a completely blank expression, seemingly incapable of reading a single word. At those times I could understand the people who diagnosed the child as feebleminded. It took him hours to focus his eyes on the words and read them. In our house, there were no friends to distract him, to give him an excuse not to do his work. By the time he got through his work and helped with the dinner dishes, it was time for him to go to sleep.

He had no friends except us, no gangs to join, no kids to get in trouble with. On weekends, he would visit briefly with his family, and on Sunday he would attend Mass in a church near our house, and visit with us and our friends.

A different Anthony began to appear. He was a gentle child, always ready to help if he liked you, always sensitive to your needs and to your moods. He was able to control his rage. If he wanted to hurt anybody, he did not do so, as he was immediately sorry and full of compassion for the intended victim.

His delinquency now was something he talked about, rather than acted out; something that still made him a "somebody," but much less so. It became more obviously a pose. In the time he lived with us, he attacked no one.

Anthony was a profoundly religious Catholic. He was terrified of the Church, and felt that he was completely accountable to it. He was convinced that his crimes would condemn him to burn in hell forever. Confession was of great importance to the child.

I remember watching him out of my front window on many a Sunday morning, seeing him go, full of evil and an ardent desire for retribution, his head bent already in prayer, his knees buckling from the heavy weight of his load of sins on his way to "c'fession," as he called it. Later, through the same window, I would see him return, cocky, full of the devil, stepping lightly, filled with gaiety, puffing on a cigarette he was smoking on the sly, already starting off to accumulate a new load of sins.

His Catholicism was filled with dogma and superstition. I remember a Seder in our house while Anthony lived with us. He was very engrossed in the preparations for the meal and enjoying them thoroughly. His father came bearing gifts as usual, lots and lots of beautiful fish; and his mother too came with gifts of many kinds, and pastries that she had baked herself. Anthony ran from store to store shopping for matzos and other Seder foods. His curiosity about the meaning of the different dishes was endless. My husband and I explained it all to him at great length. However, once the Seder dinner started and the chanting of the story of Passover began, it was a different story.

The child was convinced that the matzos were made from the bodies of Christian children, and that the wine was the blood of Christ. He refused to taste either. So there he sat at the Jewish table laden with Jewish foods, among many Jews, proclaiming that since the Jews had killed Christ, he could not sit at the same table with us, the killers of God.

I remember the conversation we had, Anthony firmly insisting that Christ could never have been a Jew, that the Jews killed him. The evening was saved by a phone call from Jonny's mother,* a devout Catholic, and to

* See "Jonny" chapter.

54

Anthony the final authority on Catholicism. She assured him over the phone that Christ was indeed a Jew, and that indeed it was the Romans who had crucified him, not the Jews. And she went on to tell him that the Romans were Italians. Anthony's shock was beyond belief.

After being reassured that the Jewish wine was not Christ's blood but made of grapes from the vineyards, and that the matzos were not made from the bodies of Christian children but of flour and water, and finally that the Last Supper was itself a Seder, he seemed to settle down to enjoy the meal.

But although the intellectual realization was there, the emotional lagged behind, and Anthony, after eating the matzo and drinking the wine, passed out at the table. Despite what Jonny's mother had told him, his terror and emotional conviction were too strong for him. We saved the day by saying that he passed out from drunkenness—from one glass of Christ's blood.

Anthony's identification with Hitler was dying, but slowly. He no longer was Hitler, as he had felt when we began working together; but his admiration and envy of the man lasted. He had long admired Hitler because Hitler had acquired great power and effectively expressed his great hatred.

Jews were just something that Hitler could vent his rage on, show his power over, destroy. They were an abstraction to Anthony. In his mind he separated "the Jews" from us who were Jews. He, too, wanted to express his hatred, wanted to vent his rage on all those who did not give him what he wanted.

But Anthony grew taller and stronger, and as the "bad boy" became a "good boy," the Hitler in Anthony began to die.

The relationship with my dog, Dobie, changed in time. At first, Anthony thought of Dobie as a big, fierce, all-powerful protector, endowed with magic powers, who was going to smell out all the terrifying people who were out to get Anthony. Living with Dobie, feeding

55

her, playing with her, sharing his bed with her, helped him to see Dobie more realistically, and Dobie gradually changed in Anthony's mind from a fierce protector to a pal.

I often think of the fire in our backyard. Anthony was cooking a steak for himself, us, and Dobie. Suddenly, the fat from the meat caught fire and flared up. The child stood hypnotized, making no attempt to put out the flames, which were beginning to burn a corner of the house. We smelled smoke and ran out to put out the blaze. Anthony acted as if he had been unconscious of the crisis. Thinking back, I can see that this was a sign of things to come.

The following summer, Anthony's mother recovered from her operation, and my baby was born. Anthony seemed ready to try to live at home again. We continued to work together, but our relationship was not the same as it had been before he came to live with us. Now he was a member of my family, and we treated him as such. My baby, Kivie, was Anthony's brother or cousin, depending upon the mood he was in. He carried the baby's picture around in his wallet, and protected him at all costs. Dobie was Anthony's dog; our home was his home.

Throughout the year, Anthony continued to improve and grow. His father groped for a new way to live with a son who did not provoke any more. At school, Anthony seemed to have declared a truce; in the neighborhood, the gang did not seem to satisfy him any more.

The summer after that Anthony came to Camp Blueberry* with us as half camper and half employee. He worked as a waiter and earned some money, and he was wonderful with the children. He knew how to reach them, how to relate to them. With them he was unafraid, accepting, patient, and protective; but with most of the adults he was defiant.

He matured at camp. Many of the children were completely withdrawn, nonverbal, self-destructive. With

---

* See Appendix A.

these, Anthony was gentle and protective. The children who acted out he handled with firmness and true understanding. He had always been afraid of these autistic, self-destructive children, as if they held a mirror up to him. He was afraid of the self he saw in them. He "was afraid," as he used to say, "of becoming like them, like Jonny, like Gary, like Billy."

Anthony's experience of actually living with them took away his fear of these children, and at the same time, helped him to understand and accept some of his own autistic features.

Anthony was growing fast. He was sixteen years old, very tall, very handsome, well read, bright, but he still had many of his old problems. To part from his bowels was difficult, to work well at school very hard. At home, his relationship with his father deteriorated and his feeling of being nobody increased. He decided to leave school and find a job. He felt this would make him somebody. But in order to be interviewed, he had to play hooky from school, and as a result, the merciless beatings at home began again.

I decided that in addition to the very good relationship Anthony had with me, he also needed to experience a profound relationship with a man other than his father. I asked my husband to work with him, since the seeds of their relationship had already been sown when he lived with us. Anthony admired my husband very much.

All through that year, we both worked with Anthony, separately and together. My husband became a father to him, and it made growing up a little easier.

Of course, Anthony put my husband through all the paces, provoking him incessantly, testing the limits constantly, trying to make sure that my husband's response would not be the same as his father's. In an attempt to divide and conquer, he also provoked situations between my husband and me.

The next year, Anthony decided to join the Marines, trying to follow in his father's footsteps in the search for his identity (his father was once a Marine). Being too young, he needed his mother's permission in order to enlist. He did not get it—she wanted him to finish school first, saying that she "didn't want him to be like his father." Anthony took this as a terrible rejection, not only of himself but of all his hopes and dreams. In refusing to allow him to join the Marines, he was certain that his mother had denied him the possibility of ever being somebody.

Now his work at school got worse and he looked for friends from his old gang. He began to disappear from home again and got into trouble with the police. Then, after a few months, he began to control himself better; he decided to wait until he came of age and could enlist on his own.

As soon as he turned eighteen, Anthony tried to join the U.S. Army. This was of the greatest importance to him. The Army's acceptance would put the stamp of approval on his manhood—a stamp of approval issued by his country, his society, his peers, and his family; a stamp that said Anthony was normal, a stamp that said that Anthony was somebody.

He tried—oh, how he tried! Twice Anthony took the Army tests. Twice he failed. He was not accepted by the Army.

Anthony had failed, only by a few points, but still he had failed. I am not certain why. Maybe his fear of reaching his goal was too great. Then again, perhaps it was because he felt my silent disapproval of his joining the Army. Both his mother and I were against his going off to the war in Vietnam. We did not want him to be fodder for the guns. I felt that he could prove himself in another way than by losing his life. On the other hand, in their concern about Anthony's manhood, his father and my husband both thought it was a good idea for him to join the Army.

Anthony was crushed by this rejection. He withdrew and became listless. He took no interest in anything. He was ashamed to see the friends who had given him a going-away party to celebrate his joining the Army.

He refused to go to school. He began to drink and to

hide from everyone but my husband and me. All our attempts to pull him out of his withdrawal were useless. I failed when I tried to get him involved in helping me with some disturbed children at Blueberry; I failed in my attempt to get him involved with Kivie, my baby. I failed in my attempt to get him involved in anything. Whatever he did, he did halfheartedly. When he visited, he would just tag along, hopeless, listless, not caring if he was dead or alive.

One day, I was sitting in my kitchen drinking a cup of coffee, listening to the radio, when a news item came over the air:

OVER A HUNDRED OLD BUSES
ARE ON FIRE IN THE BRONX BUS
GRAVEYARD

The announcer went on to say that the public would be kept informed of further developments through special bulletins. The fire spread quickly because many of the buses had gasoline left in their tanks. It became a five-alarm fire.

The Bronx bus graveyard stretches along the main railroad tracks and the main highways that run through the Bronx; as a result, train traffic and highway traffic were stopped because of the fire. One hundred trains, ready to leave New York City, were delayed; 25,000 commuters were stopped; railroad service out of Grand Central Station between the hours of 5:00 P.M. and 7:00 P.M. was completely cut off. On the highway, all traffic came to a halt. The police suspected that somebody had started the fire and they were looking for the criminal.

At one o'clock in the morning, another news flash came on the air:

"A teenager has walked into a police station and has turned himself in. He says his name is Anthony Davico. He has told the police that he will lead them to the person who helped him set the fire. He is worried that perhaps a derelict has been caught sleeping in the buses or there may have been some children playing nearby. He says he must know to be sure that no one has been hurt."

So Anthony had finally done it—he had stopped New York! I was alone with Kivie, who was sick. There was no one to leave him with, and there was no way to go to help my other "baby" and do battle with the police for him.

Then Anthony's parents telephoned. His father was crying. His mother kept repeating, "What do we do now?" My husband called. He had heard the news on the radio and was on his way to the police station to see what he could do.

Next morning, the story was in all the papers.

"Front page of *The New York Times,* that doesn't happen too often, cover story in the *News,* in the *Post,* over the radio and on television," as Anthony said to me later on.

Anthony, in his rage, had tried to burn the world down. In the end, however, his attempt at being "bad" had been destroyed by his compassion for the children or derelicts who might have been hurt. Anthony's brothers and sisters ran around buying up all the newspapers with articles about him, and he stuffed his wallet full of clippings about himself. He got the recognition and the notoriety, but the sweet smell of success was not there. Anthony's parents mortgaged their house to get him a lawyer who was able to set him free, with records destroyed. His father looked at him with a new-found respect, his mother felt greater sorrow than ever before.

No one had ever paid any attention to Anthony. His parents had always rejected him; he had failed in his attempt to join the Marines; the Army had rejected him. No one listened to him—Anthony had never mattered.

Now, at last, Anthony counted. For six hours, he had affected the lives of hundreds of thousands of people. Anthony had stopped the trains. Anthony had closed the highways. Anthony had made the front page. The Fire Department had mobilized its forces. The Police Department had been frantic to find him. Anthony's rage counted; his pain counted; his compassion counted. Anthony's love counted. Anthony counted!

A few months later in my house, Anthony took his news clippings out of his wallet and left them on my table forever.

Then Anthony came to live with us. He was changed. Now he was a young man, the big brother to my small son. Now he was the big son to me and to my husband, and to his parents. Now at last he was growing up.

Later, he got himself a job. Then he got an apartment. Then he joined a union and got a better job.

One day, Anthony brought a girl home for me to meet. She was Polish, Jewish, a musician. They were married in a Polish church. The bride and the groom walked proudly down the aisle. Just as he passed me Anthony stopped. He took hold of my hand, looked at me, and then he walked on.

Today, Anthony has a good job, a good wife, and a beautiful child. He is a good husband and he is a very warm, understanding father. Anthony has compassion, he has integrity, he is quiet. Anthony is somebody.

THE HAMSTER

Katy Kill Falls is a residential treatment center for emotionally ill children. It is a large and depressing institution, which cares for, treats, houses, and molds 150 children from all walks of life, from all social strata, all with one common denominator: mental illness. Some children are sent there by courts for offenses committed against others or offenses against themselves. Some children are sent by psychiatrists, parents, and/or agencies for offenses thought about though not yet committed against others or against themselves. All are sent in a hope of curing them and preventing any kind of major irrevocable hurt to themselves and others. The children range from age eight to eighteen. The symptoms range from delinquency to childhood schizophrenia.

Picture a small city. A replica of a large city, with all its misery, wretchedness, loneliness, fear, hatreds, angers, rages, and loves. Exaggerate it. Amplify it a bit more, as under a microscope. This is Katy Kill. I was hired in June 1952—the first young woman teacher to work at Katy Kill with these children. I was to work with the younger ones, ages eight to eleven. I signed the contract and then anxiously waited to get to work. I was to start a month later. Many of us teachers commuted from New York. I still remember that first morning at Grand Central Station where some of the other teachers working at Katy Kill met me, so we could make the trip together. I was all nerves, excitement, curiosity, and anticipation. They decided to play a trick on me. As soon as the train pulled out, they told me that I'd work with the big boys—sixteen, seventeen, eighteen years old. I panicked and was ready to turn back at the next stop. The men confessed it was only a joke. "It would be crazy to put you with the big ones," they said, laughing at my gullibility. "They'd rape you the first week you were there."

When we arrived at Katy Kill, Mr. Rastinow, the principal, called me into his office. My assignment, he said, would be mornings with the younger boys, eight to eleven, and afternoons with the big boys, sixteen, seventeen, and eighteen. I stared at him in disbelief. My colleagues were as bewildered as I, and guilty that the joke had turned into this ugly reality. "But my contract says I was to work with the younger kids . . ." I began. Mr. Rastinow didn't let me finish. "A man is a man for all that and all that and all that," he said. "Same goes for a woman." I hated him, but I was there, and that was that.

I remember glancing at my reflection, as if compelled, in his glass door, as I was leaving his room. I seemed even smaller to myself than my actual 5 feet 4 inches. I recall unintentionally feeling my arm muscles to see how strong I was. My findings only increased my terror. And in my head the refrain "A woman is a woman . . ." was going around and around with no relevancy to anything else at all.

Katy Kill

Children: Labels. Categories.
Rape, assault, murder; some reached out to the world in this fashion.

Withdrawal, inaction, regression; others removed themselves, withdrew into their shells, and waited—waited for the world to reach out to them. They reached out in this fashion.

Then the ones in between; they did both.

Katy Kill. Always erupting or ready to erupt. Seething with greed from so much deprivation, with hate from so little love, with rage from needing and not getting, with love hidden deep and yet right on the surface. Seething with terror. Seething with sorrow deep and pain so potent that when the eruption comes, it has the howl of pain that it is driven by, rather than of the rage that it expresses itself through.

Katy Kill. Have you ever heard the sound of rage when it seems noiseless? It roars with an intensity. It grumbles with a desiccating rhythm. Its voice is dry and throaty. Sometimes it sounds like hell. And its color is white.

Have you ever heard the sound of terror when it is noiseless? It rustles helplessly, like a leaf in a hurricane. It breaks hard, like the thunder. And it has a smell, a smell that shrivels your skin, a smell that makes you break out in a sweat so cold it freezes you. And its color is blue—deep, dark blue.

Have you ever heard the sound of pain when it is noiseless? It howls the loudest and it whines the quietest. It sounds as if it comes from the deepest bowels of the earth—that is you. It shakes with intensity and trembles with its own resonance over oceans of nothingness. And its color is black.

Have you ever heard the sound of loneliness when it is noiseless? It has a blast of thousands of trumpets. It has the howling of hyenas waiting for their prey. It has the howl of herds of starving wolves. Its melody is neither nice nor pretty. And it is gentle and full of fury. It is deep and somber, threatening and pleading. And its color is gray.

It shouts at you and echoes over all eternity. It reverberates over the whole world and echoes in every cave, cavern, and mountain. It has a frightful sound; it has a howl. And the plea is: "Love, come to me." Its basic ingredient is: "Give, give to me." And the other ingredients are pain and terror, hate and rage, anger and tears, and: "Do not leave me, love me, and oh, it hurts so much."

And the search. Have you ever seen the search for "that" which one no longer knows by any rightful name, but "that" or "what" or "Oh, God, help me!" or then no longer even that, but the burning ashes of a long, long, long ago fire?

Have you ever seen and felt and smelt and heard them all together? They have cold, sweaty hands. And eyes that sometimes burn and sometimes weep, red-rimmed, sleepless, hopeless. Eyes that try to hide deep into the sockets of the head, and finding the futility in this, just stare—nowhere. And the body, no matter how straight or bent, or fat or skinny—something just about the shoulders—a little tilt, which in spite of all its bravura and all its bravado in a very, very small voice asks: "Protect me."

A child. Any child when abandoned. But all these children feel abandoned. It is the world versus the child. The child versus the world. In all, the impotence of both. In all, the fear of both.

And sometimes this loneliness of theirs takes you by the shoulders and says, "You are going to give." And sometimes it kills because you didn't give. And sometimes it kills because that is a giving, too: their giving. And sometimes it just withdraws and waits till you come and give, and in its waiting it often dies. It stops. It doesn't talk and doesn't walk, and sometimes doesn't move. It waits. If often dies, and in its strange perverted way it makes you give.

Sometimes there is sex to fill this void. And the sex is then strange. There is little giving, but there is taking, there is devouring of you and whatever you can give to fill this void. The exquisite giving and taking is no longer. The balance is disjointed. Because it is to take, to calm, to quiet this awful howl of loneliness and the hunger that derives from loneliness. To feed, so that for once, for this one short while, the need, the plea, the want is filled.

One doesn't cry, with tears.

One doesn't sob, with sobs.

One doesn't ask, with pleas.

One waits, one watches. One is ready. One is tough. One pushes away. Except in the dreams. One doesn't talk about the dreams. That is the way to be, out there in the world that is a jungle. One hurts. One fights. One kills. So that one does not get hurt, get killed, one withdraws. In order not to get refused, one doesn't ask.

The price of the ticket for a lifetime is high. One pays. But one sees to it that everyone else will pay it too.

I heard rumors, but I did not know enough and believed not enough of what I heard. And that was my good fortune. I didn't know that they honed their buckles as sharp as razor blades. I did not know that they sneaked in knives. I did not know that they ran away. I did not know how they fought. And I did not know their laws and rules and their justice.

Mr. Rastinow was right. "A man is a man for all that . . . Same goes for a woman." I knew the kids only for what I saw them to be. It wasn't hard to see beyond the label, and I treated them for what I felt was in them. I gave what I could, and did not touch what I felt I had no right to touch. They were human beings. In a sense equal, in a sense needing more. And there was no shame in being human, and no shame in being hurt, and no shame in needing. I afforded them the dignity of their feelings. I respected them and expected and demanded their respect. I put up with no nonsense. I gave them none. I was a woman, weaker than they— and I expected them to respect that. And expected their protection, as a woman. I demanded manners, and I gave them manners. And that, too, gave the kids limits. I demanded what was the best in them and they gave it to me. I recognized their strengths, positive or negative. And once recognized, they didn't constantly need to test them or prove them to me.

And so it came about that the boys learned to love me and respect me and trust me, and protected me against themselves and each other. And in doing so, they grew stronger, became kinder, and less hateful of themselves and the world around them.

I had two groups. The morning group of my little kids, and the afternoon group of my big kids. They all did quite well. To my utter surprise, the big ones were even littler than the little ones, at times; and at times they were either very, very big or as little as my little ones. As long as I allowed them to keep and respect their bigness, as long as I responded to their littleness, we could get along and love each other. I could read "Little Red Riding Hood" to the little ones in the classroom, but the big ones only accepted it miles away from the classroom, where, after building a lean-to or having a picnic, they could relax and let themselves enjoy the story.

But all that became even easier after they "adopted" Justin, an eight-year-old boy who could not get along in any other group, a very sick little boy whom they helped me protect and take care of and love. Then, not only "Little Red Riding Hood" but all the other fairy tales were avariciously devoured "for Justin's sake."

The competition over me between the two groups at the start was frightening. But after a while the competition lessened. It lessened almost to the extent of the sharing of a hamster. Almost.

I still remember the beautiful sight of my little kids and my big kids waiting for me at the bus stop one morning when I arrived at work. Shuffling from foot to foot, uncomfortably expectant, self-consciously excited, and so bashfully hopeful. I had been commissioned by them to bring two hamsters back from New York. I still remember the scramble and lunge toward the bus stop as I was coming down the steps with the box. I still remember the wide-open eyes of all of them when their "dream come true" arrived. And once again I realized the tragedy of them: what they really want that no one will ever give to them. They hadn't believed that I'd really bring it. And then the transformation. The blasé and not-caring look—"Oh, you brought . . ." which quickly covered up the warm, magnificent feelings of a moment before. They were not going to be caught un-defended, with their love showing.

And then the shock and horror in their eyes, which came through past their protective wall of smugness. I was carrying a 3-foot-long wooden box, with big black letters printed on it: "DANGEROUS SNAKES." As I explained to them, the pet store had no other box. I still hear their hearty laughter ringing in my ears, when I told them how I got an empty car in the New York subway in the midst of the morning rush hour, the passengers reacting to the sign with the same horror as they did.

They loved the two hamsters very much. They built a cage for them, fed them, gave them water, took care of them. They played with them, and said things to them they did not dare to say to the others.

One hamster died, however, on the fourth day. The other one got the love stored up for the two of them. And that was a great heap of love. But one day he died too.

On a Tuesday morning, after the long Yom Kippur weekend, when the "morning kids" and I got to the classroom, the hamster was dead. The sun was beating through the windows, and the hamster lay dead in his cage. The stench in the room was unbearable . . . the dead hamster, the apple jelly which we had left half-cooked in a pot, the dozens of flies, the rotting leaves, the closed windows. And it was a humid day. The hamster lay dead in his cage. We threw open all the windows.

"Hey kids, the hamster is dead," Timmy howled in a broken voice. And all the kids were beside the cage, touching and nursing the dead hamster. Donny, who had an exaggerated terror of germs, was petrified. "Why did he die? He died naturally, didn't he, Teach? He did." Jumping up and down on one foot in a panic, he sought reassurance. "Sure he did," I said.

"Am I gonna get sick from him? Am I gonna get polio?" he screamed.

I called them back to their seats. "You know all living things die," I said, trying to be casual. "There is spring, summer, fall, and then winter, and then all over again. Each stage is beautiful. Did you ever watch a blade of grass break through the earth? It is beautiful. It grows, gets bigger and greener, then it is yellow, then it is dead, and then a new blade of grass comes up. Like the tomatoes you picked yesterday. Same with them. What makes them die, I do not know. A law in nature, something wonderful in nature that makes things live and move, makes them rest and die, and then again new things rise up and live. And so it goes on. Nobody really understands it. It is one of those wonderful, beautiful mysteries, secrets that nature has."

The kids were all quiet, mesmerized by my droning on and on.

"What do you want to do with the hamster now?" I startled them out of their trance.

"Bury it."

"Yes!"

"Let's give him a funeral!"

They began to get excited and yell.

"How shall we do it?"

"Hey, Mira, come on, how?"

The kids outshouted each other.

"There are many ways," I resumed my droning. "Some people, when there is a death, dance and sing and feast and sort of celebrate the going away of their friend. Others I've seen get together and wail and just let themselves go, howl and cry for days and days until there are no tears left to cry. Some get their family together and sit shiva. That's my way, you know. Some make fabulous funeral processions, burn their dead, and throw the ashes into a river or scatter them to the four corners of the earth. So you decide what you're going to do."

They decided. And I can see them now . . .

Lenny, excitedly: "Hey, kids, let's make a funeral."

Jimmy: "And a procession."

Roy: "And a casket."

Jeffry: "And I'll make a sermon and we'll put earth on him."

Jimmy: "Hey, Timmy, put him in that box and wrap him up in cloth—that's good."

Roy: "Hey, Timmy, is it okay if I put clay around that box so worms don't get him?"

The box is covered with wet clay.

"Jimmy and I are gonna carry the casket!" Roy announces, and puts string on both ends of the box. The box slips out of the string and falls down.

"Hey, you! Don't hurt him! He's gonna be dead twiced, now, you motherfuckers!" Lenny curses.

"Hey, guys, here's a piece of wood. Carry the box on that. Looks more dignified," Mat says.

The kids do it.

"Okay, fellers. Line up behind us," Jimmy and Phil command.

Timmy: "I go first 'cause I carry the monument."

Jeffry takes out a harmonica and begins to make sounds that are monotonous and sad. The line is forming.

First, Timmy with his "monument."

Then Jimmy and Roy with the casket, which is carried with great dignity on a board.

Then Jeffry and his harmonica.

Then Mat.

Then Ricky.

Then Lenny, with an empty pail and a stick with which he beats out a rhythm on the pail.

Then Donny.

"Okay, Mira. Let's go. We gonna bury the hamster," says Donny.

"Do you have a shovel?" I ask.

"Don't worry, Teach, we'll dig a hole with somethin'," Lenny assures me.

The procession begins.

Down one flight of stairs.

Down another.

Onto the lawn.

"Let's sing somethin' sad. You know, somethin' 'propriate for the funeral," Lenny says, and they begin to hum Mendelssohn's *Wedding March*. The harmonica and the pail-drum accompany.

71

"Where do you want to bury him?" I ask.

"Where the grass is high," I hear.

"Okay. Come on, fellers, I got a spot," Timmy says.

"No, let's put him next to the old hamster so he won't be so lonely," Phil says.

They search for the spot. Nobody finds it.

"Oh, you dumb jerks, it's 'cause you didn't put no sign on him. How in the hell you 'spect to find him with no sign on him, you motherfuckers?" Lenny curses.

I sit and watch. A fistfight breaks out over a rock to be put on the grave.

"Hey, fellers, here's a spot and a rock." Jeffry saves the day.

The procession stops there.

The kids like the spot.

They dig a hole with their hands, and put the box in.

"Okay. Now everybody put seven handfuls of earth in the grave," Jimmy says.

"Okay. Come on. Next. Next. 1-2-3-4-5-6-7. Next. 1-2-3-4-5-6-7. Next. 1-2-3-4-5-6-7. Next. 1-2-3-4-5-6-7. Next. 1-2-3-4-5-6-7. Next. 1-2-3-4-5-6-7. Next. 1-2-3-4-5-6-7. Next. 1-2-3-4-5-6-7. Next. 1-2-3-4-5-6-7."

Jeffry comes running with a pail half-filled with sand. "Hey, don't you bury him yet. I got here somethin' beautiful. Beautiful sand. Special." Jeffry pours the sand on the grave. The boys surround the grave with rocks. Donny brings some flowers which he has just gathered and sticks them into the sand on top of the grave. Timmy gently puts in the monument.

Lenny sees the Star of David that somebody put on the monument. "Hey, what's that? A Jewish hamster?" he yells out, belligerently.

"Sure, you wanna make somethin' out of it?" Jimmy, red in the face, puts up his fists.

"It's okay with me." Lenny shrugs.

"Quiet, I'm gonna make a sermon," Jimmy says. He stands motionless. Everyone is quiet. Not a word is said, either by the sermonizer or by the mourners. The quiet lasts a few minutes. One child brings over a wooden box. "That's for everybody who wants to visit the grave, so he can rest a while."

Mat: "Teach, how do you like the grave?"

I bend down and read the inscription on the monument: "Here lies Tiny the hamster of Katy Kill kids. Died October 30, 1952.

"It's truly a beautiful funeral.

"Okay, fellers. Now let's go picking tomatoes," I said. "Got the baskets or extra shirts or something to carry them in?"

"Sure!" exclaims Jeffry. "The pail! Oh, shit! We buried the hamster in the box. We could've carried tomatoes in it."

"But when are we gonna visit the hamster?" Jimmy insists.

"Yeah. We got to every day," the kids whimper.

"Okay," I say, "every day."

And we went picking tomatoes for our country fair. But they did not want another hamster yet.

It was different with the big boys. I neither anticipated nor understood what I got. It was a shock.

At 12:30 in the afternoon, I went to pick them up—at line-up—as usual. Against the red brick wall of the gym building they waited for me as usual—eleven of them. Against the geometric pattern of the brick they stood, their bodies making their own strange design, with their grotesquely exaggerated posturing of defiant independence. Together, and yet separate.

Tall, ominous, frightening, the boys loomed before me. Each taking on the appearance of his own crime. Each taking on the appearance of his own label. It was standing between me and them.

"Hi," I said, as usual, ignoring that something, the "it" between us. "Put your cigarettes out and let's go" (to the classroom I meant).

They do not move—unusual.

And then, "So your morning class killed our hamster," Joe says. Slowly, deliberately, enunciating each word clearly. Each fell separately, cold and sharp, like strokes of an ax.

I make a face. The joke isn't funny, it is distasteful. I turn to go to the classroom. No one moves.

"It is your morning class that done it, Mira," Art

73

starts out, calmly. "It is Jeffry. Your nice little Jeffry," the voice gets higher. "He always kills animals, that's why he pets them so hard." Something new now creeps into Art's voice. Something old-new. "I'll kill him. Whoever done it, I'm gonna kill him." His voice is hoarse now. And the old-new quality of it makes my throat feel tight.

Is this all real? is my thought. Impossible. But no one moves.

"Who? Who killed him? Come on, fellas! Let's get him!" Buddy jumps up and down, itching for action, like a puppet ready to strike as soon as the string is pulled.

It is real. My friends are enemies now. They seem hysterical, and yet deliberate. I stand flabbergasted. I try to reach out across the abyss.

"Nobody killed the hamster. The hamster just died," I say, reaching out my hand toward them, physically trying to bridge the gap between us.

"Oh, yeah? If they didn't kill him, she must have done it."

"She killed him! Yeah!"

"Yeah!"

"You killed him."

I cannot believe my ears. Billy's pimply face is very close to mine as he points his finger at me. The accusation falls like a stone in a well. It echoes inside me, all around me. I am afraid. I become part of their nightmare. They are making me part of their nightmare, and my fear helps them to do so.

I must get them into the classroom. Somehow this thought and my determination make me more secure. The four walls; within the four walls I am king. I must get there. I begin to walk. Now they follow me. In the grumblings, I hear, "If they didn't do it, she must have."

Up one flight of stairs.

Up the other. A flight of stairs is so long.

I have to shake this picture out of my brain. It comes again. The same as at line-up. No longer my boys, I can see only their crimes.

Art is from Chicago. He is in for beating women. How many? I never wanted to know.

Buddy and his grandmother. Did he kill her or just hurt her, or just wish her to be dead? Suddenly it makes a difference.

Billy set fire to his house. His father and mother burned up in it.

Big Bob, he likes to write and add columns, long columns of figures. He had to kill his brother. He was still adding.

Adam. Adam couldn't hurt anyone. He was too disjointed, too "retarded" to do anything. Until the day when he becomes "jointed." One day he will. When will the jointedness come? When he is sure he won't be hurt? Or in order to hurt?

And Joe. I can't remember his crime. My Joe.

Enough.

We are in the classroom. The four walls give me limits. I am assured of myself. The nightmare is gone. I am in control. They all sense it; they all get into their seats automatically.

Little Justin joins the group. In his constant state of excitement, twirling and jumping, he picks up the thread. "Who? Where is it? Who killed it? Let's look for it. Maybe he ain't dead. Maybe he's hiding." And with that special immunity little Justin enjoys as the mascot of the big boys, he begins his search by crawling under the desks.

"He is dead," I say. "We buried him this morning."

"How do you know when a hamster is dead?" Art asks, in anguish that looks like disdain. "Maybe he's just asleep for the winter, you know."

Justin rekindles the hidden hope.

I say, "You mean hibernate," hoping to calm the rising excitement.

"Okay, okay!" Artie yells. "Whatever you call it, and anyhow what do you know about hamsters?"

"And where did you get your teaching license, in Macy's bargain basement?" Joe yells.

"She's a witch," Billy says. "Witches have magic, to kill, to bring back to life."

I say, "Look, fellows, I know what you are talking about, and I know it hurts. But this animal doesn't

75

hibernate. When an animal hibernates, it looks as if it is dead, but it isn't. It is asleep for the winter. But this one wasn't. He was cold. He smelled. His heart didn't beat. He was stiff." I was trying to hold them.

Art lets out a shriek. Right out of his guts. Then covers his pain: "You go to hell! You don't know nothin' and you probably done it." And then, "I'll kill that morning class of yours. Your nice little brats."

And then again, "Anyhow, how do you know he is dead?"

I say, "If you doubt it, we can go and look at him again."

Joe, surprised, says, "Okay, let's dig him up."

Brave excitement all over the place.

"Yeah."

"Okay."

"Okay."

"Yes."

"Sure."

They lurch out of their seats, and we all go down. We get to the burial place in no time. The kids tear up the carefully built grave.

"See. Those sons of bitches, they even made him a grave, those bastards."

"And he ain't even dead," Art says, stubbornly.

"Look at that. First they kill him, and then they bury him," Joe yells out.

"Look at the bathtards. Who told them to make that grave?" Buddy lisps.

And they gently take the hamster out of the box. Art and Joe both look over the animal carefully. It is quiet all around. Suddenly, Artie looks around with an expression of fierce determination on his face, lifts up the dead hamster so that each kid can see it better, and then lays it down into the first outstretched palm. The kids are strangely quiet—the hysteria is gone. The hamster is passed on from hand to hand, until the circle is completed. Everyone held it once.

I get a funny feeling down in my stomach.

Joe comes over to me and says, "Sorry, Teach, we

was rude before. We didn't mean it. Thanks for digging up the hamster."

I relax. But not for long. It's still strangely quiet.

Then Artie says, "The hamster was killed. His neck is broken."

He parts the hamster's lips and I notice that the animal's teeth are bashed in. I look closer and I see its eyes bulge. The air is hard to breathe. My knees are full of nothing.

"Okay, Teach, now you just take yourself a nice long smoke, then get a drink of water. In other words, get lost for ten minutes. And when you get back, we'll know who done it," Artie says, in a businesslike voice.

Joe explains to me, "We'll have a Kangaroo Court."

I say, "What's that?"

Joe answers, mockingly, "That's when you beat the guy over the head till he tells you he done it."

"First bury the hamster and make sure the grave looks nice," I say.

Artie parts with the hamster, reluctantly. It is reburied, and we all go up to class.

"We'll find out who killed him, don't you worry, Teach," Joe assures me on the way up.

"And you ain't gonna recognize the fuckin' bastard, neither," Billy adds, laughing.

"Oh, no you don't, fellows, not unless I'm around," I say.

"If you don't let us, we'll just do it in the cottage, later on," Artie says, matter-of-factly.

I know he is right. And I know I must avoid that.

"You can have your trial," I say. "And we will all find out how it happened. But it'll be a real trial, with a judge, a jury, a prosecutor, and a lawyer for the defense."

And I hope and pray.

To my astonishment, Joe says, "Okay, but you ain't in it."

I have caught their imagination. Suddenly their cry of vengeance sees the need for a semblance of justice, or, at best, a pathetic imitation of it.

"And we'll have a Bible, too," Joe continues. "And witnesses."

"Like a real court."

"And we're gonna ask Jeffry, too. You hear?"

I say, "Okay, but why just Jeffry? After all, you ought to ask the whole morning class."

"Huh?" Billy asks, caught up in the excitement of it all.

Hoping to divert them from the lynching feeling against one to a more rational search for justice against many, I continue: "And I'll send out passes, one at a time, so you get them out of their classroom. And you call them to the witness stand one at a time."

"Okay. You gonna do it, ain't you? Or you kiddin'?" Art looks at me unbelievingly.

"She better, ha ha," Billy laughs, unpleasantly.

Joe: "I am the judge. Art, you be the watchamacallit, the one who says you done it."

Me: "Prosecutor."

Adam: "Billy and I'll be the witnesses."

Paul: "I'll be the witness, too. No, I'll be the lawyer."

Buddy: "And me?"

Me: "You take notes, court stenographer, you know."

Buddy: "Okay."

Adam: "I want to be the judge."

Me: "Okay. You'll have your turn."

Ronnie: "I don't want to be nothin'."

Joe: "You'll be the court audience, and you got to take the stand. Maybe you done it. And you, Simon, too."

Simon: "I wasn't in class then."

Art: "So what, who the hell knows? Maybe you got in somehow and killed him."

Justin, whining: "And I wanna testify."

"Sure, sure. You bet you will, you little bastard," Artie assures Justin affectionately. And ruffles the hair of the small boy. The boy who loved Justin most, protected him most unselfishly, was Artie. The leader of this group. Art and Justin had become inseparable. Justin looked up to the bigger boy, admired him, worshipped him, and listened to him. In Art's heart, Justin was as precious as the hamster.

Me: "Everybody else has a job. Couldn't I just be the defense for the accused and kind of keep order in case the judge needs some help? Come on, fellows, it'll be awful boring for me."

"Okay. He's sure gonna need a lawyer," Simon says. Billy adds, "When we find him, we'll kill him."

"You bet we will," Art says. "A poor little critter, the motherfucker. Jesus Christ, I'm just going to crush the bastard!"

The atmosphere is tense once again in the classroom. The boys look at each other suspiciously. I arrange the desks. It is safest to keep busy.

Joe is the judge. He sits in front. The jury sits on the side. The prosecutor sits separately. And we have a witness stand. It is quiet in the classroom.

Joe takes the dictionary. "This is the Bible and you gonna swear on it, just like in court, and if anyone lies, God's gonna punish you," he says, menacingly, and he believes every word of it.

"Okay. Court come to order." Joe pounds the desk with his fist. I give him a mallet to pound with.

Joe: "Paul is first."

Paul gets to the stand.

"Raise your hand. And you swear to tell nothin' but the truth, so help me, God?"

Joe turns to me and whispers, "What hand does he raise?"

I say, "Right."

Joe screams, "What's the matter with you, you fuckin' bastard. Don't you know you s'pposed to raise your right hand?"

Paul: "I am."

Joe: "Oh, okay. You killed the hamster, we know it."

Paul: "I wasn't in school Friday, just got in from New York today."

Artie jumps up, grabs Paul by the throat. "I'm gonna choke it out of you, if you don't tell it by yourself," and proceeds to choke him.

"Hey, cut it out! No choking! This is a court! Joe,

what kind of judge are you?" I yell, enraged. "You just ask questions and keep order! You don't accuse. You don't tell him he done it. You listen to him. And Art! Do you want a fair trial or don't you? I thought we had a real court."

The kids are taken aback by my rage. Paul is let alone.

"Do you fellows want a fair trial or don't you?"

Joe, angrily: "Well, it is fair. That's how the judge acted when I was in court."

Me: "That's too bad. Did you like it?"

Joe: "Go to hell."

Joe raps the mallet. "Court comes to order. I renounce you . . . hey, Mira, how you say it?"

"Pronounce."

"I pronounce you not guilty. No evidence. Next, Simon."

Simon gets onto the stand, raises his right hand, swears on the Bible.

Joe, red in the face, shaking Simon: "You done it, Simon. Come on, you bastard. O, 'scuse me. What the hell did you do with the fuckin' hamster? Did you kill it or not?"

Simon: "No."

Art jumps in. "When did you see it last?"

Simon: "Friday, about three, before we all went to recess."

Art: "Did you touch it?"

Simon: "No."

Art: "Did you see anybody touch it?"

Simon: "No."

Joe: "Where was he when you saw him last?"

Simon: "On Art's desk."

Everyone looks at Artie.

"Hell, you pricks know he was settin' there while I was doing my 'rithmetic," Art says. "You know he always did that." He seems fed up with this waste of time.

"Okay," says Joe. "Art, you next."

Art gets on the stand.

Joe: "Swear on the Bible."

Artie swears.

"Where did you see him last?"

Art: "When I put him in the cage."

Joe: "What time?"

Art: "About three."

Joe: "Did you touch him?"

Art: "Sure. He was settin' on my desk like usual, and then he was creepin' under my shirt."

Joe: "And then."

Art: "Then he was creepin' up my leg, under my pants."

Joe: "Where was he after that?"

Art: "Back on the desk, and then Mira made me put him in the cage 'cause I was readin' to her. That witch. And the hamster was climbing over the book."

Joe: "See anybody handle him after that?"

Art: "No. Maybe Sonny. But it's Jeffry who killed him!"

Me: "If you handled him at three o'clock, Art, and at four you fellows saw him in the cage, right?"

"Right," I hear an answer.

"It was Friday. You were the only kids in the classroom all afternoon. Right?" I continued.

"Right," the answer came.

"Then there was the weekend. And I've got the key to the classroom. You haven't. Jeffry is in the morning class so he could not see the hamster after 11:45 Friday. Right?"

"Right."

"The next time Jeffry was in this classroom was this morning, and the hamster was dead and the windows were locked from inside. Bring Jeffry in," I said.

Jeffry comes in.

He waltzes in, this pretty little child of eight who looks more like a cuddly puppy dog than a boy. Hat askew, hands in pockets, whistling a tune. Giving himself bravado. Grins at me. Jeffry is most comfortable with animals. He loves them so. But the rumor among the kids is that eventually he kills them.

The trial continues.

The tension rises. Fists clench.

Joe: "Jeffry, you better tell the truth."

Jeffry: "And if not?"

Joe: "You get the shit beaten out of you."

Billy: "It is the Bible you swearin' on."

Jeffry: "Oh, okay."

Joe: "When did you see the hamster last?"

Jeffry: "This mornin', when I buried him."

Joe: "I mean alive."

Jeffry: "Why didn't ya say so? Friday about eleven."

Art screams, "What did you do with him? Come on. We know you done him in."

Jeffry, cool as a cucumber: "I chased him."

Art: "And then you killed him!"

Jeffry: "No. I caught him and put him in the cage, and then you killed him, in the afternoon."

Art jumps up, grabs Jeffry by the throat.

Me: "Look, Art. If you played with him at three o'clock, how could Jeffry have killed him at eleven in the morning that same day?"

Art, embarrassed: "Okay, okay, okay, just checkin'." Sits down.

Joe, the judge, whose usual feelings for fair play have got the better of him, spits out, "You dumb bastard!" to Art, while at the same time he puts a reassuring hand on his friend's shoulder. Joe becomes one with the role he is playing.

Joe: "Okay, Jeffry, go back to class. So far, not guilty."

There is angry grumbling in the classroom. Dissatisfaction. The judge is not pleased.

"So far not guilty," Joe repeats. "But we'll call you again, Jeffry. Buddy, you next."

Buddy swears.

"Look, honeth, Joe, I didn't touch him," he says, in fear. Then his face takes on a crafty look and he continues, "But I know who done it." And he whispers in Joe's ear.

Joe: "Okay, Ronnie next."

I am caught up in the trial completely. The rotten informer, I think, his best friend Ronnie.

Ronnie: "I didn't see the hamster. I didn't touch it and I'm not interested," in his slow deliberate way.

Art: "You wanna get the crap beaten out of you?"

Joe: "I hear you killed the hamster, Ronnie."

Ronnie: "Go to hell," very slowly. "It's sheer nonsense. I don't bother with hamsters."

Joe: "Did you or didn't you?" losing patience with the deliberation in Ronnie's voice.

Ronnie: "Of course not."

Art: "Can't you see he's too busy with that fuckin' number writin' of his? He's even too dumb to hurt the hamster."

Joe: "Okay. Not guilty."

Justin: "Hey, what about me? I wanna go on the witness stand."

Art: "Forget it. Adam is next."

Adam: "I swear I killed him, then burned him, and anyhow I want to be the judge now."

Me: "Adam's turn to be judge."

Joe: "Okay, Adam, let's see. What you gonna do?"

Adam giggles. "What shall I say? Who wants to be judge anyhow?"

Joe: "What did I tell you? See, you didn't do nothin'. That's Adam!"

Justin: "I wanna testify. I wanna testify."

Art smiles down at him and shushes him. Art seldom smiles—he smiles when he loves.

There is a commotion in the back of the room. Bodies are scrambling all over the floor, picking up papers, tiny pieces of paper. They are notes. Billy reads one of them aloud: "I killed the hamster, but I am scared to admit." The spelling is atrocious. Everyone is puzzled and angry all over again. The pulse of the courtroom is faster. There is heated discussion as to who wrote the note. Suddenly, Buddy runs across the room, very pale and shaking, gets on the witness stand, and with all his courage summoned lisps out: "Honeth, fellowth, I done it. I wath juth dethperate."

Art: "Get him quick. He done it."

Buddy: "Yeah," relieved, "I thwear I twithted hith neck off."

Me: "Buddy, this is no joke."

Buddy: "I ain't jokin'. I done it. Come on, fellowth, beat me up. I done it."

Nobody moves.

"Anyhow, I wanna get beat up. Come on, all of you. You yeller or thomethin'?"

Everybody lunges.

Joe, the judge says, "Oh, don't bother with him, he's screwy."

Art: "No, he confessed. Come on, fellas, we gonna get him."

Me: "Art, use your head. First Buddy says Ronnie did it. Then he spreads notes all over the place. Then he tells you he did it. Then he says, 'Anyhow, I wanna get beat up.' Just think for a minute, fellows."

Joe: "Sure. He just wants a beatin'. You fellas are just fallin' right into his trap."

Art, utterly discouraged, but not spent. "Yeah, I guess it's just one of them screwy things."

Buddy, whining dejectedly: "I done it, fellowth, honeth I done it."

Joe: "Shut up, you dumb jerk. That's enough out of you."

"I wanna testify, I wanna testify." The melodic chant of Justin is heard again. "I wanna testify, I wanna testify." He darts from one end of the room to the other. With his angelic face and clear blue eyes, he moves about with infinite grace. Like a dancer. With palms upturned, legs bent at the knees, he sways from side to side, hardly touching the ground, swift, fluid, and yet at the same time angular, jagged. Yet it is not the movement that strikes one, but the incongruity, the insanity one so clearly senses, which permeates the very being of this child.

"I wanna testify, I wanna testify."

I turn to the child.

Artie, accompanied by Joe, jumps over the desks to me and whispers, "It's no good, Mira, whatever you're thinkin'. He's real sick. He belongs to K.K.* or Belle-vue. He shouldn't be upset. He's just a little kid."

Justin is crying now: "I wanna testify, I wanna testify. You all did. I want to, now. What's the matter, ain't I important enough or somepin'?"

Me: "Okay, Justin." And I whisper to Art, "You've got to let him testify, too, but go easy on him, boys."

Joe: "Okay, Justin next. Swear."

Justin is delighted. He raises his right hand and swears solemnly. "Now ask me all the questions," he prompts.

Joe, routinely: "When did you see the hamster last?"

Justin: "Oh, Joe, about three thirty, after recess."

Joe: "Did you play with him or something?"

Justin: "Yeah. I had him on my desk."

Art: "Then you put him in the cage, right?"

He is trying to get it over with.

Justin: "No. That I did later."

Art: "Whaddaya mean?"

Justin: "First he fell on the ground."

Joe, nervously: "Jus, how did you play with him?"

Justin: "I was huggin' him."

Art, excitedly: "How? How?"

Justin: "With my fingers."

Art: "Where did you squeeze him?"

Justin: "Around his head."

Art: "And how did his face look when you squeezed him? Did his eyes bulge or somethin'?"

"Yeah," Justin replies, completely unaware of the implication, overwhelmed with his importance.

Joe: "Did his head fall on the side or somethin'?"

Justin: "Yeah. And then he fell on the floor. And then I picked him up, careful 'cause he was restin', and put him in his cage."

The room is silent. The veins on Artie's neck look as if they could come right out through the skin.

Justin: "What's the matter with all of youse?"

Artie whispers to me, "Teach. Send him out. Quick."

* K.K.—is a house for the sickest children at Katy Kill Falls.

Me: "Justin, run over to the office and get me some paper."

Justin goes, and hell breaks loose around me.

"You know what that means?" Artie shrieks. "Justin killed him. Only he don't know it."

I am just as bewildered, and I turn to them for help. "Remember what you told me, guys. He is very ill, he doesn't know what he's doing."

Joe: "That's right, you guys. He is real sick. We can't punish him. He'll go crazy."

Billy, perplexed: "And you can't tell him that he done it, neither, 'cause then he'll go crazy for sure."

"That's right," I said.

"Oh, my God. What am I gonna do?" Artie stares into space.

I wait, motionless. I look at all of them, especially Artie. Time is running out. Justin will be back any minute.

Then it comes. Artie says, desperately, "You just can't punish him. And you can't tell him neither. What are we gonna do?"

Everyone is suddenly acutely aware of Artie's tragedy.

Joe: "Let's just all stare at him for one minute. Whaddaya say, Art?"

I, in terror of having to make a choice between Justin's and Artie's sanity, turn again to the boys for help. "But remember what you told me. You can't let him know he did it. You cannot punish him."

Artie, pale and tense, through his clenched teeth, says: "Leave it to us, Mira."

Me: "Okay, guys. I trust you." And I hear a ring of truth in my voice. But then I start praying.

Justin walks in. He has a box of cookies in his hand which he stole meanwhile from the dining room. Everyone rushes at him, fighting for the cookies. Justin gives them out in an orderly manner. Each boy gets one. When the cookies are gone, Joe says, "Justin, sit down."

The child sits down. Each kid gets into his chair. It is very quiet. While sitting in it, each kid takes hold of his chair and moves it closer to Justin. They form a circle around the child. Together, in utter silence, they move their chairs with their bodies on them, closer to Justin. In unison. In silence. As if they are one body and Justin is in the middle. The silence gets louder. They move closer, closer. They all stare at Justin. Justin stares back at them. They move closer, silently, staring at Justin. Justin looks down at his shoes, searching. The silence gets louder. Closer, closer. Never taking their eyes off the child. Terror has a sound. Here it is the heartbeat. Mine and Justin's. And the chairs go on getting closer and closer and closer. Until there is almost no room left between them and Justin. I look on, petrified, as if hypnotized, moving my chairless body in their rhythm.

Justin yells out, "What's the matter with you all?"

No one answers. They move closer. Suddenly, Justin jumps up in the tiny space left to him, gives a blood-curdling scream, and runs out of the classroom.

I shout to Artie, "Remember what you told me!"

Artie looks at me. No, through me.

"Art, I trust you," rips itself out of my guts.

And after the deed, the thought: Art has to choose. Life or death. Sickness or health. Sanity or insanity. For himself, for Justin.

Art runs out of the room. A minute passes, maybe two. Two are an eternity. To us an eternity. No one moves. Everyone understands the stakes. But Art will have to make the choice. They do not interfere. But we all live, die, live, die, for Art, for Justin, for ourselves.

Art returns with his arm around Justin. Justin is weeping.

"I know it was nothin'. I knew you guys was just kiddin'. But it was so horrible," he is saying, between sobs.

"Sure, sure, Justin. We was just kiddin', and you take it all serious! Nice kid, Justin." Art rumples Justin's golden curls, and Justin looks up at him, through his tears, with eyes full of trust. But you can't see Art's neck for his veins.

I put my hand out to Artie, but it isn't taken. I know he has to finish solving this all for himself.

That evening Arthur Schurtz ran away from Katy Kill Falls. Next afternoon, the police brought him back to school.

"What happened?" I asked him.

"I just got lost," Art said. We smiled at each other.

He had walked all through the night.

His face was pale, drawn, but at peace.

"You must be hungry," I said. "You didn't eat the whole evening, the whole night, and the whole morning. For a guy like you, that must be awful."

Artie smiled. "Yeah," he said.

I gave him a pass to the kitchen. "Fill him up," it said. And Joe, the chef, told me that Art ate ten eggs, six bars of cream cheese, two quarts of milk, and a loaf of bread.

Art took, after giving so much and giving up so much. It takes a lot out of you to grow up.

They did not get another hamster.

Three months later, Justin hanged himself.

THE GIRLS

"Hush, little baby, don't say a word.
Mama's gonna buy you a mocking bird."

The girls up at Katy Kill are very beautiful. That is, past the makeup, past the grimaces, past the defense.

Carla, the sixteen-year-old murderess, the gangster's moll, who threw the bodies of people she helped kill out of running cars. Carla, the Spanish Jewess, with eyes full of tears, full of love, full of loneliness, so rich with honey and sweet tenderness. The gangster's moll, with a mouth that stubbornly belied the cruel outlines of the lipstick. The sensuous yet delicate mouth of half-child, half-woman, slightly open in awe and surprise at the world. Carla, the cruel one.

Annie, the seventeen-year-old leader of a gang of prostitutes. A mother forced to give up her newborn child. Annie, who always struck me as a wild cornflower swaying gracefully among the golden wheat, who drove people like a herd of cattle. Annie, with eyes so full of pencil, so full of mascara, so artfully made up that even upon careful examination you still looked into the eyes of a rattler. But when a child was around, a change would come over her. Her body would take on the ample, giving form of a magnificent woman with a bottomless compassion. The endless sensitivity of a woman, and an almost holy bereavement would change this girl into a mother who still grieved for the loss of her child.

Mary, the mute one. Gray, massive like a boulder and just as impenetrable.

A boulder precariously balanced. Ready to crush all in its path.

She couldn't talk. She wouldn't talk.

Some say she saw her mother and father and brother killed. Some say she did it. No one will ever know, unless Mary speaks.

And, too, there were Patty and Sally and Bonny and Cybelle and Molly.

During a summer, I was asked to "take over" some of the girls. The institution's approach to the treatment of their disturbed adolescents was then undergoing a change. And I was the symbol of this change. Being the first young female teacher brought in by the director (against the better judgment of the powers-that-were and most of the staff), with some innovations and a nonpunitive approach, I was in contrast to the other few females on the staff—the middle-aged prison matrons who until then were inhabiting the place. And so, along with this change, the girls' program was being reorganized, and from a male institution, Katy Kill was changing rapidly into a co-educational one. I was to work with the older girls, sixteen-, seventeen-, and eighteen-year-olds. I knew how rough these girls could be. I knew some of their histories—they were frightening. I remember the director asking me how I would feel about working with such a group, and I remember my own almost instinctual recoil. I remember my cool and haughty, self-satisfied reply: "But I work only with boys. I do not care to work with girls." And to his persistent "Why?" I replied, "I do not care to look deeply into the soul of another woman." And his answer, "You will never be really a woman yourself until you can look deeply into another woman."

My haughtiness was gone. Yes, I did not care to look deeply into another woman. I knew why. Like them, I had been hurt into the depths of my femininity. Like them, I carried the hurt and rage and pride inside of me. But I denied it, while they acted it out. And they would know it. To them, I would not be able to deny it, as I had been doing to myself.

At first, the girls and I got along "great." We were cool, detached, and, what's worse, courteous. It was obvious that we were waiting each other out, I biding my time, they, theirs. I felt as if I had all the strikes against me. My own fears were great. Then, too, I wasn't old enough to be their mother. We had to meet as sisters, and they were going to show me how frighteningly sisters-under-the-skin we all were. And I knew it, and waited terrified for this revelation.

I was also their competitor for the boys, since I worked with the bigger boys who were their boyfriends and contemporaries and with whom I was rather successful. The point had been made that one didn't have to be rough, tough, and ready to be admired by these boys, and this they couldn't stand, since they themselves didn't know yet how to be this way. They were caged in; I was free. They had all the bad breaks; I had gotten off easy.

The waiting ended soon enough.

A fight broke out between two of the girls in an isolated bathroom. I walked into the middle of it. One was violently hitting the other, while the rest egged them on. A few more minutes and they were digging under each other's nails and pulling out eyelashes. I insisted that they stop. The obvious thing happened. Enemies became friends, and all converged upon me. I am terrified of physical violence. The sight of all these hands going after me made me back up against the wall, and whatever feeling of self was left within me quickly dissolved in terror. Suddenly, I heard a calm voice say, "I know all these tricks. I've seen women fight in greater desperation than you. You don't know what women can do when they fight for their lives. Your nail and eyelash gimmicks are nothing in comparison." The voice was mine, but I hardly recognized the words. The girls receded. We both won. Somehow we were more equal. In spite of my politeness, I would fight. I, too, knew about not having all the breaks.

The first hurdle over, we became closer and they could even begin to talk to me. Some facts became clear. Eighteen girls lived there among 160 boys. No program was set up to suit their needs. They were used, abused, and brutalized, both by the kids and by the staff.

They had no identity, often no name. They were referred to as "the whores." And treated as such. They were beaten, cursed, spat upon, neglected, seduced, overpowered, and at times raped. They were in a men's institution—a men's world. Treated as an adjunct. A heap of garbage.

They were surrounded by men teachers and men correction officers. Whatever women staff were there were tough, bitter, hardened, sadistic, ugly old women, who themselves became caricatures of the brutal male correction officer.

I wanted desperately to show the girls that they were human beings, just as the boys were. To be respected by others and by themselves. That they could do work as the boys could. And that at the same time they were women, separate and different. To be respected and recognized as such, for it and because of it.

Our activities took on a different direction. We worked mostly physically, but always my idea behind it was to recognize and accept their femininity. I was going to show them that I respected the woman in them and the human being that is a woman, so that they could learn to do so too. They were going to have an identity, their *own* identity.

I was a teacher, yes. I was to teach them to read and write and other academic subjects. But it was nonsense. They were strong, raging, volatile, violent, energetic teen-age girls, entrapped in a corrective institution that was "worse than a jail."

They needed to move, to do. And to do for themselves, not for others. To do things that would recognize and answer their own needs, not those of the institution or of the boys. They were important; their needs were important.

So with this goal in mind, the girls and I set up a program together. A great deal of physical activity was planned. The girls had no place where they could get together with the boys. So we built fireplaces out of brick and cement, cut down trees, and made tables and benches in order to set up an outdoor entertainment area where the girls could have cookout parties and entertain the boys openly rather than sneakily in the bushes.

We also helped build a beauty parlor, which we painted in "soft, lovely colors." There the girls could enjoy making themselves prettier for their dates on "campus," just like any other teenagers, without the disapproval and connotation of whoring.

I got them a beautician teacher, who taught them how to use makeup and hairstyling so they could not only improve their appearance rather than make themselves look grotesque (without love), but also use these skills later on as a profession.

We also made jewelry together, knitted stoles for ourselves, cooked out together, and all along talked, talked, talked, getting closer and closer and closer to each other, with a beginning of trust. A beginning.

I was an enigma to them. We built together, we painted together, we talked together about personal and intimate things. They saw me cut down a tree and mix concrete, use hammers and saws, and at the same time still be a woman. They were bewildered by this combination, by the fact that one can use strength and yet not be brutal, that one can be vulnerable or even helpless and not need to defend it by cruelty.

But the trust was beginning. I came to the feeling it was time to take a chance on the trust by celebrating the "finishing of the knitting of the stoles."

I suggested we go to a show in the next town.

It was inconceivable for the girls at Katy Kill to go "off grounds," outside the institution, except when they "took off," which means when they ran away. And so after countless dire predictions by my fellow workers and the administration (except for the few who trusted me), "They'll run away the minute you leave the grounds," or, "They'll kill you if you get in their way, or each other if *they* get in the way," we drove off in our best finery, all wearing the white stoles we had made, to see the show.

Of course it was walking on a tightrope. I knew that and so did the girls. Neither I nor the girls were certain that they would come back. I believed they would, and I desperately wanted to trust them and wanted them to trust me—that much they knew. Yet I also knew that the girls needed to "scratch my surface" and at the same time feared what they would "find under the surface," that it would belie the outside. That need was very strong. I knew that they'd have to chance it and find out; but I hoped it wouldn't be this time. They all knew I was risking my reputation, my job, and the trust put into me, and so, any hope of changing their program if they ran away.

We drove off to see the show.

It was a good show. At the theater, the girls kept walking in and out throughout the whole performance —either to get candies or to go to the bathroom. Mostly, however, to enjoy their freedom and to test it, and me with it. I tried not to show my fear. Toward the end of the show, I sensed a tension among them and noticed that they were passing around a note to each other. My impulse was to count them. I restrained myself.

When the lights went on, Annie said, "Two of the girls are missing." She searched my face, saw that the desolation in it somehow reflected her own, and through clenched teeth whispered, "Don't worry. I'll find them."

The rest of us went into the station wagon and waited. A few eternal minutes later, Annie and the two missing girls appeared. I was too spent to be happy, and I was watched too closely for reaction. For a long while we drove in silence, smoking, and outwaiting the tension.

Suddenly, there was a shriek. I looked around and

saw that Annie had the car's red-hot cigarette lighter smack on one of the runaway's hands.

"That's for breaking faith," she said.

"A torch never taught anybody anything," I said.

We could smell the burning flesh.

We "kept faith." The price was high. The trip was hailed a success and the few people who bet on us won. But I wondered "what price glory?" The girls had shown that they could be trusted, that with an honest relationship they could begin to change their picture of themselves and their world. But what was most important to me was that these girls who wanted so desperately to believe but were so hopelessly afraid of believing could begin to have some faith in me.

Yes, I knew it was only a beginning—a rather lopsided one. I knew that only the surface was scratched. And I wondered how far we all have to go to become human.

After that, there were many other trips, but only one that answered my question.

One hot day the girls decided to take me on a trip. It was to be a treat, an outdoor restaurant, "French style" —Hot Dog Joe, their favorite spot whenever they "took off from Katy Kill."

The day was beautiful, the spirit free. We all decided to walk the 2 or 3 miles. We were all dressed in dungarees, some of us in work boots, all in gay-colored shirts. As we walked through the fields, we picked flowers and put them in our hair. The sun kissed us all equally and we all liked each other well. We sang songs and laughed and felt good. The seed of trust was sown between us. The warmth helped it grow.

After a while, we got to the highway, where we walked single file by the edge. We noticed a cop on a motorcycle close by. The girls waved to him, and we walked on. A few minutes later, there were two cops on motorcycles. Again the girls waved. It was a rare and proud thing for them to walk freely "off grounds" and not need to run from a cop for fear he'd catch them and cart them back to Katy Kill or to jail. This time, the cops waved back and stopped their sirens. The girls felt important and thrilled.

"Where are you all going?" one of them asked.

"To town," Carla answered him, gaily.

"What you gonna do there?" he continued, smiling.

"Eat hot dogs and ice cream," I told him.

The girls delightedly invited him to come along. Such friendly conversations with policemen were not the usual thing for them.

"And how come you are alone?" the other cop asked.

"Oh, no. We are with our teacher," Annie said, surprised, in a most dignified manner.

"And which one of you girls is your teacher?" he inquired.

"She." Bonny pointed to me, pleased with the policeman's joke.

"Aha," he said. With that, he turned to me, looked at me with disbelief, and asked, "So where are you going, teacher?"

"To Hot Dog Joe," I told him.

The two cops saluted, and then drove away. We continued on our merry way.

Hot Dog Joe was all that it had promised to be. We had a great time, a wonderful and gay time. We sat there timelessly, inhaling the free air, gorging ourselves on hot dogs and Cokes and ice cream and cakes, and marveling at the number of police sirens in the vicinity.

Then it was time to go.

Satisfied and content, we left the "café" and fell right into the arms of the police.

"Could we give you a lift, girls?" a cop asked.

"No, thanks, we'd rather walk." I told him it was a lovely day.

The police car followed us for a while; it was a nuisance. We decided to ignore it, suspecting the cops to be "on the make." Suddenly, a paddy wagon appeared out of nowhere. The door opened up right before us, and a cop yelled out roughly, "Okay, girls, get in. We're giving you a ride. Where the hell do you think you're going?"

"To Katy Kill Falls, if it's any of your affair," I said angrily, "and we do not care to ride with you."

In a flash, there were eight cops surrounding us, their night sticks out, their faces full of rage. They looked menacing.

The girls stared in disbelief.

"The cops think Mira is one of us," one of them whispered. "Can you beat that?"

My fury at that point had no limit. I felt only for the girls, remembered what it was like to have a stigma, to be always guilty unless proven innocent, to be haunted, hunted down like an animal. Because of what?

I remembered once more what a horror being different can be, how one hates the difference, and what an insult this can be.

"Of course I'm one of you," I said. And I was ready to fight with them unto death.

The girls had no time for hurt. They were too absorbed with my reaction. They had to protect the uninitiated. This was no longer an insult against their human dignity, against their innocence. They had more now. They were above it. It was as if suddenly I became the symbol, the embodiment of their long-ago repressed, forgotten innocence, of their dignity, their hurt, and their helplessness in all its purity. I was all that was sullied in them, tramped on, and they weren't going to let it happen to me, to them all over again. And unknowingly, through protecting me, they protected and recaptured some of their own lost innocence.

To them, it was more simple. They had to protect me in my stupidity versus the stupidity of the policemen. And they knew the score.

Carla got me by the elbow, and said, calmly, "Now, climb in, Mira. We don't want trouble and we don't want to see you beaten up. It ain't worth it."

Like a wave, all the girls plunged into the paddy wagon, sweeping me along with them. I was too angry for that. I jumped back out, refusing to allow the cops to humiliate us like that.

One cop grabbed me and threw me violently kicking and screaming into the van, spitting out after me, "Get

97

in there, you filthy fuckin' bitch!" Then he proceeded to malign the girls with the usual: "Those fuckin' whores! How do you like them? A teacher! Ha! That's a new one."

They continued the abuse, trying to intimidate us with threats of various punishments and abuse, once they got us into jail.

For a while we all sat very quietly in the wagon, exhausted and spent from the experience. Some of the girls seemed bewildered, some astonished. But all looked as if a heavy weight had been lifted off them.

After a while we began kidding, and we all broke into songs.

Then one cop turned to me and asked, pointedly, sarcastically, "If you were really going to Katy Kill, which way should we drive you?"

I innocently showed him the shortcut through the field. The one the girls had told me about.

He laughed, and said to the other cop, "This just shows you. Now I know she ain't no teacher. The only ones who use the shortcut are the runaway girls." Then, viciously, "Only, this time you didn't make it. Ha!"

Then he asked me, "Since when do they have young women teachers at Katy Kill Falls? You should have made up a better story."

We all burst out laughing.

"All men are created equal" kept ringing in my ears. Freedom, equality. The girls got an inkling of both on this trip. Yes, under the skin we were sisters. We were equal. Their stigma didn't stick out all over them. I could be mistaken for them and they could be mistaken for me.

The cops brought us to the police station and booked us and put us in jail. Then they proceeded to notify Katy Kill Falls that they had caught eight of their runaway girls, and unless the girls were picked up, they'd have to spend the night in jail. Katy Kill in return notified them that they had caught seven of their girls on an authorized trip with their teacher. And, they added, the police better quickly bring them back to the institution.

We arrived at Katy Kill in style, in a paddy wagon, with motorcycle escort. In front, a police car, another one in back following us, and the sirens going full blast. All of Katy Kill was awaiting us. The administration tried very hard to keep from laughing. I've never seen so many red-faced policemen. I'd very seldom seen before what I now found in my girls' faces. They'd discovered some more faith, some more love, and a happiness. The trip was a success.

Next day, a big bouquet of flowers arrived at Katy Kill, with a card signed by the Chief and his eight policemen. It was addressed to me and to the seven girls, mentioning each one of us by name. The girls and I felt victorious. They had dared to scratch my surface and their own and under it had found equality.

CHAIM

"And God created man in His own image."

Once upon a time, there was a little boy called Chaim. . . .

They came from the camps—Treblinka, Dachau, Auschwitz, or Buchenwald, no matter . . . A sea of bodies with souls seared, scorched, and in some, extinguished forever.

They married in a repatriation camp, had a child, and came to the United States of America. The promised land—no camps, no persecutions, peace.

It was too late for peace. The mark of Cain was on their foreheads. The brand of the conqueror on their arms.

And forever the conqueror remained within them.

In the United States, they had another baby; a warm, lovely baby. They named him Chaim—"Life"—for their dead ones. A free baby, in a free country, where freedom rings.

The baby, Chaim, grew and developed normally. He was loving and lovable. But when he was four and a half years old, his world stopped, and he "forgot" almost all that he had learned during those four and a half years, and arrived upon a different truth, a truth of his own. Chaim stopped his speech, his hearing, his urine control, his bowel control, his ability to eat with a utensil, his ability to dress, his capacity to understand what was said to him; and turned into a primeval, wild animal with one aim in life, to attack in order to defend himself.

He had many ways to achieve this end. When spoken to, Chaim cocked his head to one side, closed one eye, and looked at you out of the corner of his other eye, with a look of cunning, fear, mistrust, and murderous hate, and then he walked away as if he had withered you with this one look and turned you into nonexistence so that he wouldn't have to fear you any more.

At other times, when approached he let out a heinous shriek, and then attacked you with force and strength and rage and fierceness.

In 1963, I saw the child and took him into Blueberry. Chaim's father, Stefan, was short and squat, of tremendous strength, with arms that could lift boulders, with hands that could tear the world apart. He was a bagel maker—proud of his work, proud of his union, proud of his strength. He wore a short-sleeved shirt and you could see his concentration camp number very clearly.

He was a Polish Jew. When he said, "Mira," he rolled his "r" the way only Poles do it, with rage and vengeance and a fierce pride. I wondered where the pride came from. Perhaps from his experience in the woods of Poland with the partisans. His face was flat with burning eyes, yet at the same time extinguished: brute strength, no soul, no compassion, no love, no tenderness, except at times when, for a split second, his guard would fall, as our eyes met, and I could see his soul's nakedness. Then he would just say, "You know," and he would add, "there." "There" was Poland, as we were both from "there." But "there" was also the place where all-encompassing human pain, humiliation, reprisals, betrayals, hates, revenge, loves, and courage lived and died, or perhaps were strangled, slowly, deliberately, torturously. To him, it was a camp in Poland; to me, it was "another" place; to you, it is "the other." But when one naked human howl meets another, the walls are gone and "there" is just there; a place within oneself where no one ventures of his own free will. He must be forced, either through compassion for another, or because of pain and terror. One is rooted there, forever.

He did not talk much, and when you asked him about his child, he would look down at his arm where the number was branded and, as if a fearful oath had sealed his lips, would say nothing.

Chaim's mother was short and buxom, with blue eyes and blond hair. She looked Polish by birth, Jewish through experience. Her name was Channa. Too stout, with eyes too placid, she "wanted to do well," "to seem fine." Yet, there was something in Channa that intruded and forced her "to seem not fine."

"To seem fine," and "do well" meant not to remember the horrors and the pain that she had lived through, which drove her to become what she was now.

No matter how she tried, they would break through and she would remember. Then, suddenly, she would lose the trend of thought and start to speak about her needs, her terror, and her nightmares. Her eyes would lose their placidity and dart wildly from object to object, and one could sense how much she needed to flee, what an effort it was for her to remain still, with what superhuman power she did not flee.

Then, just as suddenly, she would forget once more, and tell about the shock treatments she demanded and got at least once a year, how "great" she felt after each one, and about "the pills," how good they made her feel.

Whenever I focused the conversation on Chaim, and asked her directly what happened, who cast the spell and made him give up life, she, like her husband, would look down at the brand upon her arm and become silent. The numbers then would swell up in my mind's eye; each one spelled another horror too heinous to be mentioned. Then they all just melted into one big word: silence. It was forever there; silence.

Channa was in an extermination camp for four and a half years, part of the time in the death house. What she did the rest of the time she would not talk about.

She was young and pretty, a well-developed adolescent when they took her. She remembers being liberated in May 1945, but she cannot remember when she was incarcerated. Everyone else in Channa's family died in the camp.

Stefan fought with the partisans for a while before they took him to camp, where he spent almost five years. Everyone else in Stefan's family also died in camp.

Stefan and Channa met in a Displaced Persons camp after they were liberated, and they married there.

I remember being told that Stefan had to examine the remains of the Jews as they were spat out of the oven in order to collect the gold teeth—or was it shoes? —or maybe that was Channa's job.

Stefan and Channa had three children. Joseph was born while they were still being repatriated. Chaim was born nine years later in the United States; and then came Bernie.

Joseph was an angry, sensitive, guilt-ridden adolescent when I first saw him. Bernie was a chubby, self-indulgent five-year-old.

Chaim was different. Chaim was a caged-in, terrified, terrifying animal. Chaim was Channa's baby, Channa's soul. He was her fierce hate and her self-pity, her degradation and her terror. He was her self-indulgence and her pain. He was her love, whatever strange forms it took, and her destruction. He was her life and he was her death. Chaim was all that had been done to Channa, and all that Channa wished to do in return. Chaim and Channa: he was her legacy. Thus, autonomy for Chaim was an impossibility. He was Channa's extension.

The last words Chaim spoke, before he stopped speaking, were: "They are knocking on the walls. They are coming to murder me."

When Chaim misbehaved, Channa put his hand on the burning gas range. When she pulled him by the hand, she broke it. To teach him a lesson, she would scald his hand in boiling water. When annoyed, she would sink her teeth into his flesh, and when angry, she would beat him with a buckled belt. When he touched his penis, she would threaten to bite it off. When he masturbated, she told him she would cut it off. He slept in her room until he was nine years old, he slept in her bed until he was eight.

She often complained, "He can touch my breasts, do things to me like a man, but then he soils himself like a baby." When he was eight, Channa told me, "I only live for Chaim." Then she would add that Chaim was her "unhappiness," her "sorrow," and her "pain."

Every May, Channa needed shock treatments, and sometimes also in September.

We would find Channa walking in the middle of the night in her nightgown in Prospect Park. We would see her clawing her clothes off her back, screaming in incomprehensible agony.

During the night, she relived her extermination camp experiences. She yelled, she fought off attackers, she screamed vile curses, she whimpered pleas until finally, she was beaten down, until finally, she succumbed to the conquerors. She fought for her life in her bed with Chaim beside her.

During the day, like an automaton, she went about her chores, moving in and out of consciousness with Chaim always there beside her. She did not allow him to go outside to play with other children until he was three and a half years old.

In 1963, Chaim was brought to me. I remember that a friend of Channa's, another ex-concentration camp inmate, brought her little girl along. What I can never forget is that the friend kept her daughter tied up with ropes in the trunk of her car, like a hog for slaughter, "because she is so wild."

Chaim was wilder. Coming into the room, he leaped for my face, scratching and clawing before I realized what was happening. Then Chaim smiled. It was a grimace, the most horrifying smile I ever saw, because it was so vacant, so cold, so unsmiling, inhuman, dehumanized, and so dehumanizing. Then Chaim moved away. His whole expression changed. He closed one eye, cocked his head, and looking out of the open eye —as if I were some monster to be conquered, with terror, with cunning and curiosity—searched for a new way to "kill me." Having sized me up, he shot an arm forward, his fist tightly clenched except for the pinky and the index finger, which pointed sharply at me: the "magic" method.

Like lightning, he jumped and shoved these two fingers in my eyes, screaming so fiercely that I knew it was to frighten me away. But since that did not frighten me away, nor did it kill me, Chaim ran to the other end of the room and back to my end of the room, then started to run in circles. Round and round, round and round, howling.

The fierceness too strong, the pain too great to be anything else but human; and yet, the fierceness was too strong and the pain too great to be human.

Suddenly his mood changed again, and in an instant, he had stripped and stood before me naked, his head shaven clean and white, his body shaped like a woman. He defecated and urinated all over the floor, angry and defenseless.

All this transpired without one word from Chaim, as there was neither speech nor hearing nor, seemingly, any comprehension in this child.

Chaim was seven years old, and I accepted him for treatment at Blueberry. The name of the person I assigned to work with Chaim was Ron, a teacher-therapist I could constantly supervise. Ron was very patient, very understanding, very devoted, terribly involved, with an ability to be sustained by very little gratification from the child.

For four years, Chaim and Ron worked together year round—at our day school, at our residential camp, at Ron's house or at Chaim's house, or at our residence, very often day and night.

Ron nursed Chaim through sleepless nights. Ron nursed Chaim through foodless days, through violent rages, through hopeless pain and bottomless despair, but to no avail. The hurt was too deep.

Working with Chaim during the first year was unbelievably difficult because his provocations were endless. Chaim trusted no one, but he trusted Ron even less. Chaim wailed incessantly. Chaim shrieked incessantly. Chaim screamed incessantly. He could not be touched, unless he initiated it, and then he either scratched Ron or poked him in the eyes or beat him with his fists. Afraid of being held, afraid of lying down, afraid of being lifted or stopped in his constant motion, his safety seemed in motion as if the moment he stopped running he'd be completely destroyed. He was forever darting from one end of the room to the other like a caged-in animal trying the confines of his cage, running away yet unable to leave. His food intake was very selective, as he "was afraid of being poisoned." His brother said he couldn't be bathed, for he "was afraid of water flooding his nasal cavities."

Chaim defecated and urinated in his pants and wallowed in it. He constantly undressed and threw his clothing out the window, as if throwing himself away.

Every so often, he'd try to put his tongue into Ron's mouth. There was a great deal of rubbing against things, and against Ron, in a seeming attempt at masturbation, but I think it was most likely an attempt to feel himself alive.

Chaim only smiled when another child was hurt.

Whenever Chaim was taken to a store, he stole something—gum, cigarettes, hand lotion. He had an obsession with cigarettes. He had to touch them, hold them, have them lit for him by Ron.

His one-eye way of looking at people developed a variation. He would spread his fingers and look through them to see but not be seen.

Mirrors held a tremendous fascination for him. He

would look into them and make terrible faces at himself, as if trying to frighten himself or the other self that he might have seen there. His first words that year were said to the boy in the mirror: "Boy," and then, "Die boy," and then, "Bad boy," and finally, "Die bad boy."

Often, Chaim would turn his head and look as if he were listening intently to someone; not to any one of us, for he would shut us out and not hear us, but to some other voices speaking only to him, and to be heard only by him.

Chaim's nights were sleepless. They were either spent in his mother's bed shrieking, or running around wailing.

After a year, Chaim improved. He became attached to a baby doll and made an attempt to show us what he wanted. He rocked the doll gently, but then stuck a cigarette in her mouth. Next, he became attached to a toy stove, but he kept shoving the doll into the stove. For a while, the stove was the focal point of Chaim's day. He guarded it. He ate on it. He tried to get in it.

Chaim's next word was related to the stove. First, the word was "Naki," then "Nati," and finally, "Nazi." Was Chaim guarding the stoves of the camps so that no one could put him inside? Or was he going to make sure that no one burned his hand or put it in boiling water? Was he perhaps doing the same job his mother did at the camp?

March 2—Chaim drank some milk for the first time. He learned to relax when riding in a car. But he also began to beat other children with a strap, showing us what was being done to him at home. We stopped Chaim's parents from doing this.

March 6—Chaim continued to communicate with Ron through scratches, bites, blows, and punches.

April 7—Chaim did an "E" during school work. After four days of continuous teaching by Ron, Chaim nestled it in Ron's "E" like this: ⊏⋿. It seemed like the beginning of some trust or a rebirth.

April 12—Chaim knew some twenty words and phrases and repeated them voluntarily all on his own: kill, die, gun, bad boy, ugly boy, baby, die bad baby, die baby, die doll, doll, die boy, murderers, nazi, no, burn, mirror, go, go away, milk, Ron.

In the spring, we began to prepare Chaim to go away to our summer camp. This was to be his first separation from his mother. It took us a while to realize that to Chaim, "camp" meant concentration camp, and the very mention of the word put him into a frightful panic. He would roll on the floor until he knocked himself unconscious, and thus die before being killed.

Camp for Chaim was a brutal, but at the same time, a beneficial experience. During the first week of camp, he refused to eat or drink. He stayed up all night, making frightening sounds and frightening faces, as if trying to overcome his own terror by terrorizing the others. He defecated constantly, and would not leave Ron alone for an instant.

Ron, who spent night after night with Chaim, believed that Chaim was not only expressing his own terror, but was imitating his mother. His mother's nights must have been like this.

But Chaim's terrors and his mother's were the same. When a child and his mother are so fused together that neither knows where one ends and the other begins, there is no imitation. There is only identification—and the horror of one becomes the horror of the other.

Toward the end of the summer, Chaim went in the water and played. His fear diminished. Chaim began to sleep. He allowed Ron to lift him, carry him about. He ate better and his speech increased to around twenty-five words. "Good" and "good baby" and "good boy" were among his new phrases. Chaim looked better, more like a boy. His face developed some expression. At times, he even lost his vacant look. His hair grew. We found that he had lovely blond curls, which he enjoyed touching and looking at.

September 15—In the fall, Chaim returned home and for a while his camp improvement continued. He slept well. He did not attack his family. His shrieking diminished and he used language.

October 17—However, a month after being back, Chaim went back to his old ways, only this time with greater violence than ever before. Now, Chaim would hit his mother instead of only biting her. He hid his clothes, threw silverware out the window, grabbed people and tore their clothes off, ripped pillowcases off pillows and scattered the feathers all over. Whatever could be taken apart, Chaim took apart, and hid the many pieces so that they could never be found and fixed: lamps, toasters, locks, doorknobs, irons, radios. Chaim bit and scratched and shrieked at anyone who entered the house.

In school, it was the same. Chaim's first month back showed progress, then, as if all Chaim's hopes collapsed and total terror took over, a new dimension was added to his agony—a search, a desperate search for something. Whenever Chaim saw a car, he would grab Ron's hand and run after the car. We began to suspect that Chaim might be searching for something he thought he had lost at Blueberry; perhaps his self.

Our hunch proved correct. Ron drove Chaim to camp, where the child immediately ran to his cabin, checked his room and all the surroundings, sat on his bed, and then with a sigh of complete relief got into the car and returned to New York.

After finding his lost self, Chaim seemed to find peace again. His violence diminished, his speech increased, and he slept better.

But Chaim's peace was again short-lived.

January 7—Ron reported that "weekends at home are impossible. His tantrums increase, he bites ferociously, takes chunks out of his mother and brothers, either with his teeth or his fingernails. Again, wakes up every night, screaming."

Soon, Chaim's mother began to speak of "putting Chaim away." She "can't stand her own suffering, nor her family's suffering, nor Chaim's suffering. She is also afraid of Chaim physically, as he is bigger and stronger."

January 20—Ron moved into Chaim's house in the

hope of better controlling the child, in the hope of saving him from a state hospital.

In school, Chaim lost his bowel control again; very violent temper tantrums; constant physical attacks on other children and on Ron; constant shrieking; constant throwing things out of windows; constant wailing; "violence beyond my control," said Ron.

January 25—"Lately Chaim, when angry, lets out a half scream and half growl and takes a swipe at you like a cat," said Ron. And his brother Joseph: "He makes sounds like a wounded lion." Whenever he walked in the street now, he stopped every few steps to press his index finger against the ground or the fence or the wall, made a frightening grimace, and screamed, tensing his whole body so that he appeared, almost, to take off from the ground. People ran in terror. We stopped taking him outside. He also guarded his stove incessantly. Wouldn't let anyone touch it, and would leave it only for shortest times.

February 2—A little relaxation of his terror. His bowel control had improved again. He only let go of it when angry at Ron. Slept better. He had again resumed his mirror fascination, and seemed to be looking into it for longer times.

Ron continued to stay at Chaim's home.

March 12—Once, Chaim said the word "love," but afterwards, for days on end he yelled: "kill," and "murderers."

April 19—Chaim's speech improved and he began to play with other children, sometimes imitating their actions, sometimes competing with them. Coupled with this was an increase in his violence.

April 29—Chaim began to "strangle cups" and objects with his hands. He grabbed Ron's head, screaming, "Break, break," and all the time growling fiercely. Then in a violent panic, he rolled on the ground shrieking, beating his head on the floor while also trying to strangle himself, and yelled, "Kill, kill, kill!" Nothing, but nothing, would quiet him down. Finally, when he did quiet down, stripping himself, he stood before us naked, straight as an arrow, beyond fear, beyond humanity, repeating one word over and over again, "Ugly, ugly, ugly."

The night before, we had found Chaim's mother naked in the park, running across the lawns yelling, "Kill, kill, kill!" The next morning, she was hospitalized and given shock treatment. It seemed that Chaim and his mother were one. When she died, he died. In this matter, Chaim had no choice.

In Chaim, as in his mother, nakedness was an attempt to stay alive. Perhaps, by stripping and submitting, his mother somehow saved her life. Chaim, too, by his stripping and submitting to the fate, made his mother conscious of his body, and thus caused her to save his life rather than kill him.

The next spring, we began to prepare Chaim for camp again. His reaction was the same as the year before. "They're going to kill me!" he shrieked. Chaim stopped his speech, his sleep, his bowel control, his eating, and once again, he acted like a primitive beast.

During the first week of camp, Chaim tried desperately to obliterate himself—to die before he got killed. He began to devour himself, feeding off his own flesh, eating chunks out of his lips, his tongue, and the insides of his cheeks. He refused all food and drink. He began to run away. His running seemed in response to the voices he heard. One could see him hear the voices. One could see him listening to them attentively, and then, as if in response to the command he heard, one would see him run. The aim was always self-destruction. He ran into the road under cars; he ran into the pool where he could drown; or he ran into the woods where he would be lost.

His nights, again, were filled with horrors, and the only way that Chaim could get some rest from them was either by Ron sleeping in bed with him, or Ron walking with him through the night.

In the midst of all this destruction, the child learned how to dress himself, and how to say new phrases. Incessantly he would repeat: "I want to go home," "No camp," "Take me away in the car," "Take me home, car keys," "Take me away from camp in the car, quick," and, "I got you the car keys."

After two weeks, Chaim relaxed and began to believe Ron's assertion that he was not in concentration camp; that nothing horrible would happen to him at camp; that he would not be killed; that his separation from his mother would not mean that Chaim would die.

Chaim began to show Ron what he needed. He kept pointing to a picture of a baby bottle, and to pictures of infants. He also became very involved with and interested in my little boy, Kivie, who was then two years old.

Chaim needed, wanted, and was ready to become a baby. Ron responded to the infant in the child, and became the mother. He nursed Chaim; he fed Chaim; he took care of Chaim. Chaim would only accept milk, and only from Ron, and only in a baby bottle. Chaim insisted on being carried by Ron, swung by Ron, lifted by Ron, and rocked by Ron. Ron could not escape. He couldn't get out of the child's sight at all. If he did, the child wailed desperately.

Chaim's demands on Ron were so overwhelming, for the child's "starvation" was so complete, that at times Ron became terrified that he would be engulfed by Chaim. Chaim lived, breathed, and ate Ron. Ron said, "When Chaim permits himself to be a baby, his needs are endless. I often feel when I'm so close to him, he could and would eat me up."

Ron finally took a halfday off. Chaim threw his bottle away and became enraged.

The nursing period lasted about a month, till one day Chaim gave up the bottle and in his new role as a boy, asked for food. He played with other children. His vocabulary again increased. He called his new friends by their proper names; he ate different kinds of food; he began to swim and to sleep through the night. He grew to like Gretchen—another child at the camp whom he played with, relied upon, talked to, and to whom he came for protection.

This lasted for a month; then came the last week of camp, and with it Chaim's terror and the withdrawal.

113

He refused to eat anything. His body changed. He became tight and shriveled and pale. His anger grew ferocious, intimidating. He began to look like his mother. As he got close to Ron during the nursing period, so now he began to pull away from Ron, psychically and physically. He found a belt which he put around his body and that quieted him, as if the belt would keep him in one piece, and no part of him would be left behind, like last summer.

On September 12, 1965, when Chaim's parents arrived to pick him up, he wore the belt around his hips. Calmly, he walked into the car and gave up everything he had gained at camp.

September 14—Two days later, at the day school in the city, Chaim withdrew completely. He stood by the stove and guarded it; forever. Every now and then he stuffed his doll into his stove. A few days later, Ron took Chaim from his home, because Chaim's mother could not cope with him. She herself had broken down again and was about to go to the hospital. And so Chaim began to live with Ron in Ron's home.

September 17—"Chaim was like a keg of dynamite ready to explode. His intensity was unbearable. He could neither relax nor stand still for a moment.

"He was forever in motion. Forever busy. Running and jumping, instead of walking, and screaming incessantly. His intensity was almost unbearable. At first, I thought he was trying to drive me crazy by being so absolutely 'insane' himself. But then it occurred to me that he had become his mother more actively, and was going insane like she had. He began washing dishes and cleaning like she had, thinking that by becoming her, Chaim would save her from her insanity and from going to the hospital"—Ron.

In October, Chaim's parents spoke again of sending him to a state hospital. His mother's last breakdown and hospitalization had made her angrier with the child and herself. By now, we ourselves began to wonder what to do with Chaim. The one-to-one relationship Ron had had with the child—the intensity of which Ron finally couldn't bear—didn't work. The one-to-two relationship, when we included another child, Jimmy, in the group to save Ron from Chaim's intensity and Chaim from Ron's, again didn't work. And including Gretchen, Chaim's favorite playmate, in the group didn't work.

Ron's complete involvement over the three years with the child (which finally put him into analysis), watching, feeding, nursing, and nurturing Chaim, didn't work.

Days and nights together, terrors and pains together, trying to give, trying to understand, trying to structure this child's life, did not work. Medications given intermittently—thorazine, Miltown, and so on—didn't work. Each medication, like each psychological approach, worked for a while, and then the child became immune and returned to his original state of being—schizophrenia.

We asked Chaim's parents to give us and the child one more try.

Dr. Loomis, our chief psychiatrist, suggested narcosynthesis: an injection of various chemicals that would create a metabolic reorganization of the child's chemical process in the hope of allowing Chaim to tell us what had happened that one memorable night to make him stop his speech, his life, and turn his world upside down.

How naïve we all were!

Chaim's parents consented. Proper releases were obtained, and on Wednesday afternoon, October 23, 1965, Ron brought Chaim to Dr. Loomis's office.

Two physicians, a heart specialist, a nurse, a social worker, and myself were present. Chaim was examined by the doctors. He was made comfortable and then gently, oh so gently, given sodium pentathol intravenously, and—oh my God, I never want to be a party to anything like that again.

It looked as if the child faced all his horror and was thrown into the infinite abyss of his pain. He became pale, then green, and the eyes sank deep into his skull, as if to hide from what they'd seen. Then he grabbed the mirror which was placed there and began to look into it with his terrifying intensity. I spoke to him. I spoke to him in Polish, in Yiddish, and in German; to no avail. He looked into the mirror and whatever he saw in it was neither pleasant nor friendly. Stark horror appeared on his face. He reeled, fell to the couch, and began to yell at the top of his lungs: "Murderers, murderers, murderers! Kill, kill, kill!" Then he fell into what seemed to me unconsciousness—the kindest state to him.

He got another shot. He rose up like a bull, injured unto death, but with the final desperate fight still in him. He reeled, trying to keep his balance. It was horrible to watch. The expression on his face was total abandonment; a child lost, hopelessly, helplessly lost. Then the rage took over. Reeling and fighting, hitting as if blinded, not aiming at anything: the screams and shrieks and screams again. And then he ran to me, as we were friends, and grabbed me with a plea to save him from that horror that was so clear within his soul. His Horror. He held me and looked for a place to run. But like a caged animal with no place to run, restricted by the cage's bars, he hit at me as if I were the bars, as if when he broke through me he would break into his freedom—freedom from terror, freedom from pain, freedom from want—oblivion. His Oblivion. But, as there was nowhere for Chaim to run, there was no freedom for Chaim. He folded up and collapsed.

We carried the child onto the couch. He awoke and in his half-awakened state, he spoke of murderers and killers. And he spoke about that certain night when his brother Joseph had frightened him; then he spoke my name, and Ron's name, and passed out. Chaim's terror was too much for him.

We stayed with him for hours. Ron took Chaim home with him, and they stayed together for many days, and Chaim talked incessantly of the murderers and how they were going to kill him, and how he was a bad, ugly baby, and how he would be put into a stove and burned. And talked of how the walls were being knocked down so that they could get him, and of how he would die, die, die.

He talked to Ron most, but at times, he spoke to his voices. To them he mainly answered with his, "No, no die," and called them murderers and hid behind Ron for protection against them. Whether it was fear of the narcosynthesis, which could have meant execution to Chaim, that propelled this kind of behavior in him, or actual breakthrough, we did not know; only time could tell.

Dr. Loomis proceeded with the narcosynthesis. Each time our hopes were raised, and each time they were broken.

Second narcosynthesis: afterwards, Chaim withdrew into complete silence. There was no relationship with Ron; no relationship with me, nor with anyone else. Chaim was shapeless and weightless. Like air, he slipped through your fingers and disappeared.

Third narcosynthesis: Chaim showed interest in his stove. He scratched, he bit. No relationship with Ron. No speech.

Fourth narcosynthesis: Chaim was wilder. Still no speech. No sleep.

Fifth narcosynthesis: Held onto his doll. Mouthed doll. Licked doll's mouth, trying to put his tongue in its mouth. Held, protected, and shielded the doll as if from attack. Silence. Insisted on folding clothes and throwing them out the window; guarded his stove.

Narcosynthesis had failed. Another torture had been inflicted on the child; another attack; another murder.

We had watched him see his terror and we had been helpless to protect him against it. Chaim's terror was greater than Chaim; greater than our strength and knowledge to shield him from it.

We were ashamed—ashamed of being witness to the crime, ashamed at our impotence—and horrified. Chaim's terror rendered chemotherapy as impotent as it had rendered psychotherapy.

A thought began to creep in. Perhaps there are children who have incorporated into themselves the absolute need to be dead. For whom the need, command, to be dead, as ordered by their parents, has invaded so great a part of their personality that no matter how much nursing, how much nurturing we give them, this need, this order, this command, defeats us. For the child knows of nothing else.

Anyhow, so it seemed . . .

March 1966—Chaim's parents once more wanted to put him away, forever, in an institution. We were defeated, but we were unwilling to give him up. And once more, we convinced Chaim's parents to give us a last chance.

In utter desperation, we came upon an idea we called survival. We based this idea on our first Blueberry camp experience. Three of us adults and eleven schizophrenic children had set up camp on an unfriendly and remote island. Under rigorous conditions, where often food had to be gathered by all of us, where the older children had to protect the younger, where wilderness, danger, and hunger were a way of life unless we all worked together, both the children and the adults grew. The children made amazing progress. The responsibility they carried, the respect they received, the dignity which they learned, brought about an understanding and a change that we had never seen repeated.

We decided to try this with Chaim.

We had the place: 130 acres of mountainous, stream-ravaged woods, far from our main camp.

There was one problem—staff. We needed two people who could spell each other with Chaim on a twenty-four-hour basis, seven days a week, for seventy days. Two people who were secure enough to withstand the isolation; strong enough physically to withstand the child's attacks, and to protect him against outside dangers; strong enough emotionally to withstand the seduction of the child's terror and pain and the cruelty of his self-destructiveness; compassionate enough to work with an unworkable child; and patient enough to be able to wait and wait endlessly, and still not give up.

We found two men. One was Sadik, a Turk, who

had two Ph.D. degrees, one in physics, one in engineering. Studying history and philosophy were his pastimes. He had hunted and camped in Turkey and in the Caribbean since he was a boy. He was headstrong, brilliant, creative, sensitive, with no time left for wasting.

The other man was Yasser, an Arab from Syria who was taking his degree in English Renaissance literature. Yasser had lived most of his life in the desert. He was brilliant, gentle, contemplative, and he knew how to wait.

Together these three—the Turkish conqueror, the Arab poet, and the Jewish kid from the concentration camp—were put on top of a mountain and told to survive.

They had a tent, a water bag, axes, basic tools, sleeping bags, clothes, and food. After trying three different mountains, they found themselves the right mountain with the most convenient water supply, the least mosquitoes, the fewest raccoons. Here they dug a latrine, built a cable connecting them to the camp where food and medical supplies were sent to them, and settled down to the long hot summer of surviving.

Being Eastern, Yasser and Sadik set up for themselves different time schedules than we are used to, schedules dictated more by their needs than our labor laws, and proceeded to take turns with the child. Sometimes they worked for twelve hours; sometimes for sixty-two hours. Sometimes they worked for five days and nights at a stretch, depending upon their endurance and upon Chaim's needs. They refused to allow their work to be interrupted.

Chaim, suddenly exposed to these two different, untiring, and highly disciplined personalities, was at a complete loss. These men demanded cooperation and could wait. They had their own conception of time. They knew pain and terror, but were neither subdued by it, nor intimidated by it, nor indulged in it. To them the law of survival was unquestionable, and that of life and death elemental.

The first few days were rough. The child went on a hunger strike. Instead of food, he began to eat the inside of his mouth. He refused drink and he began to dehydrate dangerously. He soiled himself. He attacked his counselors and he howled all through the day and the night. The two men fought Chaim back when he attacked them. They let him lie in his soiled clothes, and they cooked thick steaks in front of him, and let him starve. Then, after the first week, Chaim opened cans with a can opener. He learned to bathe himself in the stream. He learned to take care of his clothes. He ate. He drank. He lived.

In two weeks, Chaim began to collect wood. He made fires. He cooked his own steaks. In three weeks, Chaim began to use a knife and fork while eating. He learned to use a knife and an ax. He climbed mountains. He operated the cable which brought food up to the mountaintop from the camp below.

In the middle of the summer, he began to ride a bicycle.

I met Chaim and Sadik in the nearby town, 6 miles away, where they had walked. I could not believe my eyes. Chaim looked trim, put together, in command of himself, knapsack on his back, a flask and a knife hanging from his belt, keeping step with the Turk, answering obviously in response to a question and then smiling with pleasure about something that Sadik was saying. And Sadik was a great talker. Later, I saw Chaim sitting cross-legged in the tent in the setting sun, listening to the Arab read him stories from *A Thousand Nights and a Night,* as Yasser called it.

July 3, 1966, Sadik—"The boy's eating his mouth. I offered him food. He ran away. I did not chase him. You do not chase a frightened animal, but wait till he loses his fear and comes to you." July 4, Yasser—"The child was lying in his excrement. I showed him where to wash it. He refused." July 5, Sadik—"The child took steak and wood, showing that he wishes food. I cooked them for him. He ripped it with his teeth like a ravenous hyena. It was his first food." July 9, Yasser—"I washed Chaim's mouth and tongue with the solution. It is still sore where he bit it off. I hope no infection sets in as it looks as if it would." July 15, Sadik—"Chaim used

120

a can opener to open his food, as I refused to do it for him." July 19, Sadik—"Chaim and I took a one-and-a-half-mile hike. We investigated the flora and fauna of the region. He enjoyed it as much as I did. We took along axes and chopped down some dead shrubs. He still is awake all through the night." July 21, Sadik—"Chaim and I built a raft out of saplings which we chopped down. He still runs in circles when he's not busy." July 23, Yasser—"Chaim and I made a fire. I talked to him a lot and told him of my desert. He seemed very interested, but I don't know if it was in the content or in the movement of my lips. We ate our dinner which we cooked. Then we washed his laundry and we watched the raccoons watching us. Chaim was fascinated by the animals." July 27, Sadik—"The raccoons stole our food. I went looking for them saying, 'I will kill them.' A great excitement entered Chaim's face. He joined me and looked ready to kill." July 29, Yasser—"Chaim operates the cable very well. He was the one giving signals today for more food. He likes to lie next to me at night, listening to me talk and tell stories from *A Thousand Nights and a Night*. He makes the fire with me and we are both warm. I wish he could sleep at night." July 30, Yasser—"Chaim has changed since yesterday. He was not quiet and lonely, but communicated with me and sat beside me most of the day. He insisted on my smoking. He went back to walking in circles, only now he did it in a peculiar way and at certain times, that is, when he was desperate and demanding something. Once he pointed to the water and I insisted on his saying the word, 'water.' Then he began moving in circles with signs of anger and crying. Again, he did it when he wanted to go to sleep. I think he's making an effort to say words. I tried to make him say 'smoke,' 'water,' 'meat,' 'woods,' and he tried to say them all. But when I asked him to say 'Daddy' and 'Mommy,' he was furious and refused to say them. Now, I'm going to put the food and drink so he cannot reach them, hoping to force him to ask for them. In the afternoon, he collected wood and put it in the fire pit, brought the gasoline, poured it on the wood, lit the fire and pointed to the meat. Then, taking me by the hand, forced me to put the meat on the fire. When I told him that he must ask for the food before getting it, he started to steal it. I gave him the food after this." August 2, Sadik—"Chaim bathed himself in the stream and did a good job of it. He also swam in a pond we discovered." August 3, Sadik—"I love this strange child who is so much more animal than child. I want to take him with me." August 4, Yasser—"I am very disheartened and very tired. We have only one month left to make him better, but we cannot. It is all so deep rooted. He understands all I say, but then a mask goes over his face and he hears and understands nothing." August 12, Yasser—"Chaim screamed all night long again; this time in his dream, 'Murderers, they're going to kill me!' When I woke him up, he ran away into the night with fear." August 18, Sadik—"We have built a small playground, Chaim and I. We cleared the ground and built some benches. He is a good woodsman, but lazy. We threw knives into the ground for sport. He is a good marksman." August 21, Sadik—"Today, Chaim tried to ride a bike in town, on his own." August 25, Sadik— "Chaim learned how to ride the bike." August 27, Yasser—"Today, Chaim was strange and new to me. He seemed to be living in a world by himself and would not let anyone disturb him. Whenever I tried to talk to him or play with him, he got mad. Most of the day, all he did was sit alone with hardly any motion, gazing at the ground, playing with some branches in his hand. He did not insist on my smoking as usual. He stopped walking in circles; his comprehension seemed slower. He ate well. I took him for a long walk in the woods, and while I was tired, he showed no signs of tiredness." August 30, Sadik—"Chaim, Yasser, and I sat and ate together. This confused Chaim as we do it seldom, for he does not know how to act and who to choose to listen to. He got up and began walking in circles." September 2, Sadik—"Chaim retreated completely for the day. He would neither see me nor hear me." September 6, Yasser—"We met Chaim's parents. It was an unusual experience. They took him home. He exhibited no fear, no anger, no pleasure. What now?"

Sadik decided to continue to work with Chaim in the city. All his doctorates notwithstanding, Chaim was more interesting than any academic study. Sadik, like the rest of us, could not take failure. The compassion and love for this unlovable child and the constant seduction of Chaim's salvation were too much for the Turk. Religiously, he came to the day center. For five days a week, sometimes for seven, Sadik worked with Chaim. He even built his weekends around the child's needs. In spite of this profound involvement, the child began to revert. Although, every now and then, he would still smile with affection at Sadik, Chaim's terror and pain took over again, and outweighed completely the connection between the two. Slowly, and then not so slowly, the child began to lose all that he had won. Again, he growled like an animal. His shrieks and his screams reverberated throughout the building. His violent attacks on everyone else around him were uncontrollable. His aimless walking in circles resumed their dizzying effect. His nights became sleepless again, full of terrors and attempts to get away from his terrors.

He burned more and more doll babies in his oven. His fascination with smoke and smoking again took over, and his coercion of everyone to smoke became unbearable. Chaim's speech disappeared, except for a few phrases: "Murderers," "Kill the baby," "Bad baby," and "They are knocking on the walls," which he repeated over and over, in the sing-song rhythm reminiscent of the chant, "Shma Israel," which the Jews sang before their execution. After saying this, Chaim would suffer a strange loss of gravity which affected only the top half of his body. He would fold over like an orangoutang in captivity, defeated. Grunting and howling, hopping and leaping, arms hanging at his sides, rigid with terror, he ran in hopeless circles, ready to trample and kill, terror etched in his face so deep that it became arrested forever. After a while, he would fall to the ground in a stupor.

Soon Chaim refused to eat and drink, and he began to devour himself.

And finally, he attacked, and attacked, and attacked.

Being a large boy of eleven, and strong as only a cornered animal can be strong, Chaim became a menace at home and at school, and so he was put away; forever, to rot, to vegetate, to die . . .

And it is said, "Let the dead bury their dead."

But if the dead are still alive, who shall bury them? Is it not the legacy of the living?

It is ordained by nature that the child feeds off the mother. But when the mother feeds off the child, it is against nature and it destroys the child. The mother carries the fetus in her womb where the fetus is an integral part of her, where the fetus lives off the mother. When the mother gives birth to the child—when the child comes out of the inside of the mother—with this very fact, the mother begins to give the child his autonomy.

Chaim's mother could not do this. From the depth of her grief, her terror, and her loneliness came her need for Chaim to remain an integral part of her, and so she devoured Chaim.

Day after day, she proceeded to "devour" the child, to incorporate him into herself, and thus to obliterate him. This emotional cannibalism of the mother toward her child cannot and will not let the child grow. Neither can it fulfill the need of the mother, as the child as her sustenance cannot satisfy the "hunger."

By the very nature of this kind of relationship, the child is little more than an extension of the mother. She never sees the child's needs. She never sees his rights. She uses and abuses him with hardly any understanding of what she is doing.

He is her happiness and her unhappiness; her curse and her undoing. He has to breathe her air, eat her food, drink her drink. To give him identity is beyond her capability. If she is persecuted, so is he. If she is killed, so is he, and sometimes in the midst of her rage, she will mistake him for the persecutor or the killer, and kill him.

If she dies, he must die with her, psychologically, but very often, physically.

The child is entrapped in this horrible web and cannot break loose, and there he is finally devoured. He can only live one life: hers. And can only die one death: hers.

SARA

A little girl came into my playroom, looked around in terror, pushed up her sleeve, and with tears in her eyes and determination in her voice said, "Okay, doctor. Give me an injection. I'll cry a little. Then I'll go home. I'll be all finished."

This was Sara.

"I'm not a doctor. I don't give shots. How about a candy?" I asked.

"No, thank you. You really don't have to fool me. I just want to go. So finish," she said with trembling voice, eyes full of tears. She was a determined little girl and her terror was not going to be disappointed.

Then, deciding that I was drawing out the torture, she said, "You are mean."

She settled down and began to cry bitterly. After she had seemingly allowed me to quiet down her fears, she began to look around the room. Resolutely, suspiciously. Neither trusting nor believing me. Just waiting.

She noticed all the toys. And for the first time moved from the one spot in the room to which she had been rooted.

Still rigid with terror she began, haltingly, to touch the toys.

She was a pretty little girl, too small for six, with the grace of a wildflower and the nimbleness of a fawn.

There was an unreality about her sensitive, sensuous little face and her doll-like body which at times gave her the appearance of a wood nymph, while at other times that of an old woman.

Sara was brought to me with a diagnosis of mental retardation. No if's, no but's, no maybe's—the opinion was unanimous. Every physician, every hospital, and every clinic came up with the same diagnosis: "Retardation." The only one who sometimes questioned it was her mother.

"I know she's stupid," Sara's mother told me. "I know she's retarded; but then there are times, and they seem to come out of nowhere, when she's so bright, so wise, so precocious. But it's so fleeting and so elusive. It disappears before you notice it, or can hold onto it. And there she is—stupid Sara—all over again and no one believes me, what I've heard.

"Sara developed normally," she said, "doing everything a bit precociously. But at two and a half years she changed and became impossible. Her brother was born then."

Impossible was the only way her mother could describe her. Impossible was truly the way she was.

Sara hadn't slept through a night since she was two and a half, she hadn't eaten a proper meal since she was two and a half, hadn't gone to the bathroom since she was two and a half, except when she could not hold her eliminations any longer. They would fall out of her or run out of her, wherever she was standing. She hadn't focused her eyes since she was two and a half. She hadn't gone to a window since she was two and a half, nor had she looked in a mirror since she was two and a half, and she had not let her mother out of her sight since she was two and a half. "She always wanted packages," her mother continued, "wrapped, tied packages." And whenever any of these requirements weren't met, which was often, because of the impossibility inherent in the nature of the demands, Sara had terrible rages, terrible screams, terrible tantrums.

Lately she had developed something new, her mother was saying. She stretches out her hand in front of her, looks at it, and has long conversations with it.

When I asked her father if there was anything he could add to this account, he said Yes.

"She's like a leech; no, like a tick; no, a demon. She burrows into you and doesn't let you go. She doesn't let you live. She sucks you dry and then drives you mad by her persistence."

There was a poem in this child, and I wanted to find it. Sara and I began to work together immediately. I did not believe she was retarded. But I felt that she was so frozen in her terror and her agony that she could not move, and therefore appeared retarded.

It was a specific terror, a specific agony, although I did not know what. But there was a singleness of purpose in her, a resoluteness, which made me feel that she had gotten herself organized for one purpose only, to circumvent the deep and unbearable pain that consumed her. She would do anything to escape that pain— to never, never be exposed to it again—and to avoid any of the landmarks which reminded her of it.

But the landmarks were all around her and so many that to walk among them without feeling them was increasingly difficult. In order to avoid them, Sara's world was becoming smaller and smaller, and she was more and more frozen in within it. And the preoccupation with this avoidance and with protecting herself against the terror became greater and greater. There was no choice for the child but to appear limited, retarded.

At the beginning, working with Sara was like walking through a minefield. There was a mine buried under every bush and the field was full of bushes.

Sara and I were forever stepping on the mines; the explosions were endless. And she expressed the explosions through incessant crying, wailing, or raging until she'd become breathless.

If we walked past the window—explosion. If there was a mirror in the room—explosion. If we talked of

Mommy or Daddy—explosion. If I offered her food—explosion. If she saw the bathroom—explosion. If I mentioned sleep—explosion. When I mentioned her brother—explosion. If anyone looked at her—explosion. If she accidentally focused her eyes and looked at anybody—explosion. When you mentioned bowels—explosion. When there was no package—explosion. If the package was wrapped—explosion. If it was unwrapped—explosion . . . And if you asked her why she was exploding—explosion. These were just a few.

And once Sara began her tantrums and once she began to cry, she seemed to forget how to stop. The agony and the isolation in her wail were limitless.

It was impossible for me to help her at the start, for by necessity she froze me in as much as she froze herself in. As she was afraid of physical contact, I could not touch her, and any words that I tried to use to comfort her created just another explosion. They were invariably the wrong words for they would touch on another fear, at the time still unknown to me.

The extent of Sara's isolation was so devastating and her terror was so great that it precluded letting anyone in to give her the security she needed to help her out of her dilemma. So Sara resolved the dilemma for herself. She made herself a friend, a friend she could control completely—her hand.

It was her friend; it was also her enemy, her confidant, and her betrayer; but it was always under Sara's absolute control—and therefore safe.

She had lengthy conversations with her hand, but you could seldom make out more than snatches of what she was saying. "Is it okay?" she'd ask her hand, and the hand invariably would give her the approval or disapproval that she searched for.

The hand could even stop her crying and her rages—"Okay, Sara," it would seem to say, "you've cried enough."

Sara felt so disconnected, so disjointed and scattered, that she truly felt her hand had an autonomy all its own. But at the same time she could only feel complete by having her hand join her. Since she gave part

130

of her own autonomy away to her hand, she needed the hand to complete her own autonomy.

Sara would stretch out her hand before her, look at it intently, with eyes focused, and in deep concentration converse with it for hours on end.

The hand was safer, more predictable, more reassuring than anyone else, including me. It could neither frighten her nor pain her, save by her own command.

Her isolation and her terror forced her to control her world by controlling another part of her body—her eyes.

She was afraid to see. To see what she was seeing and to see again what she must have seen that frightened her into her present state. So she put her eyes out of focus. (The sight was grotesque.) One eyeball would wander off so far into the outer corner of the eye that only the slightest part of it was visible, not merely eliminating the world from its view but hiding itself from the world's view. The other eye would wander off into the opposite direction, but would not run away so far, would not hide itself so much. After all, Sara needed to watch. She had to continuously size up the situation, to see what to eliminate so no harm would come to her. Her eyes reminded me of a ship disappearing behind the horizon, beyond the realm of our vision. We can see it no longer, but we know it is there, and that it sees us.

Sara gave her eyes an autonomy just as she had done to her hand. And she controlled them precisely by giving them autonomy. Yet she was controlled by them, too, and had once had an operation on them to correct them—needlessly, I might add. It did not change them.

Control, control, control. It was this need of hers to control and arrange her life situations so completely that enabled me to help her get better in a comparatively short time.

I saw Sara for over a year, once a week and sometimes twice. I worked with her at Camp Blueberry for ten weeks of summer where I was with her continuously, twenty-four hours a day.

In this relationship of ours I always felt that Sara was my teacher. I never understood how in so short a time she improved. The initiative in Sara's treatment was always Sara's. So was the method and the way. So was the pace. I only loved her and enjoyed her, appreciated her and respected her. And whatever I understood, I shared with her. This resolute, lovely little girl laid down the terms; I followed them. She did the rest.

The second and third week she came to my playroom, she still tried to get me to give her an injection. However, during the fourth week her insistence waned; instead, she threw one of her tantrums. It lasted over three hours. When she finished, she asked me for "a present"—"a package," she told me. "It has to be put in a box, wrapped in paper and tied with a string."

When I complied, she took the "present" under her arm, looked at me with her non-seeing eyes, and left without further ado.

I knew I had made the grade with her.

Literally and figuratively Sara wanted everything in a box, wrapped in paper, tied with a string. A neatly wrapped package. A present. Up until then, nobody's "package," nobody's "present," was good enough. Now mine was.

One of Sara's mother's chief complaints was about the packages.

At all times, she told us, Sara wanted everything wrapped in a package. A spoon that she was to eat with, a sock she was to wear, an apple core she was to throw out. "Wrap it in a package" was her constant demand. "Did you bring me a package?" was her eternal question. "Presents," Sara called it. But no "present" was satisfactory enough. No package ever good enough. So Sara threw tantrums—one continuous tantrum, her mother said.

The fifth time Sara came, she came looking for and determined to get her answer.

"Okay. You are not a doctor. You are Mira," she said to me. "So I am going to be little and you will be my Mommy. You must do what I tell you. You must put me down on the bed."

I did.

"And now cover me. With a blanket."

I did.

"And now I am a tiny weeny baby," she continued, lapsing into baby talk. "Give me a botty."

The artificiality in the situation was quickly gone; the feeling that I was part of a poorly organized stage set disappeared. There was a strange reality; the child, though acting, was really not. She was being. And I followed her commands to the letter, feeling that I was invited into this child's most private and desperate world. I filled a baby bottle with milk and handed it to her, touching her lips with the nipple the way one does with an infant. Sara immediately began to suckle the milk vigorously, every now and then biting and pulling the nipple. When she finished it, she said, "Now burp me. Over the shoulder," she directed. I picked her up and, as one does with an infant, patted her on the back to get a burp. To my amazement, Sara burped.

"And now the baby must go to sleep," she continued. So I laid her down on the bed, again covered her, tucked her in, and began to sing her a Yiddish lullaby which her mother had told me Sara liked.

Sara yawned and rubbed her eyes and fell asleep immediately.

Sara, who never trusted anyone enough to sleep.

She slept for about fifteen minutes. It was a deep sound sleep. Then she woke up, shook the sleep out of her eyes, and said, dropping her baby talk, "Okay. Now Sara will go to the kitchen. I am bigger now. But carry me there because I am not that big yet," she continued. "Put me down in a chair and give me food. Food that is for bigger babies."

I did so.

Sara ate and I ate with her, at her request. "Okay," she said, when she had finished. "Now I am Sara six years old." She jumped off the chair, took a pencil, and drew a picture.

Then she ran out to the waiting room, where her

ever-present mother was patiently waiting for her, and announced, "Okay, now you don't have to wait for me any more. Just bring me here, then go away and when it is time for me to leave, come pick me up."

Her mother was so stunned that she could not move.

"Go," Sara said. "Go already."

Sara, whose demand on her mother's wakeful presence, be it day or night, was incessant, suddenly said "Go."

Sara, who needed to see, feel, and touch her mother at all times, said "Go."

Sara, whose constant need was to be connected to her mother, through words and deeds, said "Go."

However, freedom for her mother lasted only as long as Sara was with me. At all other times the child's terrifying need for total connection with her mother continued.

Sara insisted that her mother always be within her sight. She would not let her mother go, physically or verbally, for her constant fear was that her mother would disappear. "And what might happen then to Mommy? To Sara?" was Sara's rhetorical question. Who knows?

Thus a devouring, leeching, draining of her mother had gone on forever. Twenty-four hours a day, every single day for four years.

Sara asked her mother questions continuously, questions to which the answers were never satisfactory, since they were never the answers that Sara really wanted. Still, she would repeat the questions over and over and over again. To hear the answers, to reassure herself of the sameness of the answers, to keep the connection. (Which gave her some kind of security, consistency, even if the answers were wrong.) But really not wanting those answers at all.

She was forever looking for the one and only answer that nobody had given her yet. That her mother could not give her with words alone. The answer was mainly that her mother's love was there for the child. Strong enough, wise enough to help teach the child to become her own self, in her own right, complete, fulfilled, independent.

Sara must have found some of this answer with me. At the child's demand we continued to act out the play of infant, baby, and child every time she came. For over three months.

We used the same words and the same gestures each time. ("It has to be like that," Sara insisted, "otherwise it will be no good.") And every time before she left, I had to give her "something wrapped." Most of the time she accepted the "present" from me without ado. However, sometimes this routine would get interrupted by a tantrum, or by repetitive questions. The tantrum I'd wait out, as I did not know what would calm it. To the repetitive questions I only had one answer—"That's all. One answer is enough. I don't have to repeat the same thing over and over again. Because you know what I mean." And that would suffice.

After these three months Sara's relationship at home improved. She nagged a bit less and demanded less.

It was then that she began to tackle her bowel problem.

Until the birth of her brother, Sara's toilet training had proceeded normally. However, a few months after he was born, she became incapable of separating herself from her bowel movements. And defecation caused severe temper tantrums and endless weeping spells. She held back her bowel movements for days, often for weeks at a time. There were times when this would extend her stomach so much that she looked absolutely pregnant. Then when the muscles couldn't contain the excrement any longer, it would drop out, wherever she was at the time. This loss was always accompanied by wails, shrieks, and moans—those of fear, pain, and rage.

One almost had a feeling that in addition to her emotional pain over her loss, the physical pain accompanying the loss was as unbearable.

I began then to suspect that not only was Sara afraid that separation from her bowel movement meant a

135

separation or loss of some parts of her body; it also symbolized pregnancy and birth, her mother's pregnancy with her baby brother, whose birth Sara possibly witnessed and which had robbed her of her infancy and her mother's love. Therefore she tried to undo the whole thing. She would be pregnant, but never give birth; there would be no brother, for she would carry him within herself. And by not giving birth, she would never give up to her brother her place in her mother's heart. There was also another possibility. Perhaps she was pregnant with herself, in the hope of becoming reborn and so getting the love that she felt her brother had gained instead of her. However, since birth was such a frightening thing, it was in Sara's mind equated, confused with death. The horror to a little child of witnessing birth itself cannot be overlooked.

Therefore, the bathroom as a word in the vocabulary or as an actual place was an off-limits topic for me and for Sara. And the words "bowel movement" or any reference to them were just as taboo.

Then one day Sara took me by the hand and led me into the bathroom. She sat me on the toilet seat and said, "When you make, does anything happen to you?"

I said, "No, but I feel better."

"Do you flush?"

"Yes," I said.

"And when you flush, are you still there?"

I said, "Yes."

"All of you? You don't flush any part of yourself away?"

I said, "No."

"Do you flush the baby away?" she asked, half hopefully, half terrified.

"There is no baby. It is only waste, food that your body doesn't need any more."

Sara took me off the seat and sat herself down on the toilet seat. She tried. She tried very hard but the fear was still too great. After that, every time she came to me, she tried. Sometimes with a slight degree of success, most often with none.

136

Each time, however, she'd ask me to sit on the toilet to see if anything happened to me.

And then one day her mother called me and told me that Sara had taken a diaper and stretched it out on the bathroom floor. She had moved her bowels in it. After that, she moved her bowels more often and more regularly in the diaper.

Her mother's understanding was remarkable. "I know she is going through her toilet training period," she told me, "which wasn't so good then. Perhaps she also came out in the open with her competition with her brother. And she relived the whole thing. Her problems began when her brother was born. Was it that she thought she lost me when I bore him?"

With me, however, Sara never wanted to use a diaper. She went to the toilet, successful or not, until success became more regular.

Sara was getting better, more acceptable to and accepting of her parents. She was even changing at school. Although her teacher still considered her mentally retarded, she began to take an interest in Sara's "remarkable improvement" and to help her with it. She could not get over the fact that now Sara actually dared to go over to the windows at the school. That Sara even dared to look out of them. She, of course, did not know that it took Sara three months of talking about it to me, three months of consulting her hand about it, three months to build up her courage to look through the windows and not scream.

Summer came and I took Sara to camp with me. It was her first time away from home. Her parents were quite happy to have her away—to have their first full night of sleep, their first meal without packages, their first respite from Sara's control, their first vacation in a number of years. And the knowledge that I would finally get the burden of Sara—her tantrums, her nagging, her controlling, her sleeplessness—added to their pleasure, for they were contemplating "putting Sara away" in some residential institution and were sure that I did not fully appreciate Sara's demands on them when I advised them not to do it. They were quite right.

In camp Sara was quite a little girl—oh, such a terrified little girl!

For the first few days she refused to eat. It wasn't safe. At mealtimes, she would hide under the dining room table and just sit there. Our coaxing did no good. The first couple of days the child actually starved herself. Since the food was not prepared by her mother, it might be poisoned. If it wasn't mother's food—and it couldn't be because Sara was separated from her mother—then Sara had no right to eat, to be, to live.

On the third day Sara again crept under the table, but very close to my chair. I took the food in my hand and lowered it under the table, feeling that if the child was to give in to her hunger (and take the risks entailed by eating), she would not do it openly. She could neither admit to herself nor to the others that she had eaten.

So I held the food under the table and Sara, like a hungry little puppy, would take it out of my hand and eat it. I did the same with milk. But if I looked down, Sara immediately turned away and refused to eat or drink.

After a few days of this sort of behavior, Sara became more daring. Every now and then a little hand would reach out from under the table and find my plate, and the food would disappear as if by magic. After a week or so, Sara crawled out from under the table and sat herself on a chair, looking as if she had never left the table. From then on, Sara ate.

From the moment Sara got to camp, she took the pillow off her bed and began to carry it. Wherever she went, she took it along. She rarely let it out of her sight, nor out of her arms, and, if she left it anywhere for a moment, she'd run back to get it.

Every now and then she carried it in her arms the way one carries a baby. At other times she'd hug it and squeeze it terribly hard with a strange expression on her face—part hate, part delight, and part tremendous energy. She would accompany this with a strange, terrifying squeal.

Sara would not fall asleep without the pillow in her arms. She would not go for a walk without the pillow in her arms. She would not eat without the pillow in her arms, nor would she go to the bathroom without the pillow in her arms. It must have been her brother, herself, her love.

The pillow was in a pillowcase. And the pillowcase became terribly dirty. I wanted to change the case. Sara would not hear of it. It was a difficult struggle since Sara was determined to defend the pillow and its dirty pillowcase against any intruders. Still, somehow, after a while she gave in. "But I will change it," she said, determined. She turned the pillow upside down. Food began to fall out of it.

It was obviously food she had stored up from the day she came to the camp. A jar of peanut butter, a bottle of catsup, leftover bread, some old rolls, lumps of sugar, old cookies, a few candies, a pear, half an apple, a salt shaker, and various other leftovers. A veritable grocery store. When I looked at the child in amazement, she looked right back at me and said, "Didn't you know?"

When I said, "It's the same as with the packages, isn't it?" she said, "Yes."

"Is it the same as with the bowels?" I asked. The child again said, "Yes."

Through the pillow, Sara was "pregnant" again—carrying the baby inside her, the love inside her, the promise of eternity and procreation inside her: good things, things of plenty. She carried them in her pillow, in her packages, in her bowels.

Was the pillow her brother, who stole her security and her mother's love, so that she had to become an infant again in order to survive? Was she carrying him around with her, and her in him—her lost babyhood and her lost giving and protecting mother?

Poor little Sara, always incomplete, never fulfilled. Her inner emptiness was as limitless as loneliness.

Sara had to survive. If there was no food, there was no love, and Sara made sure she had food with her. That way she would never be alone; that way she would always be complete.

She changed the pillowcase and piled all her belongings back into it.

Sara's eyes could see straight, but it happened so seldom and for such short intervals that before you realized it, they were out of focus again, and you thought you'd seen a mirage.

If you got in front of her, quite low, you could see her eyes focusing when she talked to her hand. You would find out then that Sara could keep her eyes quite straight. And there was a simple fact, which was hard to discover since people just didn't get down that low: Sara had beautiful eyes. Often, the trouble in our understanding of others comes because we hardly ever go down, or up, to their level.

Yes, Sara had beautiful eyes, with long, long lashes, dark and thick, like seaweed in the water. I told her so. I told her something else. That when she talked to me, she had to look at me. And if she looked at me, she had to look at me straight, with both eyes. Otherwise I would think that she was avoiding me, that I frightened her. That there was something horrible and frightening to Sara about me. I knew that she didn't look straight at things, I told her, because they frightened her. Because there was something horrible or frightening to Sara about them.

Sara tried. Oh, how she tried! At first, she succeeded best when she was angry. When she really wanted to convince me of something, her eyes straightened, since she knew that otherwise I wouldn't listen. "Mira is not sure that I'm really talking to her if I don't look at her," she explained succinctly and bitterly to her hand.

As time went on, Sara looked more and more directly at the people she was talking to.

I've often wondered what the horror was that this little child was trying not to see. What was the badness or goodness she was trying not to show, through

140

the "mirror of her soul"? What was the fear? The primal scene? The birth of her brother? Was it a thousand other feelings transposed into pictures? And I tried to imagine what the world was like in Sara's eyes.

Packages, packages, packages. Food eaten but mostly stored for later. Everything had to be wrapped in a package. If we wouldn't do it, she did it herself. There was no electricity because Sara had the fuse wrapped and stored for later. No shoe; Sara had it wrapped. No slicing knife; Sara had it packaged. No mercurochrome; Sara had wrapped it. No soap; it was with Sara. No raincoat . . . Try to wrap blueberries in a package and tie it up with a string—or a glass of milk.

If she couldn't make or get the package, Sara threw a magnificent tantrum. Sure, she used it to get her own way. But there was much more to it. There was an urgency, a feeling of life and death in it.

Whatever she saw, she had to acquire, make it her own. She was a compulsive collector. But it was a collection with a price value that was irrelevant. The more objects she had, the more assured she felt. Of what? Take, take, but do not give.

There was a desperation in her need to acquire and a despair if she could not do so. I once saw Sara put on six dresses, one on top of the other (most of them did not belong to her). Then and only then did she consider herself pretty.

Even the food she collected was mostly not out of her plate but out of all the children's plates. If Sara went to pick berries, she had to pick all the berries, everyone's berries. If any berries were left on the bushes, she would not leave until she possessed them all.

How frightfully inadequate this child must have felt within herself, how incomplete unless she had everything of everyone's. There was never enough to make little Sara complete. Never enough love, never enough packages, never enough food, never enough berries. More of more would give her the sort of love she wanted. More of more would guarantee her need to be protected. More of more would take her fears away.

141

More of more would satiate her cravings, her starving for love. Yes. Or would it?

Yes. All of Mama. All of Mira. All of everyone. So she wouldn't have to be afraid of them, of everything. And then the fears, the terrors, and the pain of being so alone and incomplete would go away. If she had everything, she would never disappear. Then she would be she. She would exist. She would not die.

And the badness would go out of her. The evilness would be taken away. She would be good. And she would be able to give up her excrement with ease.

But now, how bad a child she must be, for wanting so much, for needing so much. How awful she must have been to be punished so severely. She did not yet have enough "more" to survive.

It was in camp that her sleeping problem became real to me. Night after night Sara would lie in bed with her eyes wide open, completely awake. Night after night I would sit by her bed, watching her, guarding her, singing to her, trying to give her sleep. If she managed to doze off for a few minutes, she would wake with a start, frightened beyond description, as if witnessing a nightmare. She seemed always to be living in the midst of a nightmare. When I asked what it was that was frightening her so, the answer was always, "I don't know." Then one night when I dozed off from exhaustion, I felt a tugging on my sleeve. Sara looked as pale as if she had seen a ghost, and, in bits and pieces, she began telling me the story.

In her usual way she arranged the stage set.

"You sit over there," she said, "in the corner on a chair, where the light is, so that I can see you and know you are you."

I obeyed her request.

"And then," she began, "there were two people and a lot of arms and a lot of legs. And they were all wiggling. And then Daddy took a knife and hit Mommy with it over and over again. He hit her in her tummy," she continued, gasping for breath. "Then Mommy started to scream and they moved like Petey [an epileptic child] when you have to put a spoon in his mouth, and then she was dead. And maybe he was dead too. No, he was just tired of killing her." Slowly, I came over to the child, against her orders. She didn't even notice, she was so absorbed in reliving the scene. She was soaked through with perspiration; it poured down her face. I took her in my arms. And like a rag doll she let herself be held—lifeless, not responding at all.

Then suddenly she grabbed me around the throat and began to scream. "Mira, I'm afraid; hold me, hold me. Don't let them kill me!"

Then she bored her eyes into mine and looked hard and long as if searching. I felt her relax. "I know you won't let them," she said, and she burrowed her head into my breast and fell blissfully asleep.

She saw. She saw what was murder to her—the primal scene.

Night after night we went through the same actions and words. And sometimes Sara would add, "But if Mommy is dead, how come she is alive?" "Is she alive?" "Is she my Mommy?" "Is she a ghost?" "Will she come and kill me, or will Daddy kill me?"

After some time, Sara finally rid herself of this memory that had haunted her all of her life. And I felt as relieved as the child. There would be sleep now—for both of us.

But no. There was another scene. It all started with a piece of liver. We had it for dinner. Sara could not sleep that night for thinking about that liver. It made her sick to her stomach, she said; it gave her a belly-ache. She asked me to hold her to make her feel better. I did. She seemed hot and cold intermittently and then clammy. Then she began to ooze out words, seemingly meaningless words, in a trancelike manner. "A big belly, liver, blood, killing the baby, killing the Mommy. The baby comes out.

"The baby is covered with blood because the Mommy killed it. The Mommy had blood because the baby killed her. And the liver comes out of the dead Mommy."

Delirium? Maybe the liver was bad and had poisoned

her, I thought. But then it hit me. Sara was describing something she had seen. A birth?

The child was shivering, her teeth chattering as if the temperature were subzero, not a 90-degree summer night. I held her tightly and covered her with blankets while she deliriously repeated the words:

"And then Mommy killed the baby, and now she'll kill me."

Little Sara, lonely Sara. No wonder she lived in so small a world. How terrified she was of everything. Because everything spelled death to her.

After this episode sleeping became a bit easier. But Sara was still terrified of any new sensation. The water, a boat ride, a car ride, a new arrival, still produced in her the fear of her ultimate destruction, and she would defend herself with a tantrum.

There was a boat that delivered mail to the island the camp was on. Every day the boat would come with packages for the children. But not every day with packages for Sara. And every day there was a tantrum. If a package came for Sara, it was never good enough; its contents were never touched, never eaten. Afterwards it was opened, in secret, closed again, hoarded in her pillowcase or trunk for later.

Then one day a package came and Sara did not hoard it. She opened the package in view of everyone and passed around the cookies it contained. She shared it. And then I knew that Sara was a little bit fulfilled, and she needed less.

As time went on, Sara became more and more fulfilled. She looked straight at you with both eyes, at least most of the time. Her tantrums diminished. She went to the toilet with greater ease, and even dared to flush the water after herself without saying, "There goes Sara." Why, she was even heard telling another child who had the same problem that, "Really, there ain't much to it. All you do is squeeze and it is all finished. Then you're nice and free and clean."

She became delighted with the feel of water on her and would spend a great deal of her time in the lake helping me wash the laundry, bathing other children,

144

or playing. She stored less. She began to play with other children and to share with them some of her storage reserves. She even helped me bake a cake for "everybody." She could wait a bit longer for things. The "now, now, now feeling," as one of the children called it, was diminishing. Her intelligence and brightness were more and more evident; they became more and more a part of her. She started "throwing parties," organizing them for herself or for the other children. She began to be more aware and compassionate toward other children's problems. Quite often, I would hear her say to a nonverbal child, "Don't be afraid to talk. It is okay. Nobody's going to hurt you. And you won't hurt nobody either if you talk. So don't be afraid."

And another time to a boy named Lee, who had the same bowel problem as she did, "All you got to do, Lee, is sit down and squeeze. It comes out, you know, so easy and nothing happens to you. You just squeeze and it's all over. It isn't really you that comes out. Just dirt."

And, "Don't be afraid, Kate. It's only water. We'll get to it and you'll have fun, like I do."

But—"Don't be afraid, Sara, it's only a hand"—we would all say. Easier said than felt.

Whenever anyone lifted a hand, either to point something out or to reach for something, Sara would fall into a heap, shielding her head from imaginary blows. Whenever I asked, "Why, Sara, what are you afraid of? Whose hand frightened you so? Did anybody hit you?" the answer always was "Just the hand."

Again the hand with an autonomy all its own. I had then a feeling that it wasn't by accident that she chose her hand to be her companion. Perhaps she was going to disarm the danger, desensitize it by making it her friend.

The hand we tackled last. Partly because of Sara's lack of cooperation and interest, partly because of our seduction by her into treating the hand as a separate independent entity. A friend.

Sara always consulted her hand, no matter whether it was something pleasant or unpleasant that she had

145

to undertake. She would stretch it in front of herself in the gesture one uses to push away an attacker. She would look at it very intently as if giving the hand a chance to speak first, and then in great seriousness discuss the matter. "Should we go on the boat with Mira?" she'd question the hand, and then answer for the hand, "Yes." "But she's such a lousy driver," she would continue, and then listen intently to the answer. She would turn to me and say, "She said that you drive okay, but it's your parking that is bad."

Then I'd say, "So, Sara, are you going?" and she'd answer, "Okay, we decided we'll take a chance, but park slow."

Whenever I tried to say anything at all about the hand being only a hand, Sara would look right past me, in effect turning her hearing off. The other children got used to the hand being part of the camp. Whenever they talked about Sara, they'd say "they," meaning the two of them, Sara and the hand. Just as Sara said "we." Not the rhetorical we, as a visitor once thought, but *we*—Sara and the hand.

The children and the staff would often say to Sara, "Ask the hand." Or, "What does the hand think?" "But I bet the hand isn't afraid," they'd say to her. Or, "Do you think the hand would like it?"

Such was the contagion of Sara's need and such was her control over the rest of us.

I would listen to them talk about the hand and think, "My God, they've all gone crazy! This child is possessed. The possession is in her hand and they are all reinforcing it."

And in the next breath I'd hear myself say, in all seriousness, "So ask your hand already and let's get going."

Then one day about a week before going home, Sara came to me giggling. With her hand stretched out in her usual fashion as if ready to converse with it, she said, "You know, Lee and Kate and Matthew and Johnny all talk about my hand as if it was a real person. Aren't they silly? Tell them it is only my hand and it is part of me."

And that was that.

How she arrived at this decision, when and what made her give up her need to make her hand into her friend, I'll never know. Because whenever I talked to her about it, she'd look at me as if I was deranged and say, "Come on, Mira. A hand is only a hand. How can it be a friend? It isn't human."

Toward the end of the summer she became quite delightful, a favorite among adults and children alike. She had become such a little girl, such a little person. Her suntan made her brown. Her beautiful black eyes, now straight most of the time, exuded health. Her sensitive features made her face beautiful and her body seemed perfect.

Her name was Sara. But we had a Russian handyman who, instead of calling her Sara, caught the poetry in the child and began to call her Blueberry.

"Blueberry Hill," Sara would say. "Let's go to Blueberry Hill. We can have all the berries we wish. Let's take a walk up Blueberry Hill. It's so lovely there." She would forever speak of that little hill on which the berries grew and where we'd all go to pick them for our dessert.

She loved that little hill and she loved the berries she picked, and she laughed there most and sang there most and was there the freest.

So she named it Blueberry Hill. And we, taking the tone from the handyman, named her Blueberry. After a while, we all forgot that her name was Sara. And along with the handyman, we'd all yell, "Hey, Blueberry? Where are you?"

And as if this name was rightfully hers, she would come running toward us and yell, "Here."

And this was how our camp was named.

After Sara: Blueberry.

DANNY

I had never loved another child
the way I loved Danny.
Danny was my baby.
Danny was the firstborn.

I once saw a spiderweb which, to me, was the most beautifully intricate in nature. I saw it when I was a child, and its complexity seemed more involved, its beauty more astonishing, its lacy workings more profound than anything I could imagine.

The understanding needed to unravel its design was beyond my young capacity. But that was how I saw it then—and how I see it still: as a marvel to look at, to admire, to try to understand. Then, as now, its delicacy and logic left me in awe of the fiercely determined artistry of the spider.

When I first saw Danny, he was a strange-looking thing, half child and half wizened old man with shoulders stooped and hunched. He had a forehead full of wrinkles; his hands hung listlessly along his body. And his body was in constant motion, as if afraid to stop, afraid of what might happen if it did stop. Disintegrate, perhaps?

His eyes were vacant. You couldn't touch him or

reach him. He was the one little star that had lost its way and kept on turning in its orbit, but with no relation to any other star, nor to the sun, nor to the moon, nor to the earth, nor to its maker.

The child just wandered about. No one could communicate with him: Danny would barely talk and was afraid of physical contact.

The only sentences to come out of his mouth, and those with no relation to the subject at hand were:

"Danny littler," "Stars and sky," and "God doesn't love littler things."

And these were said as if to himself, accompanied by a whine. The whine of a child, but so lost and so tired that it seemed he had given up looking for a path to safety any longer.

The teacher who was assigned to work with him left. And so Danny went on turning and twisting and never stopping. And then one day he was assigned to me. My first autistic child—I dreaded it. He frightened me, this whirly, fleeting thing that was a boy. His haunting loneliness and helplessness (yet loveliness) seemed too much. (Also, I abhorred him, for in some way he reminded me of myself, a self I wasn't ready to face.)

After two days of just being together in the same room, my need to see him, to know him, to understand what he was, what he really looked like, not in flight, not on the run, but stopped, got the better of me and I stopped him physically and held him tightly enough to take a long, long look. It was the last time I've done so stupid a thing. I ended up from this encounter pummeled. Black and blue. Kicked, scratched, bloodied.

He was a fair-haired boy, with a lovely little face and eyes as blue as the sky. But in those eyes that shone so brightly, in those eyes so blue, I found not the warmth that superficially one might see there, but a strange combination of excitement, depression, hatred, and terror, and a fleeting ray of pain.

And the laughter that he'd suddenly give forth was not a gay, joyous sort of laugh, as it appeared to be, but a mixture of pleasure and terror, or maybe pleasure of terror.

150

All this was there. But it would vanish in a minute, replaced by the vacant stare and silence.

For the next three months, I sat at one end of the room with him at the other, and like the hunter and the hunted we'd study each other. Since it was not clear which one of us was the hunter, the study was wary; we watched each other's every move. The only thing connecting us was a seesaw. If I tried to come over to him, he would push me away. I respected his need to be alone and to work out the relationship on his terms.

Danny hardly talked and what he did say made no sense. He did not seem to hear or to understand you, and just as often did not seem to notice you. Except when you moved. He was mostly outside the periphery of contact with you. And yet every so often I had a feeling that he'd step on this periphery and then just watch, weigh, and measure.

Always running. Always busy with something. A screw that he tried to screw in, but couldn't. A hammer that he tried to use as a weapon to destroy a box, a chair, a table, or a wall. Or his foot, with which he tried to "wreck" the wall, the table, the chair, or an imaginary something. He bloodied himself continuously. And yet there was no way of stopping him or comforting him when he got hurt. He was forever punishing himself by beating himself mercilessly, for whatever real or imaginary wrongs he had perpetrated. If he stopped, it was not stopping at all, but a different withdrawal. Instead of running away from his fear, he'd run right into the heart of it and, as he later termed it himself, "be lost." Be lost in his terror. Then he'd be unreachable again. Then he'd get into his rocker and sit and rock and sit and rock and stare out of the window for hours. However, if you looked into his eyes, you knew that he was not seeing what was there, but seeing the ghosts his frightened child's mind was conjuring up. And if you listened very carefully, you heard him mumble: "Stars," "No stars," "Little," "Danny littler," "Be lost."

If sometimes he went outside our building, he'd go as far as the stoop. You would find him sitting on the steps, with head in hands and knees supporting his elbows, looking wan, ashen, and terrified, whispering: "No stars," "Rain," "Little," "Littler things don't go to God."

If you forgot and tried to put your arm around him, he'd hit out.

If you forgot and tried to hold him or put him in your lap, he screamed in terror and pushed and kicked you away.

And yet at the same time you had a feeling that every so often Danny was on the edge of being with you. Cautiously, anxiously, watching, waiting, and daring you to come close, to break through his wall of unreality.

Danny had come to our school from a school for retarded children, where he sat and rocked for two years, doing nothing else—in the same rocking chair. He brought the diagnosis with him. Like the emperor's new clothes. We stripped it. And he, being free of it, was able somewhat to let loose.

Physically he was beautifully developed for his six years. With the coordination and control of body of a tiger cub, with the unselfconsciousness and unpremeditated innocent grace of a deer. Danny was fast like the wind—and elusive like quicksilver. One moment he was here and the next moment there. As you were beginning to think you had him, you had already lost him. His agility and sense of balance seemed to have been there for the purpose of eluding you and destroying himself. Danny could walk on a wire fence. He would balance himself precariously on the roof. He would stand provocatively on the edge of a cliff. And on the edge of a seesaw. Always on the verge, always almost —but never really—falling. Just as he was about to tumble, he'd look at you suddenly as if daring you to come to him, goading you to take up his dare, so that he'd then be forced to execute. At the same time he'd search your face for "How much do you care for me? And if you do, will you respect the 'almost' and not take up the dare?"

These were almost the only seconds of direct contact between him and me. Almost our only confrontations during these most terrible first three months.

I remember Danny standing on the roof of the school. One foot off it, ready to jump off the four-story building. Daring me to come to his rescue, or get angry, or, or, or. I died, but did not move.

"Don't do it, Danny," I kept repeating.

He watched my face for reactions. I guess he found the right one and didn't do it.

I remember his taking a nail and driving it into the bottom of his foot—just halfway. Watching me and daring me to come closer. Balancing on the one foot on the window ledge like some circus acrobat.

I brought a bucket of soapy water and a box of Band-Aids and mercurochrome and put them next to him, without touching the child—just as he wanted it, I felt. I guessed correctly. He pulled the nail out rather than drive it deeper in, soaked the foot, and put a Band-Aid on it himself.

This was how badly Danny needed to preserve his separateness. This was the extent he was ready to go to test me, to make sure that I would not overstep the boundary set up by him to preserve himself.

Danny seemed always between life and death, always flirting with death and hardly withstanding its seduction. It was as if life and death were no cycle for Danny, but that in dying he would become, that in dying he would live. Or perhaps that in dying he would be punished enough. And yet he did not dare to take this final step, either out of fear, or for some vague knowledge that it would not bring a better life to him.

So for three excruciating months I watched him. I did not get to understand him any better, but became more familiar with him, learned his ways and learned to love him.

During this time a conviction grew in me: this child had to be left alone. He had to be allowed to test me and then come to me. This child who had been so scattered and shattered, whose only feeling of self came through his seduction and defiance of death, had to be respected. Not only for what he was and could be, when healthy, but for his very way, his strange and insane way. Now I knew that this scattered, shattered, self-destructive little boy—was Danny. That was the only Danny he knew at this point, the only Danny that existed to him. The only Danny he believed in, and the only Danny he wanted you to know and love.

That was his way. His way had to be respected—no matter how frightful, frightened, and frightening it was. No matter how it hurt him and everyone else. He had a right to this self.

And so I waited and hoped and believed that one day soon he would trust me enough to be able to dare (and believe) to reach out to acknowledge himself, to show me the Danny that I began to feel existed behind his frightful defense.

The active force in Danny, as negative and self-destructive as it was, had to be respected. It couldn't be dealt with in any other way, since to him, somehow, at this time it was all he had. He guarded his inner self so well that he himself stopped believing in it. In the beginning, I couldn't challenge his defenses since they were all he had. If I were to attempt to attack them and destroy them, Danny would have felt that there was nothing left to him. And so this self-destruction that he supposedly so glibly played with was only to assert to himself that he was still alive. (Since that was the proof of his existence to him, the proof that he was.) I had to believe in it, respect it. Only then, I felt, would he let go of it and dare to look at or expose himself. Only then would he dare to see if there were really another way, if there were really anything else to him.

Cautiously, suspiciously, Danny began to trust me. He would go off to play—hammer or wreck—and suddenly come running over for a look. He'd stand in front of me, without a word, and wait. Wait till I looked up at him; then he'd look me in the face, right into my eyes, as if searching. And when finding what he wanted, without a word he'd run along again to "play." If he did not find it, he'd stand there and wait until it appeared. Whatever it was, it usually did appear.

And so day by day we learned more about each other. He learned that he could take a chance on loving and on being loved. That he could even admit it, every now and then. That he could try to trust. And I learned more about how very much I loved him, and about the particles of his fantasies, about the cruelly gruesome events that shaped Danny's life.

And so we went on and on and on, I at one end of the room, he at the other, with only a seesaw connecting us.

If I came closer, he'd run. If I touched him, he'd kick, scratch, and scream. And all along, he was testing, daring, and watching me. While he kicked the wall in, while he broke furniture, while he whirled and twirled and swung on swings so high that you held your breath for fear he'd turn over. While he sat on the chair and rocked and rocked and stared at the ceiling or up to the sky and mumbled, "The sky," "Be lost," "The stars," "Things littler," and "God." And while he got greener and greener and his eyes became more and more vacant. While he'd laugh and provoke me in a million other ways. While he'd wreck and wreck and wreck everything around him in an effort to avoid his terror—or maybe to wreck himself.

I believed in him, in spite of any logic or any sense, and began to love him very, very much. And yet, as I said, another part of me abhorred this child who, I began to realize, reminded me of me.

During this "waiting," as I called it, there were some special minutes of contact, which I was not aware of at the time, but which I realized later were quite meaningful.

One day I'd collected the seemingly meaningless words that came out of Danny's mouth—"star," "sky," "moon," "stars," "no stars," "sun," "no sun," "clouds," "up, up, up," then "helicopter." And I made up a song for him out of them.

At the time, I did not know why I gave the song the

155

meaning it had, nor did I know why it had special meaning for Danny. It was only long, long afterward that I realized how correct my hunch about the song was—that it was my thread through his spiderweb. Here is the song:

> Danny's hair is like the sun
> Danny's eyes are like the sky
> Up and down
> Up and down we go.
> Way up, up, up into the sky
> Where the wind does howl
> And the clouds roll by
> And the birds do fly,
> Way up, up high into the sky
> Where the sun is golden and warms bright
> Where the moon is yellow and lights up the night
> And the stars do shine in the sky.
> Danny's hair is like the sun
> Danny's eyes are like the sky.

The song had most meaning to Danny when it was sung on the seesaw.

There was always a board in my room with a stand. The kids or I would put it together and make a seesaw out of it. Danny always wanted the seesaw set up. If I did not set it up, he did. For a long while I thought he used it to reinforce the separation between us. But later I realized that he also used it at times as a connection between us. Every now and then he'd sit on one end of the seesaw and let me sit on the other end, using me as a weight while I sang his song.

He'd look up toward the sky and open his eyes wide when I sang about his eyes being like the sky. I repeated the song with its monotonous chant for a melody a few times and Danny would visibly calm down.

And then get off the seesaw. I noticed after a while that at certain times when he was terribly upset, he'd run to the seesaw and wait for me to get on it and sing to him. It would relax him. Then when he had got out of it whatever he needed, he'd jump off the seesaw and continue with his running, wrecking, and destroying.

His past held the usual story.

His physical and neurological development was normal—but precocious. His toilet training, speech, walking, sleeping, eating were okay—again, a bit precocious.

However, at age four, he became a "different child." Different, out of contact, and out of step. Treks and treks and treks to various diagnostic places; the diagnosis: "Retardation." He was placed in a school for retarded children for two years and then on the recommendation of an imaginative and insightful psychiatrist in Oregon, who suspected autism in the child, his parents moved to New York so Danny could attend this school.

His parents were exhausted, defeated, and disturbed. Interesting people, very bright, very idealistic. The father was a test pilot. Heroic, socially conscious, with quite a few suicide attempts under his belt.

The mother, very creative, full of "vitality" and "joy of living," which in reality was neither but rather an excitement and terror and excitement with terror. Theirs was a religious household—Catholic. Spanish and Irish Catholicism. God was accepted as a member of the household.

Neither of them was child-oriented, and a child like Danny made it impossible for them to be anything else but rejecting parents. They were both afraid of the child. Of his rage, of his uncommunicativeness, of the physical havoc and destruction he wrought, of his strangeness, of his isolation and pain, and of their inability to help him.

Some of the other events that shaped Danny's life were none too pleasant.

Danny had a grandfather whom he was very much attached to. The grandfather loved the child very much and was devoted to him, probably the only member of his family who was. The grandfather died when Danny was three years old.

There were other specific traumas. When Danny was

two and a half years old, he got lost in the forest. He was alone for two days and two nights. Planes, posses, and so forth, were sent to look for him. Eventually, he was found. At the age of three, he possibly witnessed the death of a little girl, his friend, and then attended her wake. These are a few things we know about; many others we will never discover.

Three months after I first started with him, almost to the day, on a cold November afternoon, I took him and another child to hear the ocean roar. The water seemed tempting, so I took off my shoes and walked into it. Suddenly I felt a little hand in mine. Danny walked into the ocean with me. He bridged the abyss and took my hand, with what seemed tentative fright, but at the same time trust. I looked at him for a second, unbelieving, and quickly looked away, afraid to frighten him. I remember the coldness of the water; he was pulling me in deeper than my original "up to the ankle" curiosity. I remember trying not to shiver, so as not to transmit any of my reluctance to Danny. When he got me in as far as my knees, he turned around and walked out with me. The waiting was worth it. Danny dared to trust when he was ready to.

I've never loved any child I've worked with the way I loved Danny. Perhaps that was his undoing.

I love all "my" kids, and I respect and admire their courage; but once the web started to unravel with Danny it was different. I admired and respected the fierce pride of the child, which was in whatever he did, good or bad, constructive or destructive.

There was an independence in him, which didn't come just out of fear, not just in order to control, but in order not to depend, because that was his way. I admired his need for his separateness, whether it was for better or for worse. He wanted and needed to be separate at any price. And he was so direct about it. He needed his boundaries or whatever he thought were his boundaries, even though they were only defenses—as

158

unorthodox and as insane as they were, he wanted them respected and he managed to establish this fact.

Danny was my baby. Danny was somehow my child.

Danny was like a little stallion throwing his head back and braying to the world, "This is me and you've got to love *me* the way I am."

Danny at his sickest managed to get across the idea that "that is I, that is," and, as he would verbalize it later, "that is Dan."

After the water incident Danny did not change much outwardly, but things changed between the two of us. He could look at me. And he would, for long, long periods at a time, study me intensely. He would touch me a little at a time. He would take me by the hand at times.

And he would call me by a name. Not my given name, but by the name that he, over these few months, somewhere inside of him gave to me, Miria.

M-I-R-I-A.

"That is Miria," he would say. "That is. Danny wants Miria."

From that point on, the waiting was over and more active working together began.

Little by little, Danny became more expressive. If it rained, he cried and looked up at the sky and moaned, "No sun." If it was a dark day, he'd sit on the stoop and weep and say, "No stars. No moon." If an airplane flew by, he'd look up into the sky, his little body shaking with terror and repeat, over and over, "Helicopter, helicopter."

And so things began falling into some order. Danny's father was a pilot. When it was dark, the child was afraid his father would be lost. If it rained, same fear. Part wish, part fear. And so, panic. Sometimes Danny would lie down on the floor, looking like a corpse, and say, "Danny be dead." And then more fears made their appearance and were verbalized: fear of candles, fear of fire, fear of the piano which he called a candle. Fear of "bigger things" and being bigger than himself. Fear of "littler things" and beings littler than himself. Terror of "babies," terror of dolls. Terror of being

159

touched. Terror of being helped with anything—food, an article of clothing, a screw, or a hammer. Terror of any kind of illness. Terror of suppositories. Terror of enemas. Terror of shots. Terror of adults. Terror of the other children around him. Terror of dogs. Terror of cats. Terror of water, of heights, of windows. And, last but not least, terror of being lost.

And as Danny's many fears came to the surface, I understood his constant need for motion. As long as he moved, he was safe—as long as he moved, he ran from those fears. When he stopped, he had to face them.

After Danny's reaching out to me—taking my hand, touching in the water—we both began, slowly, gently, delicately, but firmly, to unravel his web.

Any contact we had until then was never physical. A glance across the room or a symbolic touch through a song, a 12-foot seesaw between us. Any attempt on my part at physical contact produced a reaction that was either suicidal or homicidal.

After the water it didn't change that much except that he took my hand every now and then or just fleetingly touched me, like the gentlest of breezes. If I tried to touch him, he would disappear. It wasn't as actively violent as before, but it was just as terrifying. He would almost literally dissolve under my touch, as if his flesh turned into nothingness. And the feeling I'd get was— yes, I'd touched—but whom, what? . . . certainly not Danny. It was as if his very being seeped out of him, and I remained holding on to disembodied flesh, not Danny's.

The whole being of the child was telling me, without a word, loud and clear: "Go away," "I do not want you," "When you touch me, I am not there," "When you touch me, I disappear, because I do not want you."

Sometimes, almost as if he were giving me an explanation for this withdrawal, he'd say, "Danny be littler," "God doesn't love littler things," "Littler things be lost." And the only thing I could make out of it at the time was that somehow it was unsafe for him to be little, that being touched meant being little, and that little Danny things get lost.

Then one day there was an explosion outside our classroom. A tire, I think. But the noise was so deafening, the force so great, and the suddenness so unexpected, that Danny dropped the hammer he was busily wrecking the wall with and leaped toward me and burrowed into me. The suddenness of his action and his merging terrified him and he moved away very quickly. But I realized then that Danny needed so desperately to keep separate, because he so desperately wanted to merge and become one with everything and everyone. Physical closeness to him meant to swallow and be swallowed by everyone. Loss of his own self, loss of his identity. A danger to him greater than death.

Touching and being touched meant merging, meant being little and so disappearing into the other person. And yet being a baby and merging with a mother was something Danny wanted badly—wanted and needed. But the equation, merging=Being little=Baby, was dangerous to him, for it meant he was lost psychologically and also physically.

After the explosion incident, Danny avoided me for a while but forever circled me. He stared at me and studied me. I did not swallow him up. I did not take him over. I did not need him; therefore I did not use him. Then one day soon he came over and began to explore me physically. He touched my nose and ran away. But nothing happened. He returned and touched my eyes; afraid, he ran away—again nothing happened. And so he continued with every part of my face. When he got to my mouth, I knew this was the test by fire for him. If I don't swallow him, we'll make it. He circled and circled my lips with his little finger for a long, long while. Then as if suddenly he had decided to dare the most dangerous thing of all, he shut his eyes tight, and with terror and determination he shoved his fingers between my teeth. We remained like that for a while. Then Danny slowly opened his eyes and began to examine his fingers, and himself. Then me. No, I did not swallow him. He was there, all of him.

161

This was a mixed blessing for me. Danny, reassured that I wasn't going to eat him, decided, I guess, that he'd eat me. He began to bite. Bite out of love, bite out of hate. Bite out of sorrow, out of fear. Bite he did. And his teeth were sharp, like a wolf's. He bit my nose, especially, but also my arms, my cheeks, any place he could sink his teeth in. Also he would hit me, pinch me, and then kick me (I guess to see if I would wreck like the wall).

But the touching between us became very much better. There was more and more of it. He no longer disappeared when I touched him. His flesh would not "dissolve." He *let* me hold his hand when we were outside—which made it possible for me to take him for walks, since he forever needed to run under cars and especially trucks. He let me stroke his hair every now and then. Let me put my arms about him, not too often, and let me even kiss him every now and then.

Sometimes he even tried to kiss me, but that was a disaster. It started with licking and always ended with a bite—which once gave me a 104-degree temperature and the need for a tetanus shot.

Danny began to incorporate me. I was the good and the bad. I was all things to him. I became his yardstick.

Nothing else changed, however. His terrors were still the same. He continued to wreck the walls and continued to hurt himself. And "the stars," "littler," "bigger things," and "God doesn't love littler things" were still mumbled as much as ever with the same outcome: terror and withdrawal. The seesaw and the song, to which I now added a last line:

And Mira loves Danny very much

were still the only things that truly relieved his terrors.

Danny seemed to have an incessant need to be punished, to be hurt. So he constantly provoked, to evoke the hurt and the punishment.

If he did not spill the paint, he'd spill the juice. If he didn't overturn the clay, he'd overturn the garbage.

If he didn't break a dish, he'd break a bowl. If he didn't wreck a wall, he'd wreck a chair. If he didn't kick in a wall, he kicked in a table and, as if all that didn't give him enough pain and produce the punishment he was after, Danny would beat himself. He would punch himself, slap, claw, scratch, and hit himself with whatever happened to be in his hand. A block, a can, a stick, a branch, or a chair. On his backside, on the head, on the legs, on the arms, and one would hear him accompany it with a mumble: "Bad," "Bad Danny," "I am cross with you," "Naughty boy." He did it with such vengeance, self-hatred, and determination that not only did one feel the child's disapproval of himself but actually witnessed the physical execution of that disapproval.

It was painful to see this lovely, sweet-looking, fair-haired little boy, so hopelessly lost, beyond redemption, condemning himself and carrying out his sentence so methodically. He was his own sternest judge and the most methodical executioner.

For wrongs done, not done, thought of, wished for, and feared, he had to be punished. He had to atone.

How frightfully stern he was with himself—how rigid his line was between good and evil! As far as Danny was concerned, most of him was evil, little of him was good, and so he carved his image using punishment as the chisel.

I remember our first Christmas together when I asked Danny what he'd like for a present. He said very seriously, "A hairbrush." A hairbrush to beat himself with.

What is it about us, this strange thing called man? We all want to be loved. We all need to be loved to survive. And Danny did too—desperately so. We too mold ourselves to some extent to be acceptable, provided it does not interfere with our own feeling of what we are. We take over other people's values of what is right and wrong, when we are very little, and use them as a guide. But if lucky, the values are kind and we trust those other people.

Danny, too, wanted to mold himself to other people's concept of what a "good boy" was. But his concept of what was right and wrong was confused, terribly stern, terribly rigid. So most of the time to himself he was just bad. He needed to be punished, to be purified, to be good. "I will make myself what I know to be good and then you will love me. Then *I* will love me." But Danny did not trust. And so no one was to touch Danny. No one was to punish him, only he himself. "Oh, yes," he was somehow saying, "I am bad. I need punishment. But no matter how much you punish me, I shall always do it better, more efficiently." And the punishment was a must, but also a guarantee. "You may kill me but I will not kill myself (almost, but not quite). You see how well I can hurt myself. You do not need to do it for me."

Little Danny, little frightened Danny, needed—just like the rest of us—love, to be loved. Only more so. And for love, one will do a lot of things. There are very few of us, I think, who do not pay for love, some a higher price, some less. Danny was ready to pay a lot. Danny was ready to beat himself into a lovable child, so great was his need to be loved. And was it his definition of lovable—or his parents'? He was bad, all bad to himself, this little child; to be good, lovable, he had to be punished . . . by others, if necessary, but preferably by himself. Others might kill him. And Danny like all of us was afraid of dying, so he did the punishing himself. To assure himself that he would become good and lovable, he punished himself frighteningly. Danny punished himself more severely than anyone else would have done, but to him that was less awful than his imagined death at the hands of others, or abandonment.

So one day I determined to take punishment out of his hands and show him that my opinion of him could be trusted, that my punishment of him would not destroy him. That I did not consider his crimes as heinous as he, his parents, or God thought they were. That I would be his judge rather than he himself, and thus be kinder, gentler, and less punitive. That my punishment would fit the crime; that I would not kill him.

I was going to show him that Danny wasn't bad, evil, unlovable. He *was* lovable, but in spite of it and not because of it, he was punishable.

And thus, in the midst of one of his self-punishing rages, I grabbed the child in my arms, put him over my lap, and said:

"Now that's enough of that. I'm not going to let you beat yourself like that. From now on, if any walloping is to be done, I'll do it, not you." Danny looked up with astonishment, with terror, but his "flesh" did not run away. So I proceeded. I began to spank ("wallop," as he called it) his backside, counting all along, one, two, three, four, five, six, seven, eight, nine, ten, a million. Danny, with his little face all screwed up to a cry, looked up in amazement. The spanking did not hurt much, and yet I was serious, dead serious. And I proceeded: "From now on, when you are mad with yourself, when you think you need to be punished, you are to come to me and tell me and I'll wallop you. Do you understand?" I said very sternly. "Yep," the child answered, "yep, Danny must tell Miria."

That was my first definite act with Danny, where I took the initiative. He was ready. He went away, relieved and surprised. Two minutes later he came running back—"Danny needs a walloping," he told me. Again I put him over my lap and began a spanking. "You count with me," I told him.

Danny did, "One, two, three, four . . ."

"A million," I said.

That did it. Danny was beginning to be fascinated with words. "Million" was new. It took him about two minutes to learn to say it correctly. He laughed with delight when he finally said it right. He laughed and forgot a little bit about his badness.

The healing had started. From then on, we began to call it "a spanking game." The wallops were light and easy; they never really hurt. After a while, the numbers and laughter accompanying them were becoming more important than the punishment.

It was always done at the bottom of the stairs. And at

times Danny had to learn to wait for the spanking till we got back to the room from the playground. By limiting it to one place, we helped to encapsulate the punishableness of the child (Danny wasn't all bad—all punishable).

And Danny began to learn. He wasn't all bad. He was naughty (eventually good-naughty). The punishment was a wallop on his behind, not all over his body. The punishment did fit the crime. But the punishment was slight, because the crime was slight. Danny began to understand; it made a little dent. And when after the spanking he'd say, sometimes with desperation and intensity, "And a kick," "And a hit," "And a hairbrush," I'd just give him another wallop and say, "And a million. And a billion. And a trillion."

With some of the self-punishment taken out of his hands, Danny could relax a bit and allow himself to place some of the responsibility for his being and becoming on my kinder, adult world where it belonged. The trust was beginning to grow and Danny was beginning to open up more. More with his illness and more with his health. And Danny was becoming aware of the world outside his fantasy.

Words were of great importance. The longer and more difficult the word, the greater Danny's fascination. This became very useful to me. The more intense our relationship, the more he trusted me, the more I could use words to stop him from doing destructive things. *"Positively, absolutely,"* I would say, "Danny is not to bite Miria." *"Positively, absolutely,* Danny is not to wreck the chair."

He would repeat "positively, absolutely" in his own inimitable way ("posilutely, absotively"), but the magic of our relationship had transferred itself into words, and words would stop him from acting out a great number of things, would stop him from getting into difficulties.

If I said, "No, Danny," Danny would stop and wait for me to say "positively, absolutely." If I didn't, Danny would say it and wait for me to repeat it. If I cheated

166

him and said only "positively," he'd wait for the "absolutely." Both had to be.

I've often tried to imagine what it must be like to be lost. Lost in unfamiliar woods. Lost when you are two and a half years old. Lost for two endlessly long days. How many hours are there in a day? How many minutes are there in a day? How long is eternity? How long is infinity for a two-and-a-half-year-old child? As long as a night? What do two nights make? A forever, a death, an abandonment? Yet, I can't. The scope is beyond me. I cannot comprehend the magnitude of the terror, the feeling of abandonment, of impending death, of all the bogeymen when the night comes close and engulfs you. When the hunger makes your stomach ache, when the thirst parches your throat. When does it end? Ever? And the noises, real and imaginary, and the animals and the walking trees. And all the goblins and all the witches and all the all . . .

The physical discomfort is obvious, but what about the psychic one? No one to take care of you, no one to attend to you—lost. What about the feeling of being lost —losing identity, losing self in the morass of the many feelings which the child must have experienced but could not control. Danny could not find his self among all of them. The security of the self got drowned, overwhelmed by all his terrors, and Danny got lost. "And God doesn't love littler things" must have been the conclusion, as he forever reiterated it.

What is mental illness if not a getting lost of the self, for whatever reason. Danny experienced it concretely in the forest, but then forever he experienced it in all aspects of his life. "Be lost." It is a feeling both of body and mind. For when one is truly lost, all connections are severed and the vacuum this produces—the terror and insecurity—must be overwhelming.

Danny. It was in the record. Just a mention of the fact that he was lost for two days in the woods. They searched and searched and searched for him and then he was found. That's all. The parents never mentioned it. Too much pain, too much guilt. We never asked them about it. Too sensitive a topic, too frightening for them. We were delicate. But what of the child?

Lost. Danny lost for ever and ever and ever. But we were too delicate to mention it.

So one day—

As I said before, stars, the wind, the moon, the rain, the sky, and the sun seemed terribly important in Danny's universe. If it rained, he cried. If clouds rolled by and grayed the sky, all color drained out of his face. And he kept on looking up in anticipation of some horrible event. "No sun," "No moon," "No stars," he would say, and then look around desperately in search of the "helicopter." "Helicopter" was an ever-present thing for Danny. He heard them when there weren't any and heard them when there were. Planes were also helicopters—any flying machine. And he was always on the lookout for them.

All this made little sense—except for the fact that Danny's father was a flier. The preoccupation with weather conditions in this little boy was unnatural. If it rained or got dark, Danny would sit for hours on his rocker, looking out of the window, withdrawn, old, haunted, and full of terror.

Except that now he was beginning to add other phrases to his monologue, about the stars, sky, and so on.

"God doesn't love littler things," "Littler things don't go to God." "Trees," lots and lots of repetition of trees. "Go on a star," "God only loves bigger things," "Miria must not go on a star," "Littler things get lost."

So one rainy day I asked a co-worker of mine to play us some music on the piano. It was to sound like the wind. I told Danny that we would bend like the trees in the wind. Danny, after watching us for a while, climbed out of his rocking chair and fell into the swing of the thing. He forgot his hate for the piano, which he called a candle, and began to sway along with me. On a hunch I said, "Let's stretch our branches way up into the sky." Danny did and suddenly began to shiver. "No," he

168

began to scream. "No. No. No moon. No sun. No stars." He ran to me, holding on to me and pointing to the ceiling.

And then it happened, this strange awesome thing that happens between two people. No words, no conscious knowledge, but a knowledge that makes one being suddenly know, feel the other.

So I lifted up Danny in my arms and said, "Yes, but there is a moon."

And Danny said, "No. No moon. Miria is a tree, Danny is on the tree. Up, up high, but there is no moon, no lights." He sobbed, panicky. "And they will never, never find Danny again." He continued weeping hysterically. "And no Mommy and no Daddy will ever find Danny again. Never again."

And then as if he changed gears, he began to yell, "There will be a wreck! There will be a wreck!"

And I said, "No. If there is no moon and no sun and no stars, there are floodlights and searchlights, the plane will come safely to the ground. And Danny will be found."

And Danny began to weep and yell: "No, Miria must bend down, 'cause the plane will break the branches and Danny will fall off the tree and get dead."

"No," I said, "look up—up there. See the searchlights; see the floodlights?"

And so little helpless Danny, desperately looking at the ceiling along with me, saw and remembered what was always lacking in his fantasy—the lights.

"Yes, Danny can see," he said with relief, "and now Daddy won't crash, and Miria and Danny won't be dead, and Danny will be found."

The weeping stopped. Danny came to, his face looking almost relaxed. I said, "Now off the tree," as my arms were ready to fall off. (Danny looked at me as if I was nuts. What tree? And jumped off my shoulders.)

Day after day we repeated it.

Day after day I was the tree; Danny would climb up on me and look for the moon and the stars and the floodlights, when "his night" was very dark.

Day after day, he would find his way out of his nightmare and be rescued.

Day after day, I became a plane or a helicopter and Danny dared to climb into this bird of death (which was also, at times, a bird of safety) and not crash and not be destroyed.

Day after day, new words, new symbols were added by Danny, which helped us unravel his spiderweb further.

"Littler things don't go to God," he'd say with satisfaction when he was up on his "tree" (me) looking for a way out, " 'cause littler things are bad. God doesn't love littler things so they be lost and no one can find them 'cause God won't help them—'cause God doesn't love littler things."

And when he was in the "helicopter," he'd say, "Daddy will crash. Danny upset Daddy this morning and then Daddy will crash into Danny and Daddy be dead and Danny be dead. Then Daddy will go to God. God loves bigger things. Bigger things go on a star."

Then, "Danny be bad, he makes Daddy crash and then Daddy will come down in a parachute and wreck Danny."

The story began to make sense.

Since God doesn't love littler things—because they are bad—he let Danny get lost in the forest and did not bail him out. However, since God doesn't like littler things, he will not take them to him—he will not make them die. This was part of Danny's fear of being little.

Since God loves bigger things, God takes them unto himself; and if Daddy crashes, he will go to God, but he might also take along Danny, as he will punish him by taking him along with him.

Then more came out. When Danny was three, his grandfather died. The one he loved so much and who loved him very much. The explanation given to the child by his parents was that Grandpa "went to God." "He is in heaven on a star."

Grandpa was old. When people get old, God takes them unto himself. Especially if they're good.

Danny was sick quite a bit, I think, after his being lost, and was given a lot of suppositories, shots, and enemas. These violations frightened him immensely. And so, according to Danny, when you are littler, you get shots and suppositories and enemas; when you are bigger, you don't. It is bad to be littler. To be littler is to be bad, and because you are bad you get lost, because you are bad you get shots, suppositories, etc.

But when you get bigger, God takes you unto himself. You die like Grandpa and you live on a star.

So, forever, this terrible dilemma.

"God doesn't love littler things."—"You don't go to God when you are littler." But you get lost and no one finds you. "Bigger things go to God. Bigger things go to the stars."

And so, again, God is good; you should love God, "but God doesn't love littler things." There is safety in being littler. There is a guarantee of not dying, at least. God thus became synonymous with death. "Bigger things go to God," like Grandfather (and father always on the verge). "God loves bigger things," and so he takes them to his bosom, to himself, "to the stars" (synonymous with death).

And here also there was incongruity. You have to want to be loved by God—that then means you are good. And yet, if you are loved by God, if you are good, God takes you to himself. Which means death. So who wants to be good if the price of goodness is death?

The reward for living, to Danny, is to be loved by God, which to him equals growing up equals death.

You have to want to be loved by God. That is something every child is taught; and yet Danny, really, did not want to die.

So on the one hand you strove for God's love and were frightened if God did not love you. (You'll be lost and not saved.) On the other hand, you wanted no part of God. You wanted to stay little, stay bad, so as not to be loved by God and not go to God (and not die).

But if you are little, you are bad. God doesn't love

171

you, doesn't save you, and you are lost in the dark, dark forest—forever.

What a dilemma!

We continued with "the tree" or "lots of trees" and the helicopter, day after day after day. And after a while we'd be lost together and then saved together, and after a while we'd go together in the "helicopter." And finally, Danny did not need to fly any more. Danny's fantasy changed.

From the horror, when his father or he himself would go up and then crash because there was "No moon, no sun, no stars" by which to find the road back—part Danny's wish, part his fear—it changed to the fantasy where there were lights and the sun and the moon, where neither Danny nor Daddy needed to be killed.

But that took a long, long time, many, many "flights" later, as we both called it—which to Danny meant a "flight into the forest" or "into the sky," and to me a "flight" into Danny's fantasy.

As time went on, the "flights" were shorter and shorter and finally became comical. We flew into the forest in a red balloon, and in a bubble, and in the heart of a flower, and in a grain of sand, and in a teardrop. And sometimes even in the song of a bird. But by that time he knew well it was only a game. By that time he'd yell out already, "Time out for a lollipop," or, "let's stop because Danny has to go to the bathroom." But that was after zillions of trips into his horror.

As far as the dilemma of "littler and bigger things" was concerned, well, he was arrested in mid-flight. Danny was afraid to be little and Danny was afraid to be big, so we were stuck right in between—which was nowhere.

"If you get bigger," as Danny would tell me, "then Danny be old and be dead and Miria be old and be dead and everybody be dead and go to God and to the stars."

But every day meant "getting older and older," as he so aptly put it. So Danny did not want to grow.

A birthday, anybody's birthday, threw him into an

endless panic. And being "littler" was of course out of the question, because "God doesn't love littler things." Then Danny "be lost," "be sick," "be dead."

So carrying Danny in my arms—except when I was the tree or helicopter—cuddling him, or helping him with anything was out of the question, since that meant he was littler.

Danny was always wary, afraid someone would sneak up on him and put another day onto his life—added or subtracted. Only the status quo was safe; and yet that wasn't safe either.

Babies were unthinkable, they were too frightening. Dolls, too; they were like babies. Anything little and helpless was a dangerous reminder. So that every baby had to be hit, every carriage turned over, and every doll broken.

Animals did not fare any better. Cats (to him, "kitties") had to be bitten, dogs chased with the same purpose in mind, and fish squeezed until dead.

However, the longer we worked together, and the more I loved him, and allowed him to love me—as little or as much as he wanted—the greater grew his security. And then, one day, I think a bit over a year after we began working together, Danny cut his leg badly. He had to be gotten upstairs to the infirmary. I picked him up in my arms and began to carry him up.

The reaction was immediate. Shock at what I'd done, fury at betrayal, terror at what would surely happen to him (he was littler). And then, a complete reversal. Suddenly this stiff, fighting little body nestled itself into my arms with such force, intensity, and joy that he himself became overwhelmed and began to cry. Then he looked up at me with such gratitude and abandon and trust, that my love for him was almost too much for me to bear.

It was as if he had waited for it all his life—and that he did, I am sure. Christ, how I loved this child! After that I could be free to express my love for him more. After that, no cuddling was enough; he'd be in my arms and on my lap whenever an occasion presented itself to him, and if not, he created it. All the gentleness and tenderness that he had deprived himself of as a baby, he got now. All the physical loving and the cuddling, the hugging and the kissing that he had missed, mainly because of his fear, he got now. How I loved him, and he was drinking it up, as if he had been parched forever.

However, all that physicality was endlessly accompanied by the worried, "Danny be little now?" Love at the price of death. And I'd say to him, "No, Danny just feel little now." He seemed to understand the difference, for he would then repeat to himself, "Danny just feel little now. Danny not be dead. Danny not be lost."

It seemed that he was somehow quite sure of the "not be dead" but not sure of the "not be lost." Often, for example, he would gather all the adults around him in a circle and stand himself in the center and say, "Now Danny not be lost." And sometimes he would collect all the adults in a circle and place himself and me in the center and say, "Nobody be lost now."

After every physical expression of love, I needed constantly to reassure him, that he wouldn't "be lost," whether he "feel little" or "be little." And he'd constantly ask for this reassurance. "What if Danny be lost?" he'd say, and the answer was always, "Miria will find him."

As his boundaries became more secure, the questioning about his "being lost" diminished. But the fear of loss, of his self, physical and psychological—of his identity—was deep, and the memory of it seemed to haunt him.

I still remember one episode that etched itself on my very being and so pathetically told of Danny's despair.

At the time Danny was talking of "not be lost any more." Then one day something unhappy happened in my personal life. I came to school but was there in body only. Danny was obviously aware of it. He tried to reach out to me, yet found nothing there. As he was about to leave for home, he suddenly ran up to me, clutched me by my leg, and sobbed out, "Now Danny be lost. Miria is lost and she won't know where to find Danny." He sobbed as if his little heart was breaking.

"Hush, little one," I whispered. I remember my resentment. Don't I have a right to my pain? I thought. But it brought me back to the present reality. And I reassured him that even though I seemed "lost" to him, I wasn't. I was just far away for a short time. Now I was back. And he was to know that I would always be able to find him. That he would never "be lost." No matter what, no matter where, I would always know where to "look for him." Then Danny, after studying my face for a while, still sobbing, said, "And if Danny little, Danny sometimes be lost when he little." And I said, "Little or big, I shall find you."

This "be lost when little" was diminishing day by day. But the fear was replaced by the fear of "be lost when big." This I think again had a direct connection with Danny's fear that "Daddy be lost way up high in the sky—in the stars" while flying. Sometimes Danny became the father and got "lost in the stars"—went out of contact.

As he dared "to be littler" and nothing happened, and as he dared "to be bigger"—Daddy—and nothing happened, Danny began to dare to grow. He began to sip my coffee, began to stretch tall (and walk straight), and to say, "Danny is now bigger." He began to talk more, do more activities. Began to ask for help and to learn his physical limits and limitations. He began to give dolls suppositories and enemas and shots instead of shoving everything in view up his rectum and sticking nails and sticks into his arms. He said of the dolls, "They are sick and Danny is getting them better."

His birthday party was no longer ignored by him but was actually celebrated. He began to take notice of other children's birthday parties and insist on buying them balloons and presents. He began to want "bigger shoes," "bigger jackets," "bigger things" in general, for, as Danny put it, "Bigger things don't necessarily go to stars."

Death was beginning to leave his picture. "Miria was bigger and she not be dead," "The policeman was bigger and he not be dead." And, "The candy store man was bigger and he not be dead."

175

His very living, close living—living and loving—with another human being helped with all these fears.

Danny had more and more fun in the world around him. We both had fun. We loved things together, as we lived them together.

We loved the sun, we loved the rain, we loved the wind and the air we breathed. We loved each other. And through loving me Danny began to become aware of and love other children and adults.

Danny was an extremely imaginative child, I then discovered. Once he became freer from his terrors, he could give his imagination freedom.

It showed up in his speaking, where he was no longer just fascinated with other people's words but used them creatively himself. It showed up in his block building, where the helicopter and a box to die in did not dominate the scene. It showed up in his clay work, where clay was used for purposes other than throwing lumps of it on the ceiling and calling them stars. It showed up in his paintings, where the range of color and subject changed.* And so minute by minute, hour by hour, and then day by day, life stopped being a horror and became something to live, enjoy, suffer, and love. And that diminished the fears too.

We all have our wall.

Our wall of sorrow, our wall of rage, our wall of hope, and our wall of guilt. Our wall of joy, our wall of happiness—our wall—

We pray at it; we express our most secret and innermost wishes at it, and our greatest and most vehement fury. We put little pieces of paper with a hope or a

---

* It showed up in his paintings most poignantly. Initially he drew a house that had no roots on earth but stood all black and detached from it, under a dark gloomy sky. This changed into a house firmly rooted in the earth with the sun shining brightly above it. And later a man carried a bunch of balloons all of gay colors, and a locomotive and a car sped by with such feeling of movement that one wanted to get out of the way. Danny was on his way out.

wish or a prayer written on them among its stones, and wait for the wish to come true. Wait sometimes forever.

Danny had a wall in his house and he had a wall at the school. Nothing and no one could dissuade him from "wrecking" his wall. The gaping hole in his home and the basic structure showing out through the wall in his school were hard to comprehend, even harder to accept.

Almost from the day he came to the school, he picked one specific wall in our classroom and began going at it. Why this wall, no one knew. The process of selection took a week or so, during which he vehemently attacked all the four walls. He'd either take a hammer to them or a chair, or, most of the time, his foot. With shoe on or off, as if to him that was immaterial.

After the week, one wall became it. And he kicked and he kicked and he kicked until one saw a gaping hole, with slats showing wherever they were strong enough to withstand his assault.

Over the weekend the wall would get plastered up and on Monday, or at the latest Tuesday, the hole would reappear. The same was true at his house.

After a while we gave up replastering the wall and lost our rage connected with it. We just did not understand it. That wall, that specific wall, served many purposes for Danny. When he got scolded, he ran to it and stood smack against it. When he wanted a punishment, he ran to it and stood smack against it. When he wished something, he went to it and stood smack against it. When he learned or tried to learn and understand some new concept I was teaching him, again, he stood by it, smack against it. And there he would repeat what I had said to himself endless times until he understood it, or made it his own.

For the first year, though, he just kicked and kicked and kicked his wall with his feet, sometimes with shoes on, sometimes with shoes off. At times, but very seldom, when his feet were not strong enough or too bloody, a hammer came in handy. And then the child, with his pale, sweated-up little face, with trembling hands and body, as if ready for the execution, would bravely say,

"Yep, Danny wrecked the wall. Now Miria be cross." And that was as much as I could understand—Nothing.

Was it his own cage he was breaking out of, was it his own defense he was kicking through? Was it the limitations the world put on his free, wild expression of self that he was kicking at? Was it a provocation of punishment, or a reinforcement of the wish that we would not let him kick down the barriers, even though self-imposed, but would give him a security from any infringement of the world upon his very self, which he had hidden beyond the wall? (This way he could want to get out, to be free in the world, be himself, but always have the guarantee that he'd be stopped from being himself; if not by himself, at least by someone else.)

Was it that he was afraid that once he came out of his cage, he would kill? Was it that he was afraid of his helplessness or of his strength?

Or was he kicking his way out of the helicopter, or out of the forest, or out of the star—out of all his prisons?

It was painful to see this little child standing there forever before me, pale and shaking, waiting for his punishment and saying, "Danny did wreck the wall. Now Miria be cross." For "Miria" could helplessly do nothing, because she did not understand, did not know what to do.

But after many, many such incidents, the first crack in our wall of noncomprehension appeared. Heretofore Danny would go at the wall with no apparent instigation. However, one time his violence seemed to me directly connected with a physical attack on Danny by another older child named Greg. Right after the child hit Danny, Danny ran to the wall and began to kick it. "Why?" I kept on insisting, "Why the wall?" And then I added, "I wonder if Danny isn't hitting the wall instead of Greg?" And Danny looked up at me and said with terror, "Danny is wrecking Gregie. Gregie wrecked Danny," and then added, in case I did not understand, "Danny be wrecked and Greg be wrecked."

So any physical assault on Danny seemed to have

destroyed him, "wrecked" him; and any thought of, wish for, or attempt at retaliation "wrecked" the other person. Danny did not dare attack anyone else, so instead the wall went—the wall and the other person were interchangeable. Yet any time the wall was "wrecked," Danny appeared to be wrecked—he and the wall, too, were interchangeable. The murderer murders himself along with the murdered one.

So I explained to Danny, "Neither is the wall Greg nor is it Danny. Walls are just walls. And walls do get wrecked when you kick them or hit them. People don't get wrecked when you hit them or kick them. Gregie is okay. He isn't wrecked. Danny is okay. He isn't wrecked. Just look.

"And the reason people get 'cross' or object when Danny 'wrecks' the wall is not because they get 'wrecked' or Danny gets 'wrecked' but because the wind will blow in, the rain will come in, and everyone will catch cold."

Somehow it made sense to Danny. He looked at me straight in my eyes as I kept on repeating this explanation over and over again. After a while he seemed reassured. And from that day on, whenever Danny wrecked the wall, he'd run over to me and wait for the same explanation. Then one day finally I heard him stand by his wall after kicking it and say to himself word for word the explanation I had given him. And so Danny started learning at least in words the difference between himself and the wall, between the wall and others. He then began to experiment, to challenge the difference, first by hitting back the children who attacked him and then, even more courageously, by instigating fights himself. Then, he would check himself, the other children, and the wall for wreckage.

I soon realized that if Danny was the wall and Greg was the wall, then I must be the wall too. So must Mommy and Daddy, and everyone and everything in the world.

The wall was a tree with many gnarled branches, spreading itself all over the world for him, like a plague. And how to untwist that tree, how to remove it a branch at a time, I did not know.

However, I was hoping that by setting up a difference between me and him, we would come to the difference between me and the wall, me and his father, me and his mother and, therefore, between all of us and the wall. The wall, thus stripped of its magical power, would stand there impotent, alone—just a wall.

I remember asking Danny, "Doesn't your foot hurt you, all that bleeding and wrecking?"

And little Danny looked up at me with something like despair in his voice and said, "Nope, it hurts Miria?"

No, I don't think it was just symbiosis. I think Danny, because of lack of love, lack of a good concept of himself that he could absorb from his parents, almost did not exist. His body did not belong to him because no one made him feel that his body was worth anything. Whether it happened before he got lost and his grandfather died, or after, I do not know. But the groundwork must have been shaky, and after the two traumas he surely lost himself. I was convinced of it.

It therefore occurred to me that no matter how much I understood about him intellectually, how much I stopped him from his destruction and self-destruction, in the final analysis his feelings of self would not last. I had to make him feel. I had to make him feel wanted, I had to make him feel loved, I had to make him exist. His body had to exist, had to be worthwhile. His body had to be handled gently, lovingly, tenderly because "he is," as he'd say later on, "to make him be." (The suppositories that he got, the shots, the enemas violated the little self he had left and only further destroyed it, making it nonexistent.)

His wrecking himself, his destroying himself, his hopeless, helpless, hurting himself were what had to be reversed. What had to be changed.

And, therefore, my concept of him was built from my feeling about him, built from my respect for him. Whatever he was—good, bad, or otherwise—was what eventually and first of all the child had to incorporate.

Then and only then could he trust me and could we unravel the web.

At first we tried to establish the difference between Danny and Mira—and Danny had a very difficult time with it, once he broke through to me. Whenever he'd "wreck" the wall, I'd point to myself and say, "That is Miria and Miria isn't wrecked." And then pointing to him, "That is Danny and Danny isn't wrecked." Slowly he learned the difference between Danny, Miria, and the wall. After a long while and many "wreckings" of the wall, you could finally see Danny standing by his wall and repeating to himself, "That is Danny (pointing to himself) and that is Miria (pointing in my direction), and that is the wall (pointing to the wall)." Then he'd add, "Only the wall got wrecked."

Then we began to learn the difference between Miria and Daddy. One day after kicking a chunk out of it, I saw him standing by the wall and saying to himself, "That is Miria and that is Danny," pointing to himself and me respectively, and then looking around in utter confusion and saying, "That is Daddy? Daddy will be cross with Danny. Daddy will speak to Danny. Daddy will give Danny a hairbrush." Then he proceeded to kick another hefty chunk out of the wall and came running to me. This was a good time, I felt, for him to learn the difference between my anger and Daddy's. I allowed myself to get quite angry and said to Danny, "Miria is very furious."

I gave him a shaking. He looked at me in utter amazement, feeling for the first time some extent of my anger. He said, "Miria is very furious."

Then he said in a panic, "Daddy is very furious."

I said firmly, "No, not Daddy, but Miria."

He touched my face and kept on whining: "Daddy is, he is. Daddy is cross." He kept on telling me things to say which were obviously the ones Daddy said to Danny whenever the child was doing something "bad." Like "He will crash," "Come down to Danny on a parachute and punish him," "Take him with him," and so on.

I refused to repeat them. Danny cried hysterically, begging me to do so. Then I realized that this was the only anger the child knew, and as horrible as it was to him, it was still familiar and thus better than my unknown anger. I repeated everything he asked me to but prefaced each statement with, "That is what Daddy says and not Miria."

And then I repeated just what I had said before: "Miria loves Danny very much. But now she is furious." I accompanied it with a shaking as before.

We did that over and over again. That one day and on many other days, Danny would provoke my reaction on purpose so he could reassure himself of the difference.

Finally, after weeks and weeks of wreckage and my identical reaction, I heard Danny say to himself, while shielding his wall with both arms, "That is Miria and not Daddy."

And then, as if in utter despair, he said, "Where is Daddy?" It was as if by accepting my set of values he had eliminated Daddy. Then, still later, I heard him say, "Daddy is at home and Miria is at school."

After that his speaking increased, the wall-wrecking diminished, and some of the panic that would creep into his eyes began to evaporate.

We did the same with Mira and Mommy. However, that was simpler after the separation of Mira from Daddy.

Then we had to learn the difference between objects and me. If a can fell on Danny's head, "it was Miria" who "did it." And if he hurt himself in any way, it was again "Miria" who "did it." If he could not screw the screw in, "it was Miria" who "did it." And if he couldn't put his shoe on, it was again "Miria" who "did it." For all those supposed wrongs, he had to hit Mira. For a long, long time no matter how hard I tried to explain to him, using every reasonable explanation I could think of, nothing got through. Mira was all to him, the all-loving and all-punishing deity. He hated and loved it, but certainly did not trust it. Again this too worked itself out, after lengthy testing of me and finally after lengthy consultations with the wall.

And so slowly but very definitely Danny was getting some ego boundaries. And this time not by staying away from everything and everyone in order to keep his own self, but by his positive feeling that his self was not so bad or so destructible, like a wall or like a chair; that his self was not me or Daddy or Mommy, but was in relation to me and later somewhat to Daddy, to Mommy, and to things.

The less he felt threatened of invading and being invaded, the more secure he felt with me, the less he needed to wreck his wall. He guarded his wall, he stood by it and integrated there whatever new or puzzling thought process he came upon. But the destruction of it diminished. His destruction of the wall at home diminished also but I got complaints from his parents that he was breaking the windows in his house instead. A new twist. To all my questions and pleas of "why?," the answer was just "because" or "Danny, because."

His parents went from great joy with the diminishing of the wall-wrecking to great despair with the window breaking, and the beatings began all over again. Then his mother cut herself very badly trying to fix a window —stitches, blood, beatings. Danny was blamed. It all added up to nothing in my head. Danny began to kill fish and wish for me and him to go to the star—"Where Grandpa and the fishes live." We were then at the height of our "be lost" and "helicopter" game, in which time and time again Danny would go "up high" with me into fantasy, forever winning his battle with death— escaping it as himself and as his father.

He would often tell me that "when Danny be bad, Daddy will crash and come in at night on a parachute, through the window, and punish Danny." Or, as he'd say, "cut his head off." It occurred to me that since Danny was so successful at not "crashing" as himself or as Daddy (not causing Daddy to crash), thanks to the floodlights and searchlights, he had decided to test and see what would happen if he as "Danny" or as "Daddy" crashed through the window. Unfortunately, his test failed. He got what he was most afraid of—a terrible beating from Daddy. After that Danny stopped going "up up high" with me, stopped "being found" and "not crashing." But kept on staring at the window in our classroom. I knew he had to dare and break this window and so experience a different reaction from me and Charles, the male director (father substitute), from the one he got at home. And so I kept ignoring his threats of "Danny wants to break the window." This lasted for about a month. Until, one day, he broke the window.

The child was in deathly terror. I said, "Well, you did it. It can be fixed, you know. But you had better explain it to Charles." The child was in death's agony, but it had to be done. So he ran up to the director. He was shaking, his hands were cold and his face in a sweat, and he blurted out: "Danny broke a window." He sat down on a chair, shielded his head with his hands, and waited for the execution.

The director said calmly, "Oh, that's too bad because it may rain tonight and the glazier is busy now."

He then smiled at the child and said, "You should have picked another day," and offered him a lollipop.

Danny's face relaxed. He looked at the director in disbelief, took about five lollipops, and ran out of the room. He ran out to me, gave me a great hug, and sat himself in the broken window. He would not allow anybody to come next to it except the director and me. He kept on repeating the motion of breaking through the paneless window, and we both had to repeat our feelings about his behavior as we had expressed them before. We could not fix the window for a month; Danny would not let us.

A month later I saw Danny by his wall repeating to himself verbatim all we had said to him. He still broke windows at home, but his parents, after understanding what was at stake, reacted the same way we did, and soon he gave the practice up.

He then resumed his "helicopter" and "not be lost" rides and stopped killing the fish. Whenever he was about to kick in a chair or a can or wreck a wall, all I

184

had to say was "Danny will positively, absolutely not . . ." kick the chair, wall, or whatever. He would stop the wrecking and repeat to himself, "Danny should posilutely, absotively not . . ." He began to dictate letters to anyone and everyone who'd have them, and to make up songs. He became very nice to a school cat, biting it only seldom; for some reason or other he named it Lewey Screwey. And he asked his parents for a dog.

He began to take over more and more my concept of him, rather than his parents' and his own, and became quite lovable.

It often seems that the mysteries of the human race are known by a child from the moment of his conception. Millions of years are gone through in seconds, via tribal customs and rituals to our modern way. The phenomenon becomes more specific, more noticeable, more encapsulated in the disturbed child. Especially when he stops and acts the rituals out. Not for one second, but over and over again. The dybbuk of Yiddish mysticism, the numbers of the kabala, the medicine men, the exorcism. The identification with animals in search for strength and power, the magic circles, the magic of numbers, of the sky, of the stars. The magic of water.

Danny's fear of candles probably started with the day he saw his little girlfriend laid out, dead, with candles standing by her at her wake.

Ever since I'd known Danny, candles had been one of his great fears. If he saw one, he went pale and then proceeded to destroy it, moaning as he did so. A lit candle could throw him into a terror so great that the child would give one the impression of exploding from within.

Sometimes he would go off into a corner with a lump of clay and make out of it rows upon rows of candles, mumbling to himself, "That is a candle that is." And so candles, fire, and anything else resembling them were

185

removed from the child's area. I tried to understand it —with no luck. I tried to help him overcome it—with no result.

As noted, the piano to him was also a candle, and it too was treated with fear. Whenever anyone came to the piano, Danny would react strangely. He'd measure off some distance, seem to draw a mental line, and then get quite upset if anyone crossed it.

Then one day, suddenly, he took a piece of chalk and began to draw circles. One around the piano and one in the center of the room. Then busily but silently he arranged his clay candles all around the circle in the center—mumbling something incomprehensible all along. All of us had to remain where we were. When another child tried to step over the circle, Danny pushed him away fiercely, as if frightened. Then he walked into the central circle and said, "Danny be dead," and he stretched out flat on the floor within the confines of the circle with the candles all around him. I watched, petrified, not knowing what to expect but not daring to stop him.

The child closed his eyes and lay there motionless, hardly breathing. What if the child destroys his newly developing personality in this process, was my terror. I felt I had to get through to him somehow. I could not let him get too far away from me. I came closer to the circle, though feeling that I had better not cross over the line he had drawn, and whispered to him, "Danny, Miria loves you very much," trying desperately to keep the contact between us, as if his very life depended on it. Danny did not react. His breathing was as slow and as slight as before. His face was marble white and not a muscle moved. I repeated again, but very quietly, "Miria loves Danny very much," and I died in my own way with him.

After a while I saw his eyelids move. He got up as if from a tired sleep. He did not seem to be aware of what had happened. He had stepped on the line of his magic circle and so had I, with no reaction from him. I hugged him and kissed him and we went out for ice

186

cream. He repeated this bizarre ritual a few more times, each time seemingly not remembering it at all; but each time now it would be preceded by a loud banging on the piano with his feet and hands. When he stopped acting out this macabre act of "Danny be dead now," he began to light candles and make fires and became as fascinated with them as any other child. He began to play the piano, too, and would often "play out" on it the scoldings he'd got from his Mommy and Daddy.

Danny learned to come closer to the other children, adults, and animals. He had a cat now. At the start he used to bite the cat; however, they became friends. And when Danny came to school with scratches on his face, he immediately told me, "Danny and his Kitty had a fair fight, but Danny has the scratches; the Kitty has none." He called his cat Blue, painted his room blue, and liked to wear blue clothes. He learned to know what he liked and what he didn't like, and how to express it. He came to know some of his limitations and would, for instance, screw in a nail until the very bottom, but when it got too tough, said, "Danny needs some help."

And so it went. Danny became stronger and stronger, his boundaries more and more secure. In time I could say he became happier. And I loved him. He became quite a conversationalist, imaginative, vital, creative. He was so alive. Such fun. Such a joy to be with.

His running, twisting, and turning disappeared almost completely. The wall-wrecking was gone. The flights in the helicopter were finished with. His self-destruction and external destruction were done with. No need for the "spanking game" any more. No fear of stars—the moon and the sun had their place in his constellation. The inordinate fear of death was diminished; we were growing together. There still was need for the seesaw and the song, but that was mainly for the sake of remembrance.

We even changed the song together, and now it had a hauntingly happy tune with new words that Danny added:

Way up high we go
Where the wind does howl
And the birds do fly
The sun is golden and warms Danny
The moon is bright and lights up the night
The stars, they shine all over the sky.
Way up, way up high.
The sun loves Danny very much
The moon loves Danny very much
The stars love Danny very much
And Miria loves Danny oh so much.
Way up high into the sky we go
Up and down, up and down
    And down we are—safe.

He still would go off every now and then and get into
his rocker and stare, or sit on the windowsill and stare.
At those times he seemed to be completely inaccessible.
But the intervals in between such episodes were much
longer and the time he "withdrew" much shorter. Also
there was a different quality to the withdrawals and
different reasons for them, usually the facing of a new
fear and the knowledge of how to handle it differently.

It seemed at those times that he was trying to integrate whatever he had learned. At the start when I tried
to break through the episodes, he'd let me in long
enough to say, "Danny wants to be alone," or, "Danny
needs to be alone." Initially I'd try to apologize for my
intrusion, saying, "But I thought that you got lost and
I was just trying to find you." But then one look from
Danny showed me how mistaken I was, how insensitive
to his need.

After that I knew he'd withdraw because he needed
to—to integrate, to reassure himself, maybe even to
take a step backward in order to go ahead again. He
was a swimmer holding his breath in and letting it out
slowly—in order to learn what it's like under the water,
but not to drown.

Our closeness produced in him an ability to read my
mind at times. I remember the first time I became aware
of it. It was a cold day and I was going to take him

to the playground. He was sitting on the windowsill. I walked over to him and before I opened my mouth he said, "No, Danny doesn't want to go to the playground." At first, it used to startle me. (The responsibility put on me for my thoughts I felt was too great.) However, afer a week I began to take it for granted.

Was it because of his lack of boundaries? His extreme sensitivity? Or perhaps with him I had no boundaries either. I watched both of us carefully. But no— I had my boundaries and Danny was developing his.

Danny was thriving, and we both enjoyed his growing. He had such great depth and great sensitivity; it was, I think, why he was so wonderfully healthy when in his health and so frightfully sick when in his illness.

This isolated, solitary, wild, wild little animal became gregarious. He cuddled with other children, played with them, and very often anticipated their needs with remarkable sensitivity (offering a weeping child its favorite toy, for example).

His face glowed with warmth, belonging, love, and very often mischief. He had respect for himself.

Then came the second summer of our content.

Danny's parents had changed enormously with the change in him. His mother asked for therapy to help her resolve her problems. His father told me, "The boy is a pleasure and yet I am afraid of him. What do I do— what is wrong? It isn't the boy any more. So it must be me." And he went into treatment.

I loved the child more than ever. I saw the sun in his eyes, the moon and stars in his hair. He made my days. I still remember feeling how strange it was I was getting paid for helping the child I loved so much get better. To do what you are so happy doing and get paid for it—it was almost indecent. I spent six hours a day with him at school, every single day except for weekends. And on weekends I visited him often.

Then his mother, father, and sister dared to think of a vacation. I promised to keep Danny for two weeks. I thought it would be a picnic. I loved the child so much, enjoyed him so much that I was really looking forward to it.

It was fun, oh, it was great fun; but it was work, the kind of work I never imagined existed.

Twenty-four hours a day alone with the child. Alone. No one to relieve me, no one to take the pressure off. Yes, Danny was happy to be with me, and yes, he did love me, but he missed his home. He missed his parents, his sister, and the normal routine. And twenty-four hours a day was not the six hours I spent with him at school. No relief for him from me, no relief for me from him. When he got tired, he got cranky. When he had enough of me, there was no one to spell me. And the demands! On my sensitivity, alertness, strength, endurance.

I couldn't even go alone to mail a letter. Danny couldn't let me out of his sight. Then his mother found out that she needed an operation and the two weeks stretched to a month.

It was then that I learned to have respect for the parents of such children. To live with these kids is at times beyond the realm of imagination. It is at times a test of all human endurance. And at times a ripping of one's guts, a tearing of one's frazzled nerves.

It was then that I learned, at least a tiny bit, what the parents of these children go through.

I was then I learned what it means not to have a life of one's own.

It was then that I learned not to judge so glibly and not to accuse so fast, so uncomprehendingly.

It was then that I learned some compassion for the parents. It was then that I learned some humility.

And for that I shall always be grateful to Danny and his parents.

It was quite a month—and yet Danny wasn't my own. It was also a wonderful month—perhaps because he wasn't my own.

I remember a subway ride. Danny, at the time, was fascinated with the rhinestone jewelry then in fashion. "The lady has diamonds, lovely diamonds," he said in a stage whisper, pointing across the aisle to a lady's earrings. The lady's vanity was flattered; she insisted that this lovely child sit on her lap. After all, a diamond is a diamond, fake or real. Danny touched one earring and then the other and without warning gave the lady a kiss on her cheek. But as was his fashion, a kiss and a bite were still sometimes interchangeable and she got the bite. The commotion was unbelievable. Thank God the next stop came quickly. No child was ever pulled off a train so fast.

Danny's mother had her ovarian operation. Danny heard her tell me that the cyst was like a large button; a few days later, he began to go for buttons. His button collection grew immensely from day to day. All the clothes in my closet were buttonless. So were his parents' when he went home.

For Danny his stay with me was a great success. It was his first separation from home and he made it. Not only did he make it, but he continued his improvement. He grew.

By fall, everyone was amazed at Danny's growth. The psychiatrist and the director felt that the child was ready to move on, to a higher, more integrated class in the same school. There the children's disturbances were not so extreme, and they were ready for school work. Danny became more gregarious and began to relate to other adults at the school. His new teacher was picked from among these, the one he seemed to like best.

At first he was to stay with me half a day, to wean him gently. My job was accomplished. Such was the composite decision of the powers-that-be.

In my heart I did not want him to go to another group yet. He wasn't ready. "Miria will always be with Danny?" he once asked—and then answered, "Miria *will* always be with Danny." But I suspected my heart. Was I like a mother not ready to give up her child, thus holding him back?

So much was involved for me in this child.

Danny was Danny, but he was also a part of my own self, somewhere lost along the way, that I was desperately trying to find. He was the child I did not have. He

191

was my sister, my brother whom I hardly knew. He was all the hurts and joys I'd ever experienced. He was all the children I'd ever known. He was me; he was Danny; he was all. And he was being taken away from me.

How could I judge? How could I know what was for him, what was for me?

So I let my head rule my heart and agreed to the transfer.

In the other group, Danny—furious with me—became worse and worse. He had been so much better, and now he was regressing. His tantrums came back; the button tearing seemed a compulsive need; and then he began to wreck. The wall at home, the wall at the school, the window. His feet were bloody and again he went back to the rocking chair, again back to the stars, to being lost, to crashing again, again, again. I pleaded to take him back, but was told it was only a phase the child had to go through with the new teacher, that if I interfered now, he could never readjust.

The disillusionment for Danny's parents became too great. They were tired. They could not go through with another cycle. A new unit was being set up at a state hospital; they wanted to try it for Danny.

They could not take Danny at home any longer. To my constant pleas, "Don't send him away. Don't place him," eventually came the inevitable, "If he were yours, Mira, what would you do?" And "Don't we have a right to a life, too? Don't the other children?" What was there to answer—what right does one have to tell people what to do? And for how long? He was their child, but it was also their life. So they sent him to the hospital.

What right does one have to tell another how long he is to bear a cross, and how?

What right? When you cannot promise its end.

The road seemed endless, empty, arid, hopeless. And tragedy has no one face—it has a million faces, bodies, souls. It takes a million forms and shapes. No matter what course Danny's parents took, they had to live with it. No matter what they did with Danny, he would be with them every second of the day. Because he was still their child.

But he was also mine.

No, Danny, I did not find you when you "be lost." I failed.

I could not keep my promise. I came to the hospital time and time again. We'd sit on the stairs or in the visiting room, and I'd sing all the songs he loved so much:

> Danny's hair is like the sun
> Danny's eyes are like the sky.

Then he gave a small, forlorn little smile and did not want to let me leave. He'd plead with me to take him with me.

No, Danny, I did not find you "when you be lost"— "little" or "big"—because I could not find the way to you.

And then I did not come any more because impotence is terrifying and helplessness is devastating. And the heart can break many, many times and then can break no more.

No, Danny, I did not find you when you be lost— Forgive!

WINTHROP
AND OTHERS

Winthrop is nine years old and, by diagnosis, a schizophrenic child. He is removed from reality and thus
from other children. He is withdrawn, never talks to
anyone, lives in a fantasy world of his own making,
fights imaginary enemies, answers imaginary voices, and
cries because of imaginary curses.

Winthrop is an ugly boy. He is gentle, with big black
eyes and a forever running nose. With untied shoelaces,
he sometimes wears two socks, sometimes only one. His
coat is hardly ever on right; forever mismatched is the
right buttonhole in search of its mate. He has a few
possessions and he treasures them greatly. He is crazy
about his notebooks in which he keeps all kinds of
secret writings. He loves his diary in which he writes
down in the minutest details all of his movements and
all the events of the day. But his greatest possession of
all is a box filled with bottle tops. That is his treasure
and the tops are his friends, his only friends. When he
comes to class, he goes to a table, spreads out his bottle
tops, and talks to them. For them he need not fear.
From them he gets no pain, no hate, no danger. He has

over 100 bottle tops, and each one has a name, each one an identity, each one its own personality. With each one separately Winthrop engages either in a fight or in friendly play. Sometimes he makes two camps out of them. Then he is the great general, the master of it all, and when they fight he directs the operations.

One day he painted them. Some green, some yellow, and some white. And then he made three camps. Winthrop was in their midst—the friend, the king, the God, creator of them all.

They waged battle. To me it seemed a bit confusing; not to Winthrop. He made them all win. Then one day, when I came to class, the bottle tops weren't there. They weren't on the table. They weren't in the box. They weren't on the floor. And the table that Winthrop was sitting at was bare and empty. Friendless. That was strange. I was frightened. I knew from past experience the tragedy whenever one of the bottle tops was missing. I also knew how much the other children hated him and that they sometimes teased him by hiding some of the tops. But not all; never all. Perhaps I was frightened because I sensed that something was happening to Winthrop. And no matter how wonderful change is, it is always somehow frightening.

So I looked out of the window and there, in a puddle of water, bottle tops were swimming about. Green bottle tops, yellow bottle tops, white bottle tops, and gray ones. Some were smashed and some were filthy and some just stood there and stared. All his friends in a puddle. All with names, all with histories, all with battle scars. All so lovingly attended to, all so fiercely despised. All of Winthrop's playmates. So I turned around and said to Winthrop in a shakingly calm voice, "Where are your bottle tops, Winthrop?" "I don't know. They are gone," was his reply, calm and detached. "Did anyone throw them out?" I stoically asked. "I don't know. Maybe. But they are gone and I don't want them any more." And for the first time since I knew him, he looked me squarely in the face, then looked around at the children and shyly said, "I did it." He paused, standing hopelessly forlorn. "I'd rather play with the kids. Real kids," he said haltingly, and then added quietly, "I think." And with a rush of embarrassment he ran out of the room.

He came back carrying a pail of water, which he put down in the center of the room. "I brought it for the class. For everyone," he said with eyes shining and voice trembling. "For all the kids." The children accepted the gift without a comment, but there was a hush in the room. Then Winthrop took all the pencils out of my drawer and sharpened them. After each one, he said, "I am doing it for everyone. I am doing it for the whole class." And then he looked up at the rest of them and said very quietly and shyly, "And I don't want nothin' in return." The kids were so attuned to each other that they always sensed something big. Winthrop was coming back from the dead—they knew it. And though he was the butt of all their merciless jokes, they were ready to give their help to him.

I brought in the midday cake and gave Winthrop a slice. He stood there in the middle of the room with outstretched hand and the slice in it, ready to share it with all of them. And everyone knew how Winthrop loved cake. But, as I said, something happened to the kids. One child was giving Winthrop half of his piece of cake. Then another child. And another. One could see Winthrop's cheeks getting redder and redder with pleasure, and his mouth fuller and fuller with cake. With his running nose, askew-buttoned coat, and untied shoelaces. Winthrop was quite a sight. But he loved it all and the kids seemed to love Winthrop.

Lancelot. Five-year-old little Lancelot. Whose snotty dirty ugly little face was so hard to love that it left him all alone, all to himself.

Lancelot—his mother named him after the glorious knight—he was so tiny, so scrawny, so clumsy that she could not face her disillusionment and turned her love away from the child.

I called him Lance and scaled him down to size. He looked like a little sandpiper. He was always in the sandbox. The sandbox was his world.

He spent hours building his complex castles in the sand. The castles were so small that they were only visible when you came very close to them. But the moment you came that close, he destroyed them. So contaminated would any other human being make them. So contaminated would his world become.

The castles were beautiful and powerful. They had a moat, a drawbridge, and a high thick wall—they were inaccessible. They kept the world away from him and kept him secure within his own. His castles were his own and only his own.

I sat on a branch at a safe distance from him and watched him while his day away. He chased me but I did not go away. He made himself uglier but I did not turn away.

One day he forgot the wall and let another human being into his heretofore lonely world. He let me build with him. Lance let in love. And Lance got well. And became more beautiful even than Sir Lancelot.

The sixteen-year-old delinquent girls of Katy Kill Falls found a bunny.

We were working by the powerhouse, painting chairs. One girl, Gertie, who had finished her job, played ball by herself, hitting it furiously against the wall of the powerhouse. The ball landed on the roof. Gertie tried to climb up. The stone wall was too smooth. Gertie looked around for help. Bonnie and Cybelle tried to help. No luck.

"Go to the gym and get the coach," I said. "He's tall." They went and came back with Leona, who is small. They all disappeared behind the powerhouse in order to make a human chain so they could scale the wall. Suddenly I heard screams. I thought the house had fallen in on them. I ran toward them, trying to decipher the words I was hearing. "A bunny!" "We found a bunny!" "He's ours," they were shrieking, their voices tumbling over each other like a waterfall over rocks. I ran to them. In Bonnie's arms was a big black rabbit with his nose wiggling and his big eyes fastened on something—on what, no one could tell. Proudly but in terror, Bonnie yelled, "It's our bunny now." Gertie's shrieks were hysterical. "No one will take him away from us. Do you hear? We're going to keep him!"

I was excited too. A lovely small animal. Then I looked at the girls, the hardened tough girls, criminals of the institution. The ones everyone called the whores. There was something in their faces that I had rarely seen. They were all huddled as if shielding the bunny against the outside. Against hurt and rejection. They looked frightened, soft—vulnerable. They looked tender and awed as they guarded their bunny. Their tentative resentment, just in case I didn't let them keep the animal, was feeble and shortlived. It was quickly erased by the stronger feeling of warmth and pleading in their faces.

"Of course you can keep him," I said. "He's so lovely." Their faces turned up to me like flowers just opened. Open, beautiful young girls' faces, with all the resentment, bitterness, and pain gone.

Then Bonnie said, "You know, I'll tell you something. This is the first time I ever held anything alive in my arms. It is small and warm and breathes. And it's mine. You know I didn't catch it. He came to me," she whispered, the hard, tough, delinquent girl from Katy Kill. "He came into my arms, all by himself. Oh, I love him so. It's like a baby."

"Yeah, all by himself," Belle said. Like the echo of the wind amidst whispering willows. "All by itself." "All by itself," the girls repeated and repeated and repeated. And I thought, oh, God, thank you for this bunny.

Each of the five girls touched the bunny gently, with tremendous emotion, and all confessed to their love and to their helplessness in front of this little thing. Then Gertie said, "You know I'm really scared of him. I'm afraid to touch him." And Gertie never admitted fear.

Bonnie compassionately put him in Gertie's arms—Bonnie who fought with knives, clawed and pulled eyelashes at the slightest provocation. Gertie, visibly frightened, took the bunny in her arms. Then something happened to her. She relaxed, her fear all gone, and tenderly put her head against the animal's head and kissed it on the nose. The animal sneezed. Everyone laughed.

The next day a man came and took the rabbit away. It was his.

I tried to buy it from him; he refused. I offered to buy the girls another. But no, they did not want another. The hard shell enveloped their faces again. And once again they became the whores of Katy Kill.

And then there was Maria, the mute one, quick, graceful, and elusive like a gazelle, unreal like a mirage, silent and gentle like a mild summer breeze. There she is. And now she's gone! You could chase after her and you couldn't catch her. If you caught her, you couldn't hold her. Nothing worked.

But then you found it. A song. A song could entice Maria out from wherever she was hiding. It would stop her short in her tracks. It would bring her back to you. It was the only crack in the thick wall of defenses that surrounded her. The only crack which she somehow didn't fill in with the mortar and cement of fear, with the rocks and concrete of pain that she used in the wall she built. She built the wall to keep herself aloof, to keep safe and protected from life. Whatever life meant for her.

A song. A sum of notes and words. And then a fleeting ray of a smile would cross her face and she was captured. It took a long, long time, but Maria loved singing so much that eventually she was willing to sing the song with you, to begin to love you and to trust you through the song. And Maria, with her tiny silvery frightened little voice, joined you in a song and used your words.

After a long, long time, Maria learned to ask you for what she wanted through a song. To tell you of her pains and disappointments through her song. And of her angers—through a song. And you could answer only in a song. Because when the melody stopped, living for Maria stopped. Then after a much longer time, when Maria grew much bigger and much older and her trust in you and in herself and thus in the world around her grew stronger, Maria stopped the melody and used words. She became like you and me, only nicer.

Kate. Big fat ugly Kate. So very, very angry, so very, very clumsy, so very, very stupid. Forever full of guilt. Hopeless.

Looking without seeing, blinded by fear. Talking without saying, muted by pain, listening without hearing, deaf through horror. Kate.

One day as she watched me dance, she joined me. And after a while Kate began to come out from behind her walls. Bit by bit. But only when dancing. Only when dancing with me and to me. She "talked" to me through her dance. She told me her whole story.

And as she "talked" and was listened to and sometimes understood, she began to lose some of her fears and to move freely and gracefully. Her story was full of violence, brutality, and rejection, but as time went on it became full of tenderness, gentleness, and love.

It was strange to see this young child go through her metamorphosis. It was all done through movement. How she talked with her body and how her body changed! She danced with the wildest abandon, with exquisite sensitivity, with complete grace. Civilized. And so big fat ugly Kate danced her way out of her cocoon, metamorphosed into a most beautiful healthy butterfly.

It took a while.

Jimmy. The six-year-old adopted little boy. Adopted only a few days after he was born. Jimmy was so pretty, so sensitive, so gentle. He once tried to set a fire under another kid, so he "would see what burned flesh looked like." Jimmy with the golden hair. Jimmy with the face of a cherub. Jimmy who loved so much that he had to kill, be it you, be it birds, be it cats, be it other children. Lest you kill him with your love.

Love. Eyes shut, tightly shut. Teeth clenched, tightly clenched. Face contorted in a horrible grimace of terror and of pain. Because love hurt that much. Love was that dangerous. Love was that wonderful. Love and death were equal to Jimmy. You shut your eyes tightly, you grit your teeth, and you attack and kill. And then you shriek with orgiastic joy and are released. You kill. You kill a bird, a cat, a fish, whatever else you can—you try to kill a child and even an adult. Such relief after it is done! Such a need to do it.

But then punishment will come. Why punishment? You must look guilty; that reduces the punishment. But really you aren't guilty at all. You had to do what was most logical to you. The grown-ups don't understand it at all, and the grown-ups say you are guilty. So you act guilty. And you are scared. As unreal as the guilt is, so real is the terror of punishment.

"Let's kill. Let's kill a bird. So we can see the insides of it" is the excuse. The adults understand that better— better than that you must kill the bird because you love it. But then comes the terror anyhow, whether you kill or you don't. The terror makes you change.

And when the terror comes, so comes the rage at those who terrify. Then Jimmy's body changes, as if inhabited by something other than himself. "The devils live there," as Jimmy says. It becomes taut and rigid, like a tightly wound spring. And it begins to shake and sway. The arms leap out to both sides and together with the flapping hands move to and fro like wings ready for takeoff. The feet spring off the ground, touching it only by toe tips. And he leans forward like a bird ready to fly. But Jimmy can't fly; he is only a boy. So he remains arrested. Flapping his wings, hopelessly, aimlessly, helplessly. His face contorted and red with the effort, the veins on his neck protruding. He remains alone with his terror, alone with the effort, unable to flee it.

Jimmy is bright. He knows the makeup of the human body well. All the organs, especially the reproductive organs. He knows all about fallopian tubes and ovaries and wombs and vaginas. How they all come together. He also knows about penises and scrotums.

Life, death, love, death, and birth. Where does birth come in? The world is one big mother. One big womb to Jimmy—one big rejecting mother. Jimmy's parents are sure that he doesn't know he is adopted. Nobody talks about it. Few people know about it. I learned it from the child.

One day Jimmy climbed into a large cardboard crate, lay down in it, closing the flaps above his head, and said, "Mira, this is the box my real Mommy left me in, at your doorstep. Now you open the door to your house and you find the box. Now you open the box and you see a baby. Am I a pretty baby?" "Yes, you are a lovely baby." "All right, take me to your house. You found me and now I'm yours. Adopt me." Jimmy begins to whine like an infant. "Pick me up and carry me. That's what I'm crying about, don't you see?" I do see. I carry him about in my arms like an infant. He coos. "Now feed me like a baby, with milk." I do it. Jimmy relaxes in my arms and smiles with a strange blissful smile. (He is even more relaxed and more blissful than after a killing.) This goes on for hours on end, on and on and on. Then, suddenly, unexpectedly, he leaps out of my arms, off my lap, and begins to hit me in a rage. "But why did she leave me? Why didn't she love me? I was a bad baby. She was a bad Mommy."

For months and months every day Jimmy had me find the box with his baby on my doorstep. And then he went and killed a bird and a fish and a cat all over again. Because love and death were intertwined. It took Jimmy eight years to extricate love from the grips of death. But now he is okay and he rocks his own baby in his arms.

Matthew, my little Matthew. After a year of working with him, I found he had two dimples when he smiled. Before that, Matthew had no need to smile. To him the world was something to stay away from, to fear, to rage against. He wanted so much from it and got so little. His physical and psychological scars were so numerous that they were difficult to differentiate. And they all festered. A physical touch was an attack to the child; a smile or a kind word an aggression. A hug or kiss was a rape. He was so skinless, unprotected, raw.

For many many months he wore a hat pulled over his eyes with earmuffs down on his ears, a muffler around his neck, and galoshes on his shoes. And that infernal woolen coat of his buttoned up. Forever, be it summer, spring, winter, or fall; it was safer this way. This was his protection against the world. Without it Matthew felt naked, exposed, vulnerable. His need, his fear, his pain, his love were there to be hurt. So he had to protect himself with his coat of armor, literally and figuratively. Finally, when he began to trust, he dared to leave off some of his protection. He took off his earmuffs, so that he could hear. He lifted the hat up off his eyes, so he could see. He took the galoshes off his feet so he could feel the ground he walked on. He took the muffler off his neck and thus exposed his neck to murder—which he feared most. Then at last he took his coat off. "Don't yook at me," he'd say, "can't you see I am naked?"

And then much later when he dared to show more of his feelings, I remember listening with him to Brahms's *Intermezzo*. The intensity of his reaction overwhelmed him. He saw me look at him and he yelled out amidst tears and pain of exposure, "Stop yooking at me. I have no skin," so naked did he seem to himself. So intense his feeling, and so severe the pain in feeling. Matthew. I remember the first week of our working together when I bent over and kissed him on the head and Matthew, with all the savagery in him and all the fear, yelled out, "Okay, now you bend down and I'll punish you too." Then he kissed me on my head. Weeks later as he found me walking in back of him, he warned me, "Don't you touch me, not even a little bit."

And then many months later Matthew, sobbing bitterly, " 'Cause I don't want you to love me so much, Mira. I don't want you to love me at all." And then in a whisper, "Maybe just a tiny bit."

Months and months and years it took until Matthew could trust my love and accept it directly. Could let me touch him, hold him, and kiss him. Until then I could only do it either through other children or by non-verbally conveying my feeling to him. I never overstepped the bounds of his fear until he invited me into it himself.

Then Matthew on the beach. Stripped of everything but his underpants, holding them on his body under protest. Rolling on the sand, sensuously delighted with the feel of the sun and the sand, tickling mine and the other kids' feet and squealing, "It's such great fun; it's such great fun."

And all the many, many others. The Bobbies. The Frankies. The Andies.

All those who wanted. All those who needed. All those who dared to put a foot out into the world, out of their shells. And those who didn't.

Billy. Age eight. I didn't like him; he didn't like me either. We were in the same school for two years but avoided each other as if by mutual consent or by a chemical repulsion. I had my own group; he had his own teacher.

Only once during those two years did he come into my room. Carrying his bowel movement in a can—as if it were a treasure—he put it on my desk for safekeeping. And I looked after it for a whole day, knowing that it was a sign of trust and that the trust was not to be broken. Then he came and took it away. And that was that. The end of this strange mute contact.

He stopped speaking when he was four and did not speak again. Although the superintendent in his house said that Billy had spoken to him a few times, in secret, and his mother said that the cleaning woman had heard him talk in his sleep. But we never did.

He spoke through pantomime, lips moving, acting out what he meant, or using puppets. Using each of these ways separately or in whatever combination suited him.

He controlled all of us through his "non-speech"; he controlled the whole world with it. All stopped when Billy tried to "tell" us something, since all attention had to be focused on him—in order to understand what

205

he was saying. Such coercion was often unbearable to me; such control inconceivable.

He was a mean child. Always angry, always sullen, always stubborn, always hurting. He was forever devising ways of torturing others. Sophisticated ways. But he was never caught, never got pinned down. If he did not get what he wanted, he ran away, under a speeding car, down a ten-story fire escape, hanging on the back of a bus, or jumping out of a window. (What he wanted most was to get everyone involved with himself.)

He built cages out of blocks and either put himself inside them or put other children into them. He liked to trap them, watch them try to get out and not let them go. They were imprisoned as he felt he was.

He made potions out of unpleasant, often poisonous substances and was forever inducing others to drink. Then he watched their discomfort with pleasure.

Every day he would die. He built himself a make-believe electric chair and electrocuted himself daily. He'd lie there "dead" until we resurrected him.

So great was his hurt, so overwhelming his hate, so forceful his rage with life.

Until one day—

One day he dropped an iron weight out of a third-story window on the head of one of my children. He did it well. He attached a thin wire to the iron weight and the moment after it gashed the child's head, the weight was pulled up and one could see nothing. Except for the blood gushing out of the child's head.

It took a while, but twenty-one stitches later I found out. The game had begun.

Billy could never express his anger through direct frontal attack. The unpredictability in confrontation was too terrifying to the child. He forever had to arrange and be in control of any expression of rage, his or anybody else's. The expression of another's anger toward him was unbearable.

So I decided that the only way to get through to this child would be to lead him to a point where he would be forced to express his anger directly and receive another's as directly, thus exposing himself naked and undefended in his rage. I wanted to help him to face his anger and his impotence and helplessness within it; to show that he could be protected; that he could learn to be in control of his anger.

Dignity, I think. The word I am searching for is dignity. Something in his slinking, plotting, scheming way he had a right to. Dignity in his anger, in his pain, in his helplessness, in his loneliness.

I set the stage. The means was chairs. I was to defend the child that Billy had hurt.

So I grabbed a chair and slid it across the floor in Billy's direction and said, "I am angry at Billy for what he did." He stood across the room from me with a fleeting smile of success across his face because he had managed to involve me with him. But there was a ray of terror on that face because he did not know how to handle direct anger. And so he tried to pantomime his way out of it. Disarm me with this maneuver. I told him again I was angry and proceeded to slide more chairs across the floor in his direction.

I talked all along in an incessant monologue. I told him I was angry and I knew that he was angry, that I wasn't going to hurt him, but that I had to express my anger to feel better and that if he'd do it he'd feel better too. That one can fight directly and even fling stuff around without hurting the person the anger is aimed at. Each sentence was punctuated by a chair sliding across the room and each pause by Billy's bodily dodging the chairs. The monotone of my voice and the rhythm of the sliding chairs began to hypnotize the child. Finally all the chairs ended on Billy's side of the room and as I had no more left to fling, Billy was forced to fling one back at me.

Slowly and then not so slowly he began to fling the chairs in my direction. The more he flung, the angrier his flings became. Angrier and angrier he got; stronger and stronger the flings of chairs became. He threw them toward me and I returned the throws, all along engineering and controlling them.

The struggle lasted three hours, until perspiring,

spent, and relieved, the child folded up in a heap and began to weep. He looked helpless and tiny. I did not touch him. I let him settle it with himself. He did not need my help.

The next day I took my group to the sea. In spite of his terror of water, Billy followed us sheepishly. The nastiness and anger had all oozed out of the child, leaving him seemingly empty and puppet-like. When we got settled on the blanket, I began to hear strange choking guttural sounds, as if the sounds were trying to break through a stubborn barrier. I followed them and saw Billy standing by the water, bent over, as if trying to retch his guts out. All red and convulsed. Trying to retch speech out. I suddenly realized that not only had I not heard him speak; never before had I heard this mute child make any sound. He laughed without sound, cried without sound, yelled without sound.

Instinctively I took his head between my hands, the way one helps a retching child. The voice, not used to being used, would not respond. But with an effort so great it made his face purple and grotesque, some human sounds came out. It was more a croaking than a speech. But after four years of silence, even croaking has a sound of music. He tried it, over and over again, as if contorted with excruciating pain. I tried desperately to understand. He tried desperately to make me understand. Finally we both made it. "The camera doesn't click," he kept on repeating, over and over again. "It is broken."

Did he see something forbidden and then with terror record it within himself? Did he then "break" the camera speech so he would never have to reproduce it? Or did someone explain to him that the voice worked like a camera? Which was right out of the millions of possibilities?

"Don't worry, Billy, I'll fix it," I promised the child. He touched my hand gently and ran away.

The next day we again went to the sea. But this time only Billy and I. I went into the sea, while he remained

208

on its shore. I began to swim about, convinced that the sea would help him speak. Then it came.

"Mira, where are you?" I heard a child-clear melodious voice call out. He was looking right at me, but obviously not seeing me. Oh, God! Did he exchange his sight for a voice? (Was that his pact with his devil?) I began to walk slowly out of the water. As I came out of the sea, Billy came to meet me. His face was open, loving, and seeing, his hands full of seaweed. (Perhaps the blindness before was not a blindness but fear or shock and absorption with his new-found voice.)

He took the seaweed and decorated me with it, along my hair, along the edges of my bathing suit, and on my arms. After the job was completed, I got his first kiss. Then he pulled me back into the sea and went in with me. We swam around together in silence, I losing my seaweed and he picking it up for me. Then he stopped and said, "Friend. You are my friend." And then he talked about the water and the sky and his pain and his terror and finally of the scene he had witnessed that to him was murder but might have been intercourse. Or perhaps it really was murder. A scene of terror which seemingly silenced him forever. And then he smiled and said, "You see, you did fix the camera."

With us it is as it says, "From the dust thou cometh, to the dust thou goeth." With Billy it was different. "From the sea thou cometh, to the sea thou goeth." Always the sea. One day we might have to return him to the sea.

Always the sea. To the sea we went to be closer, together—to grow. By the sea, Billy regained his speech, his love—himself.

I always wondered what this child's fairy tale was that he lived by, after he excluded himself from our world. Why me? Who was I to him? Then one day when we were rowing in Prospect Park, he stopped the boat and we walked onto an island. He said to me, "You are Friday and I am Robinson Crusoe. I've waited and looked for you all my life. Now I've found you. And now I shall never, never be lonely again." Enthralled with himself, he went on: "Look at the weeping willows crying into the lake." The world lay in his new-found ability to express it all in words.

The times I spent with Billy I could count on my fingers, each time more poignant than the last, each meaningful for both of us. Each time by the water. I remember one time when we were getting our clothes off to go into the sea. He pulled out Picasso's Harlequin from his pocket. The picture looked as though he had carried it forever. "He is a clown," he told me, "he laughs. And he makes people laugh. But really he is sad. Very sad, Mira. Why?" "Maybe it is because he has lived so much and knows so much," I said. Billy then said with a smile, "It is hard, Mira, to know so much, isn't it?"

I remember another time as we were sitting by the sea, drying ourselves off—his last words, when we were to part at the end of the summer and go our separate ways—"You shall always stay with me."

For a long time afterward Billy's words haunted me. "It is hard, Mira, to know so much, isn't it?"

Why? Is it because it is hard to find words? Hard to say all one knows? A child is only a child and people don't know how very much a child knows. Or is it because people won't listen to a child, or even to an adult? Because they don't want to know, other than what they already know. Or is it because they just can't, won't understand? Maybe because they won't believe whatever doesn't come within their experiences?

Why Billy and the water? Is it an unconscious re-enacting of the beginning of the child in the water of the mother's womb? Is it an unconscious reenacting of the beginning of man from the seed? The fish? Evolution? Or is it the mythological birth of Venus fully blown, without evolution of mankind or of child into adult, out of the sea?

PETER

The antelope, the deer, and the gazelle are playing in the tall grass. The little chimpanzee is looking from the tree, enviously, curiously, at the whole terrain.

The tall grass is swaying to and fro in the gentle breeze. The birds are circling above with their melodious sounds.

The newly born colt is testing the strength of his legs —still within his mother's reach, but already longing for the moment of freedom.

Peter has never known freedom.

Peter was a little boy who could walk and who could talk, who could laugh and who could cry, and who had genius beyond our comprehension.

But—

Peter was a little boy who was desperately and irrevocably afraid of destruction. And since destruction seemed ever present, he built himself a world where he alone, the master and creator of it all, would reign in absolute power, and thus control and circumvent his ultimate destruction.

His was a strange world, a very lonely, frightening world; a very rigid, cruel world. And Peter became a very strange child.

To appease the gods of destruction, always lurking in prey for his life, he would destroy himself. However, it would never be the irrevocable destruction that his gods wanted to execute, for whatever he could do he could undo, as long as he held on to the magic key.

Through all kinds of secret ways, strange magic, and weird rituals he could resurrect himself. But woe unto him, if by some mishap he forgot any details of this magic. For then he might remain destroyed forever.

And so he lived in this strange world where danger lurked all over and destruction was all around; but Peter, through a magic of his own, escaped his fate. And everything he did in his world was directed toward his one goal—survival.

In Peter's world, memories of days gone by and years gone by and things gone by hung neatly on the twisted branches of the barren trees like fruit.

Melodies, fragmented, parts of something that was once or that is now, in their deathly, dusty, dreary monotone sang on.

Bodies walked the streets dismembered. Legs, arms, heads, and torsos moved busily about; grotesquely, with an autonomy all their own.

Multitudes of people beyond count, with little relevant identity, but with a name, an address, a birthday date, day, and a phone number, moved aimlessly about, each carrying a part of Peter.

It was a world full of graves and cemeteries, where the dead were resurrected into a living death and moved on.

A world of dust and heat and little air to breathe. A world of tears and fears.

The phantom world of Peter.

Where cats were howling, screaming, clawing, leaping, tearing, killing, and dying. Where cats reigned supreme—the cats with nine lives.

Where numbers lived with an identity, an independence, and a magic equal to none.

His was a silent world, but for the cats. Except sometimes when stillness would be broken with heart-rending screams of terror and pleas for oblivion; with yearning for union—a small child running from thing to thing, from person to person, from cat to cat, searching for the one final fusion.

At times these screams were Peter's, but they did not last too long, for it was his world. At times they belonged to someone else, but then they lasted longer, as again it was Peter's world. It was a very complex world. A catalogued, well-organized world.

His finding of his road back to life depended on its inner organization. Yet even though the child ruled in complete control, still under all of this, in him fear and destruction reigned in monstrous, absolute mastery.

Everything was marked and numbered lest he might go where danger lurked. The graves were marked, the cemeteries too. The roads and streets had names and signs and numbers. If a "no exit" sign was there or a "dead end" sign, Peter would not go, for by going he might enter a place his magic forbade him to, and thus forfeit his whole life. His exquisite memory stood him here in good stead.

So there reigned Peter, who walked in loneliness and lived in horror—but very carefully lest he forget one landmark and pay with his life.

As aloneness of any degree meant destruction to the child, out of the depth and terror of this loneliness he tried to reach out and fill his void by merging, uniting, overwhelming anyone and anything around him. But then the terror caused by this union was overwhelming, for through the union he would lose his self in someone else's and thus destroy it. And so he would run from the mazes, and thus he was trapped. Alone he could not be; it was too frighteningly painful. But merged he

213

could not exist, because the dangers of obliteration were too great. Yet these were the only choices that he knew. The only choices that he'd given to himself. Either one would bring disaster, terror, endless pain. So in order to exist he ran from one to the other within his terrifying labyrinth. Either weeping in hopeless want and desperation, or shrieking in limitless, unspeakable agony, terror, and pain.

Thus as destruction seemed ever present, so out of half truths deeply learned, out of sorrows indelibly imprinted, out of terrors tangibly experienced, out of truths never fully comprehended, he built himself his world.

The ways he chose to avoid his destruction were often just as terrifying as the destruction he tried so hard to avoid. He ran, this wretched little boy, from complete aloneness, which he couldn't stand, to complete submersion of his self, which was just as painful, knocking on locked doors, pleading for a way out of the maze that he himself had set up, with great caution, and yet not daring and not knowing where to go.

Trapped until not being able to withstand it any more he'd search for the oblivion—death—that he was most afraid of. Feeling somewhere that in this final union he would conquer all and come up resurrected, free, and unafraid.

Since most of Peter's energies went into avoiding destruction, while denying any true living, there was little left for anything else; and thus the child gave the appearance of being feebleminded.

Except for his strange gift with numbers.

From the age of two, he could add, subtract, multiply, and divide numbers of astronomical proportions. Without any effort, at just a glance, without seeming to have to go through our usual arithmetical gyrations.

When I met him, he remembered and could add columns of numbers, even written horizontally, or without having to write them down at all, merely by hearing them. It was an unusual, unspoken, uncanny mnemonic method, which only he knew (if even he did).

He could look at a handful of coins of any denominations, no matter how many, and, at a glance, tell you the sum.

He could spell almost any word.

By the age of seven he could do all the crossword puzzles in *The New York Times* perfectly.

He had a fantastic memory, from which he could reproduce all the yesterdays of his long little life, the most irrelevant details, as if they were occurring now. Nothing passed his senses unrecorded by his memory, provided it belonged in his scheme of things and was therefore necessary for survival. In his fantastic yet selective memory lay all the past and present events of his life. From hour to hour, from day to day, from month to month, from year to year, everyone and everything who ever passed through Peter's world, no matter how seemingly irrelevant to us, became collected and recallable in him.

He had an absolute knowledge of the geography of the city of New York, with all its addresses and its streets, the direction of the traffic on each street, and instructions on how to get anywhere within the city using any kind of transportation.

He needed to know the point of time of any occurrence on any day, and he had a most uncomfortable awareness of all the seconds, minutes, hours passing by—without the help of a clock or watch.

He had an uncanny knowledge of the day a date would fall on—any day, any year, 100 years in the future, 1,000 years in the past.

But all these gifts seemed disconnected from the rest of Peter—aimless, purposeless, irrelevant. And so, as a result of the mental discrepancies, the descriptions of "condition Peter" were many. "Childhood schizophrenia with symbiosis" was one; "idiot-savant" another. "Brain damage" was another; "mental retardation" a fourth.

And while debates about his condition were (and still are) going on, Peter went on his own unmerry way.

Avoiding, cruising around, peeking at, and with that circumventing his ultimate destruction.

He seemed a lonely dancer on a tightrope—always wobbly but desperately trying to maintain his balance. Not looking up or down, or anywhere around, for fear of losing his foothold, his hold on life. And while the gyrations of his arms and legs and of the rest of him seemed strange to those around him, they meant survival. The rope was taut and narrow. You looked nowhere, expended no energy anywhere else. Every ounce of energy was needed for the long and frightful dance.

So the dance went on. And only the dancer knew for a long time what the magic was that kept him from falling off the rope.

He was a most unhappy child. With pains so deep and yet unappeased, with terror so stark and unadorned, with a need so strong and all-engulfing, with an idiocy so blind and yet so purposeful, and with a genius so strange and so uncanny, that for two years—in terror, in hate, and in disgust—I stayed away from him until finally I dared to face what I saw in him, and through him in myself, and then to work with him.

This wondrously strange child, half genius, half idiot, so alone in his brilliance. And just as alone in his confusion.

The frightening brilliance I left alone, since I could never enter his world of genius. His confusion I tried to understand and let the little boy lead me there.

And thus I worked with him for close to seven years, knew him for nine. He was nine and a half when we started to work together. Toward the beginning, very intently, for five to six hours a day. Later on not so intensively, yet always the two of us together learning to understand life and to live it.

But for the first two years, I watched him very closely, not working with him, as one watches one's enemies.

And this stands out in my memory from that time:

The first time I saw Peter was in the spring of 1953. It was a warm, balmy day at a new school in Brooklyn set up for work with seriously disturbed children. I remember this force that descended on me. A sudden volcano. Or quicksand. No, both. That overflowed me, covered me, engulfed me, dragged at me. I felt myself drawn slowly, oh so slowly, into its unknown depths with a power beyond my control, never touching, never approaching me closely yet always there. Behind, in front, all around me. Following.

"Where does this 'wady' wive?" "What is this 'wady's' name?" "What number does this wady Mira wive in?" "What street?" "When is Mira's birthday?" "What month was she born in?" "What day?" "Oh, then her birthday will fall on Friday this year." "Does Mira have a husband?" "How many chiwdren?"

And so it went, on and on and on. Every answer elicited another question. The bombardment was continuous. Was it ever going to end? And those eyes looking right into mine with the feverishness and intensity of some great pain and torture, a search for oblivion or relief. It made me feel that in one more minute there would be nothing left of me but the physical shell.

I took a long walk by the ocean, an attempt to shake Peter out of me and to reassemble my self. I made a decision. Yes, I shall work at the school, but I shall never, never work with this child. Oh, God, please keep me away from temptation, from this child. He will either swallow me or climb right into me. The result will be the same. So I hated him and I feared him and for two years I stayed away from him. Incidents come to the foreground out of the discarded debris of my rememberings. The teacher who worked with Peter became my friend, so that every now and then she and I would combine our children and go on trips together. I remember once a walk into the neighborhood. It was lovely outside, the air cool, the sun warm, and the children beginning to have some sense of belonging to us. There was a little bridge on a tiny grassy hill under which the subway tracks were passing. We stopped off to take a rest. The spot was lovely, full of foliage. Sun and shadows played their games with the children. I looked around and, by an old habit, began to count the children. One was missing. I looked down and there he

217

was. Peter. Moving slowly, awkwardly, as if in a dream, toward the tracks.

Had the train just passed or was it about to come?— How coldly rational danger can make one.

By the time I got to Peter, he had managed to invade the tracks. I still don't know whether the train got there before, after, or during our getting away from the tracks. The expression on Peter's face was the same as usual. No special fear, no comprehension, no guilt. No relationship to what he had done. Just the same intense need to . . . to what? To achieve some kind of union with whatever was there.

A few blocks later, again Peter managed to get away and "unaware" almost walked right under a speeding truck . . .

The next time I remember Peter was in Prospect Park. It was another one of our group walks.

The day was late spring. The air balmy, the grass completely broken through the soil, the trees almost fully covered with new, light green leaves.

The spot we picked for a rest was by a brook. Rocks lined the brook and its shores and joined in a wreath about 6 feet above the brook. An ideal place for the children to climb about on. Peter climbed up on the rocks and was talking to himself, probably counting streets and numbers or his cats. He seemed unaware of anything or anyone around him. Little Robie climbed up after him and stood next to Peter. And then the strangest thing happened. A hand which looked as if it physically belonged to Peter reached out slowly and deliberately and pushed Robie off the ledge into the water. However, Peter himself, as if unaware of the hand's action, went on mumbling and talking to himself, remaining in exactly the same position, without any motion of the body except that the hand came back slowly to its original position, hanging loosely at his side.

I watched it all as if mesmerized. What was most frightening to me was the complete unawareness with which the child performed the deed. It was as if the hand that did it had a life of its own, and was not under the child's control. I woke up from my trance in time to see that Robie had been rescued, and with the startling realization that the deed was not done out of passivity, that there was a peculiar method to Peter's madness, which somehow I did not understand. In spite of the seeming unawareness of his actions, I felt there was a deliberateness in it. In some part of himself the child knew exactly what he was doing; the deed served a purpose no matter how twisted. To cement my knowledge, and to convey it to him—to impress upon him his responsibility for his actions from now on—I gave him a couple of healthy wallops. Thus I no longer responded to his "helplessness" and "idiocy," but kept him accountable for whatever misdeeds he allowed himself to perpetrate under the cloak of his unawareness.

Peter was often an obnoxious being who badgered everyone into desperation with his question "How many cats are there?" The cats were mostly imaginary but at the same time so definite to the child that if the right number weren't guessed, he dissolved in tears.

By the stream, I remember his cats, his meowing, and his being a cat. His constant talk about and search for cats. And the special gleam in his eye whenever he spotted one nearby and ran for it and caught it. I felt that he became one with the cat, and that this oneness, this "catness," made him complete, fulfilled, satisfied, and terribly excited. And I remember recoiling in terror, not being able to understand.

Then, of course, I remember Peter as everyone else does who came in contact with him at the time, as the child with a piece of paper in his hand, checking with anyone and everyone in sight his infernal spelling list. "Peter must know how do you spell . . ." which, of course, he knew better than we did.

Another ability drew people into him more than all the rest. Since it was beyond human comprehension, it had a quality of magic. Peter would go around asking the date of your birthday or any event that interested you, and then tell you the day it fell on in any year in history.

But what I suspected was that he used all these gifts in his demanding way with a purpose quite different from just sharing, rather as a bribery and coercion. I remember also my rage at people's fascination with it and at their offering themselves as dupes for the child's twisted needs.

I remember the plaguing, demanding kid who had to know your address, telephone number, birthday, the color of the dress you wore yesterday, the name of anyone you ever knew.

And then I remember his panics and his piercing screams of pain and terror, with no physical and no understandable emotional provocation.

Yet as time went on I began to see the child behind this fabulously intricate, yet seemingly illogical being. The wall that Peter surrounded himself with began to seem a bit transparent. The child behind it was frightened, lonely, starved for warmth, and very, very hungry. The logic of the wall was startling. What seemed to me all along frightening began to be interesting. The beautiful symmetry and logic of his defense began to dawn on me. My fear turned into anger at being fooled and into fascination at the brilliantly erected structure of his defense—the numbers, the memory, the "unawareness" of his actions—which eventually turned partly into admiration and respect for the child who could erect such a structure. I felt a need to expose these defenses for what they were, a need to know the truth about the child and to show it to the child. A need to set him free.

And a feeling for the child who wanted so much to reach out, but needed so much to push away and insulate himself against the world.

And so in 1955 I asked the director of the school if I could work with Peter.

What had changed me, made me want to work with him? I really do not know.

This idiot who was so brilliant, who could do so much and yet so little, who seemed such a mysteriously closed book to me, was so tantalizing and so hateful, so terrifying and so painful, was at the same time so familiar to me that avoidance of him became a matter of survival.

And in the midst of the avoidance, I watched him. Constantly, relentlessly. And stalked him. With a vengeance, not exactly that of the hunter for its prey, where there can be beauty and admiration and even love. But like one enemy stalking another, where the stake is survival.

When it changed for me with Peter, I also do not know. But at the end of the two years I began to see his pain and feel his need and have compassion for it. I determined not to let his need either fool me, rule me, seduce me, or insult me. Not to ever let this child again feel so helplessly absolute that he could bend the world to his need.

And so I set out to understand the fairy tale in which the child was hiding, to get to him and help him out of his morass.

For two years I'd hounded him with a vengeance. Until one day I lost the vengeance and joined forces with him to hunt the mystery of his symbols rather than the child himself.

At nine and a half—when I started to work with him —Peter was, if taken part by part, physically well developed for his age. But this searing, searching, fearing, limpid brown-eyed boy was like a lump of mud, or like an ocean wave.

The physical substance of his body always left me amazed. In spite of the fact that he had flesh and skin and bones like anyone else, one felt that he had no physical limit to him at all. He overflowed.

His walk was trancelike. Like an underwater walker seen from above, he moved effortlessly, lifelessly, as if propelled by a force outside himself. On tiptoes, body swayed forward, and yet not caring that he walked at all. Feeling no relationship between himself and the ground he walked on, the air he breathed, the world he lived in. Suspended between heaven and earth.

His body seemed disjointed, scattered, disorganized. The leg separate from the foot, the arms with no connection to the rest of the body, the head heavily supported by the neck but as if trying to establish an independence of its own. And yet there seemed to be a rhythm to it all, a purpose in this expansion and fluidity —it was creepily, frightfully organized.

He described himself. "Peter hasn't got all his parts," he said. And it seemed that way.

His clothes, when he put them on himself, conveyed exactly the concept the child had of himself. The shirt was usually halfway out of his pants, buttons and buttonholes crisscrossing each other in an unsolvable maze. His pants hung on his hips only by some miracle. His jacket was backwards and his hat covered the face instead of his head.

His voice was monotonous, with its repetitive rhythm; compelling in its intensity, relentless in its demand. Hardly any inflection in it, except for the nagging quality. Words running into one another without a breathing spell between, but nevertheless coming out slowly and deliberately.

He spoke in the third person, whether referring to you or to himself, thus depersonalizing both. ("He wants Mira to tell him how many cats . . .") Or, in the second person, "You must know" (meaning himself— *he* must know), thus mixing up your identity with his, or giving his identity up to yours.

Whatever he said seemed to have no relevance to the situation at hand, but only to his own strange "fairy tale" world.

As the child had no good relationship with the world around him, he was afraid of contact with other people. In order to avoid contact, he played dead. However, since he simultaneously needed contact, he tried to control whatever contact he did have.

Thus there was a subtle but relentless persistence in his voice from which one always tried to escape. The voice seemed to have been deadened for the express purpose of driving people away, except when Peter needed for whatever reason of his own "to know"; or "no answer" or "the wrong answer" was forthcoming. A complete change would then come over the voice. A feverishness entered it; the pitch went sky high; the slowness and deliberation would disappear, and Peter yelled his questions out. The need "to know the answers" made all caution disappear, and the former deliberateness in the voice of the hunter would change into the desperate shriek of the hunted.

He had buck teeth, and in changing all his l's to w's, he only exaggerated his carnivorous engulfment of the world around him. Yet in his own strange way he was a beautiful little boy. The big, soulful eyes, when the intensity and fear and desperation left them, if only momentarily, had great warmth.

And every now and then one could catch a glimpse of a grace, coordination, and energy in his body quite different from the Peter I knew. At those times he reminded one of a tomcat. The night prowler. Lone and lonely walking on a fence he stalked cautiously, wondering how to catch his prey, how to outmaneuver it and how to survive.

Peter was an enigma to me. Logically, I understood close to nothing. My feelings I could put neither into thoughts nor into words. So, except for setting a few simple rules for the child, I stood by and watched him closely. Hoping to get some meaning out of the pieces of the puzzle that was Peter.

Peter made little sense. His days made no sense, and one day was like the other.

"Peter hasn't got all the parts," he'd say, and then: "There are seventeen cats on the fence. What colors are they?" A little face with pleading eyes waited for the answer. If you answered with "I don't know," shrieks would result with a plea of "Peter must, but Peter must know." As if the knowledge were going to save his world.

And then—"Peter must have, must find a cat." An anguished shriek, "Where is the cat?" And then:

"Say Rugby Road."

"Say 711 Westchester Road."

"Say Bedford Avenue."

"Say . . ." He followed you around with eyes feverishly boring into yours, and "say" you must or else there was a frightful panic.

"Who is Mr. Kimmel? Where does he live? What is his telephone number?" That too you had to answer. And of course you did not know. Screams. "What are the colors missing? Peter must know." You did not know the answer, as you did not know what colors he was talking about, but to prevent his tantrum you ventured a guess—"red." The guess was seldom right, so you went on guessing. But Peter would not be appeased, so he screamed and screamed and screamed.

"Joe [the school bus driver] missed a light." Laughter from Peter: "He missed a red light." No answer is required here. "There was a dead end." The agitation begins. "A dead end. There was a no exit sign; we shouldn't go there." The voice gets higher. The mouth makes strange motions, like a fish gasping for air. "Where is the dead end? One shouldn't go there." The agitation increases—"A stop sign! The lights are green!" —screeching at the top of his lungs: "A no exit sign. You mustn't go there!" Terror, tears; and a strange excitement with the terror.

If an outsider came into the room, Peter would immediately start with "What's your name? Where do you live? What is your telephone number? When is your birthday—month—day? Do you have a wife . . . father . . . mother?" He asked for each one's telephone number, address, birthday (he'd tell you the day it fell on) until he drove the person away. Then, spent and happy, he would suddenly remember that he forgot to ask "When is your . . . ?" and the tears of desperation and intensity would roll on and on and on.

Then—"Garbage can," "8176," "7168423, and ten cents." The monotone drones on again . . .

"How do you spell . . . ?" "Mommy drove yesterday 6.11 miles; she paid . . . dollars per gallon. How much did she spend?" He gives the answer himself, of course, and laughs. "Razors in the water." "It is 11:27 and 1/3 second A.M. now." (All this could be said and done within the space of fifteen minutes, continuously, relentlessly.)

His conversation was disjointed, disconnected, seemingly idiotic. None of it seemed to have any connection with what was going on. The words were comprehensible in themselves, but together made no sense. And here, as before, I had a feeling that beyond them lay a meaning that Peter understood, that beyond this illogical conglomeration of disconnected phrases, there was a purpose and an organization.

But what? What was the child trying to convey? What was he after?

I puzzled over his use of the third person. Never "I" when he talked about himself. Always "Peter." It was as if he were expressing the words of someone else. As if he himself did not exist at all, in all this. And yet I had a feeling that his "I" was there. It was hiding in this debris of incomprehensible talk and directing this whole operation. Describing in the incomprehensible meaning of these comprehensible words what his "I" was doing, wanting, asking for, and telling.

And the question was not only what the "I" wanted, but why it was so afraid to come out directly, to say directly, "I want."

Peter was endlessly studied by various philosophical and psychiatric sages for his unusual gifts and his psychological confusion. The duality baffled everyone. All were much more involved with the uncanny gifts than with his pain.

Peter's ability to handle numbers of astronomical proportions was constantly amazing. He could do fantastically difficult computations in his head, and could add, subtract, multiply, and divide when the numbers were put on paper—instantaneously.

Everyone wanted to know his formula—how he did it. Then he baffled everyone with his knowledge of the day on which any date fell, falls, and would fall. Again, this was a subject of great interest and involvement on the part of scientists. Again, everyone wanted to know his formula—which I'm sure he did not know consciously himself.

His phenomenal memory was also studied. He remembered anything and everything that ever happened; he never made a mistake. A color, a certain date, the layout of a city, an address, phone number—whatever. And that too baffled everybody.

But what I became aware of was that he seldom talked about the specific feelings accompanying his memories. Mostly, he remembered concrete facts. However, I began to suspect that the specifics were landmarks, summations of feelings and of whole series of events. He would use one specific word, phrase, memory to sum up a mass of complex emotions and incidents.

"On December 11, 1944, Peter went up on an elevator in Kings County."

"Dr. X was Peter's first dentist."

"Mira wore a yellow dress on September 26, 1953" (when he first saw me at school).

"There was a dead end on . . ."

God only knows what Peter summed up in each one of these sentences. But I was convinced that he was expressing something beyond the facts.

What became most important to me was not that he had these gifts, but how he used them. If there was an unexpressed logic to his mathematical and mnemonic feats, and if all we got was the summation, perhaps the same *kind* of logic operated in other areas of his life, and here too all we were seeing was the summation.

Was the phrase "dead end," for example, a summation of a myriad other feelings, it being clear to him and only to him what feelings it was a summation of?

Did it mean the same to him as to us: the end of the street, forbidden to traffic; or was it something else, perhaps the end of life, the end of hope, the end of trying?

What was also important to me was that the only time Peter was in contact with anyone else was when he used his mathematical, directional, and spelling gifts. Only in these areas would he answer questions directly.

He used his gifts well. He used them to get people

involved with him, yet at the same time to push them away from him. Involved because he fascinated them, pushed away because after a while Peter's demands became too great, and, overwhelmed, they'd have to leave him.

You'd find him with a piece of paper and the five, six, seven, ten zillion digit numbers written out there horizontally, in his own fractured handwriting. Peter would tell you the sum total of it all, asking to be checked—needlessly.

At times you'd hear him just repeating sums he'd overheard and giving you again the total. Or he'd want to subtract, and plead with you to write numbers out for him so he could do the arithmetic (not that he needed the numbers set down!). He never showed you how or what he did, but the result would be there with computer-like speed—beyond belief and beyond comprehension. Correct always. This was the preoccupation for the day. If you didn't answer him fast enough, he'd throw a tantrum and scream and cry until you had to. But then it was too late, and the screaming continued until the child was spent.

He'd follow you, meet you, bump into you (you could not escape him), all along talking about his roads, dead ends, cats. Or he'd ask you questions.

At times he'd sit quietly by the window and talk to himself, about the cats, or dead ends, the roads, or numbers, or stop lights—or he'd call out the streets that Joe, the bus driver, drove on. Sometimes you saw him chuckle or become especially animated and then you knew that he'd be talking about lights, especially someone's driving and missing the lights.

And then again sometimes he'd just sit and move his lips as if in silent prayer—when you got really close you could hear him count from one up to . . . infinity. (I remember once hearing him say three and sometime later seventy-one thousand, and you could rest assured that he hadn't missed a number in between. At the time Peter could not afford to.)

Every now and then he'd throw himself on the floor and roll and scream: "Where are the parts? Where are

227

the colors? Where are the numbers?" Then suddenly he'd look at me or at another child and begin to yell: "Scat, scat, go away cat," and end it with a "meow, meow" (himself becoming the cat).

A walk with Peter was a nightmare. With the little boy's hand lifelessly in mine, we and the other two children in my group would start out peacefully—until suddenly, into nowhere, Peter would disappear.

And nowhere was a lot of places. He could vanish into cellars, buildings, and stairways, looking for his cats and forever searching for his "hidden place."

He could dart into any candy store where you'd find him poring over telephone books, reading addresses and telephone numbers.

He would walk into any real estate office, where you'd catch him engrossed in its files.

He might be in a police station, where he'd rummage through police files, with the cops too astonished or shocked by the appearance of this feverish apparition to do anything about it.

Sometimes he would throw his arms in his viselike fashion around a stranger's neck, attacking him with "What's your name?" etc.

Once he was found at the door of some unsuspecting woman, ringing desperately and screaming, "Where is your pussy?" He was looking for a kitten he saw in her window; the poor woman, bewildered, screamed "Rape!"

He would dash in the path of a truck or a car. Or, it could be anywhere! Wherever I wasn't looking.

Retrieved, and apologized for, we'd go on again, the same limp way. Until the next time he got away.

Or until suddenly he spotted a bus. Then Peter shut his eyes tight, became immobilized with terror, and began to scream: "It's a bus, a school bus!" I'd have to lead him blind and screaming, for blocks, until he was convinced that the bus was nowhere in sight.

If a cat crossed his range of vision, he would chase it, catch it, and try to drag it with him.

We were a strange sight, the two of us in the street. Me holding the child's hand, and him dragging along with me limply. Then suddenly, with a perfect coordination that seemed to have no connection with his previous disordered state of being but that suited his need of the moment, he'd disappear to sundry places. I would wander from place to place, searching for him. When I found him, we would walk again together, which was not together at all. But he would let me lead him, since that best suited his purpose.

If we went to the playground, Peter would just drop himself on a swing and proceed to stare into nothingness. He was neither able to play with other children nor to throw or catch a ball, nor to run, jump, or use any other equipment.

Until suddenly, quick as the wind and just as silent, he'd jump off the swing and attack each of the strangers who happened to be around him with "What street do you live on? What is your name?" and so on. And the intense face of the child with his ferocious demand in it would scare people into running away.

Or if he spotted someone reading a book, a paper, or a magazine, he would tear it violently out of their hands and check the number of pages in it, the author, the library due date, how many pages the reader had left till the end. Having satisfied himself with whatever he was after, he'd get back on the swing and proceed to sit and stare into his nightmare.

Needless to say, our part of the playground usually became empty very soon.

And sometimes Peter drew and sometimes Peter built.

But if he drew a picture of a person or an object, it was disjointed and looked like a dismembered body, with its parts scattered all over the page.

If he built, it was always with blocks, and always the same closed-in, boxlike structure.

At lunch he ate only chicken wings or eggs, softboiled, with bread soaked in them. Everything else he'd throw up. He never used any utensils.

After lunch, sometimes in the middle of it, he'd run to the toilet to make a "dut." As soon as he landed there you'd hear shrill screams, full with terror: "It won't come out. It's stuck there. Mira must make it come out."

The rest of his activities consisted either of "making a calendar," "adding columns of numbers," spelling out endless lists of words, "reading books" avariciously, or doing the puzzles in *The New York Times*.

This was his routine, day in and day out. His day had to have a rigid framework, a plan, a schedule, in which he had to be able to account for and to predict his actions for every minute. If anything in the schedule went off, Peter's flimsily but rigidly organized world would fall apart and the child would scream and cry uncontrollably, rolling on the floor until he got his world back into his own prearranged design.

It was all a maze to me, even though I knew that somewhere deep within the child the answer lay. Peter at this point (two or three months after we began working together) had no access to it and I no knowledge to understand his symbols. I decided not to wait for intellectual understánding but to follow my instincts and feelings, which, too, I did not understand.

But this much I knew: Peter was often diagnosed as a "symbiotic child." In his relationships he'd give up his identity and become part of somebody else's. He'd try to get the other person in the relationship to do the same. This was his relationship to his mother—each was part of the other, and neither seemed able to exist without the other—and this was the only relationship he knew. It went to the extent that the word "I" was nonexistent in his vocabulary—"I" was always "you."

From what I'd seen of Peter, there were advantages for him in this kind of relationship. He did not have any responsibility for his actions, and he could feel protected by the strengths of the other person. For if he *was* the other person, he could by some magic or osmosis take over that person's strength; and he would be protected because the other would never hurt Peter, since in so doing he would be hurting himself.

However, there was also danger in a symbiotic relationship, for each member of this oneness had to give up much of his own identity and become dependent on the other. Peter did not fully like that. So there was hate and resentment along with the love and need that fostered the union. And, as there was hate, there was also fear. Peter was afraid—afraid of the gobbling up of his self and of his gobbling up the other person's self. He was afraid to be so much at the mercy of the other, afraid of being hurt by his displeasing or being displeased by the other. So he isolated part of himself and hid it deeply in a shell, and it was this part which to a large extent directed his actions.

It was this part, too, that I wanted to find for myself and show to Peter. I wanted this part to be recognized and made aware of and made responsible; I wanted to give Peter his separate self.

I knew that to help Peter, I had to get to the Peter in the shell or "hidden place," as he called it—hurt, afraid, calculating, vulnerable, where he built around him this strange world, full of symbols—and then to nurture the child there and heal his hurt.

But as he only communicated through the strange symbols he used as a defense, his inner shell—his fairy tale world—was difficult to reach. The attack had to be both on his symbols, which were only symptoms of his fear and hurt, and on his basic fear and hurt themselves.

First, I had to teach him a new way to relate—to be. He needed to lose the togetherness which dominated him, to learn his own individuality. I'd talk to the individual in the shell, see if I could get it to come out to help me unravel the symbols that surrounded it, and thus enlist its help to eliminate the underlying hurt and the underlying fear.

I'd let him use me; I'd be his strength, his will, and his direction for as long as he needed it, but only in service of his health, not illness. I'd stop him from hurting himself and others. I'd protect him against his fears. I'd set rules and make decisions for him. I'd help him unravel his maze. But I'd never let him use me. I'd never let him drag me in into his illness.

No matter how great his pain, no matter how strong

231

his terror, I'd never join him in it to the extent where we would merge. I'd always stay separate from him, have my own identity.

I'd deal with whatever health was in him, make him conscious and responsible for his actions, and only in the service of health would we tackle his fairy tale world, no matter how fascinating it might be.

I decided to narrow Peter's world by eliminating mathematics and spelling from our relationship—two areas he used to seduce people into a relationship that required no emotional giving on his part.

I told him that as I was very bad in math, and was bored by numbers, he was wasting his time in this area with me. And, since I was a foreigner, I could never compare my spelling with his and did not even want to bother. This issue, I told him, was settled.

So by making his world smaller, there was less for Peter to run to (while running away), and thus more to face.

I announced to him that as I was there to help him and not be fascinated by him and his genius, we would have to work closely together and he would have to help me to help him. To his perturbed, "But Peter must . . .", my answer was, "But there'll be lots of things 'Peter must' from now on, and it'll be easier for you if you understand them."

I told him that from now on he could use my strength and will along with his own, but only when he joined them with the health in him. He could use me when he felt he could not find his own strength, to defend himself against his fears, to understand his fairy tale. But at no time would I let him use me in the service of his illness. I told him that I knew of his despair and his aloneness and the pain of it—but I would never let myself become engulfed by it.

Time went on. Peter was no help. He tested and tested and tested my limits set upon him, at times beyond my endurance. He still communicated only in symbols—of roads, cats, colors, etc.—which had no meaning to me. Until I learned to listen more carefully and Peter learned to help me to understand.

Then one day, when Peter again began to cry and roll on the floor and scream that "not all the colors are there and not all of the parts are there," and then added, "Peter must have them, they are Peter's," it suddenly occurred to me that he might be talking about the scattering of his own psyche or body. When I asked him if it was his own parts that he was missing, the child with great relief said, "Yes."

To my horror I realized what this little being must be feeling—that he was being dismembered. That he was being taken apart. Whether it was an emotional dismemberment or whether he felt the pain in his body (or both), I did not venture to guess. But whatever it was, the terror and the anguish this little child must have been feeling were beyond my comprehension. And then to my even greater horror came the suspicion that the mutilation was to a large extent self-inflicted. That Peter for some reason incomprehensible to me dismembered himself and suffered this pain and terror to avoid a greater and even deeper suffering: that of being completely destroyed.

So I gathered him up off the floor, took him on my lap, and encircled him tightly with my arms. I kept saying over and over again, "Peter has all his parts; Peter has all his parts." Peter's sobs and screams quieted down and he relaxed. Somehow it was as if when I held him in, within the circle of my arms, a boundary was formed which would not let him scatter all apart.

After that, any time he went into this panic, I'd just take him on my lap and proceed, with my arms around him, to reassure him of his self being all one. We would sit this way for a long while, many, many times a day, any time he felt he lost any of his parts.

After some time, as soon as Peter felt the feeling coming on, he would run and sit on my lap and like a deaf-mute look up at me and weep. And I, with my arms about him, would hold him from falling apart.

We carried on this procedure for more than half a

year. After that it was enough that we just used words: "Peter has all his parts." Until finally Peter one day decided that he could put his own parts together. "Peter has all his parts," he said, and then added quietly, "So does the school bus." And it was at that point that I realized not only was he afraid of his own scattering, of which the bus somehow reminded him, but somehow he was afraid of his wish or his "ability" to scatter or destroy the bus.

It was then that there was a visible change in the

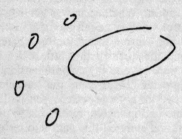

Bus moves and
is in parts—
"go to pieces"

Bus moves and
is all in one
piece.

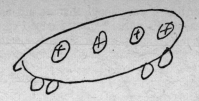

But then he drew the bus this way.

child. For one thing, he could walk on the street and upon meeting a bus not make himself blind. (Although that was still at times a struggle. One could often see the fright in the child as he forced himself to look at the bus. One could feel him stifle the scream and see the sigh of relief as he whispered, "It's in one piece.") The panics about the colors and the parts were gone.

His drawings changed, too. The dismembered bodies began to have the heads attached to them, then legs, then hands. Finally the body was no longer in parts but all together ("all in one"). The change came with the change of his concept of himself as a shattered human being to a more whole one.

However, the change was not that Peter stopped feeling he was losing parts of himself, but that, though feeling his disintegration, he was able to put himself

His drawings of bodies progressed from

to

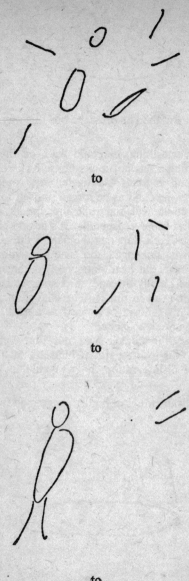

to

to

to
236

to

together again. Still, we could understand the first piece of puzzle together. Now, with his participation, we moved toward control rather than chaos.

Otherwise all was as before. The same coercion, the same engulfment, the same despair, and the same terror except in fewer areas; the same use of numbers and

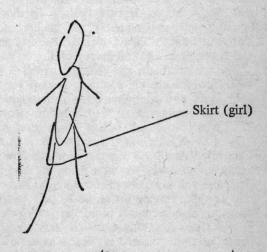

Skirt (girl)

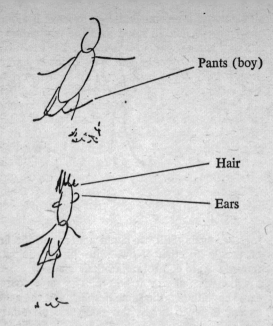

Pants (boy)

Hair

Ears

spelling, and so on, as before, with everyone else but me. He went on talking "cats," "birthdays," and "dates," "telephone numbers" and "addresses," "wrong and right turns," "lights," "exits," "streets and roads" and "cemeteries," and all the rest of it.

The streets, roads, and cemeteries routine was incessant. You saw the child coming toward you with this greed, pain, and determination in his face and you knew what was coming next: "Say Marlboro Road"—"Say 1113 Marlboro Road"—"Say Washington Avenue"—"Say 409 Washington Avenue"—"Say Mount Sinai Cemetery." And you knew that no matter how much you hated this coercion, you were going to "say" it because otherwise you experienced such screams and such panic that anything seemed better. So I "said" it, and everyone who came in contact with Peter at the school "said" it, and I saw to it that even strangers accosted in the street "said" it. I racked my brains as to how to tackle the problem, I asked advice on what to do about it; but all I got was a recommendation to leave it alone, as no one knew what it all stood for. The temptation to limit him in this area was overwhelming. Yet I felt that I had to be careful in what and how much I limited him, since I knew that the smaller I made his world around him, the more he would have to face his real fear. And the real world. For that he needed strength, and I was unsure whether he had enough. So I waited.

Then one day, after months and months of it, I decided the time was ripe. As waiting him out brought us no closer to the meaning behind it, I told Peter, "No more talking with me about streets, roads, and cemeteries," and I fortified myself for whatever might come. The shock to the child was tremendous. He looked at me unbelievingly. With terror and rage in his face, he began to yell: "Peter must. But he must," and then he came closer to me and began to repeat: "Scat cat, scat Mira, go away cat." Peter was changing into a cat and making me one too. But I was laying down the rules, and his coercion in this area was finished. Screams, screeches, wailings, pleadings were of no avail. My only answer to it all was, "We must understand what you are saying when you say it. We must know the meaning behind it." In reaction, he was constantly the cat. This lasted for about a month (most of the staff were beginning to see an ogre in me).

But then one day in the park the breakthrough came.

I saw the child running toward me as if a pack of wild wolves were chasing him. Shrieking all the way. As he reached me, Peter threw himself at me, weeping bitterly. Alternately rubbing his face and pulling at my arms, he began to scream, "Mira say Cortelyou Road. 711 Cortelyou Road. Cemetery. Cemetery," blinking vehemently all along. It was obvious that something specific was bothering him, so in utter desperation, wanting to help the child very badly, I yelled out, "How can I help you if I don't know what's bothering you and you won't tell me?"

Startled for a moment, Peter stopped his shrieking and shouted at me, "Mira, get the thing out of your

[Peter's] eye—it hurts." It was the first time I'd heard him speak of a localized physical pain.

Why Peter used such a detached and unemotional symbol as a street and its number for a highly emotional and unpleasant experience I was never able to find out. (Cemetery made sense, as a hurt might lead one there.) However, after that, any time he'd start with his "street, road, and cemetery," I'd ask him, "What hurts?" Quite often, after a lot of hemming and hawing, as if the admission of pain was dangerous, he'd give me the answer. Just as often he did not. When he did, it could be either a physical or emotional hurt he was referring to.

The constant questioning presented difficulties in addition to figuring out Peter's actual need. Here again, people's curiosity and fascination with the inexplicable, and my own discomfort with the uncanny, got in the way.

As I said before, Peter attacked everyone who came into his line of vision with his questions. No matter where—in the classroom, in the streets, in the park, in stores, at home. Quite often he attacked regardless of whether he had seen the person innumerable times before and had gotten all the information already (and once told, he would remember forever), or whether it was a first meeting.

The engulfing quality of these attacks, in which the child came very close to his victim, eyes burning into his, at times holding him down physically—by the lapels, the neck, or wherever he could reach, which was at times mistaken for a loving embrace—and demanding "the answers" from him, was astonishing and frightening. However, people would put up with it for the promise of witnessing Peter's uncanny ability. And he would tell them on what day their birthday fell, or for that matter any other day, in any year.

His powers *were* uncanny. Without batting an eyelid, with no greater inflection in his monotone than before, he'd drone out the day. It was almost unholy, and always left me with a feeling that I was invading a territory I had no business being in. On the other hand, I tried to shrug it off and ignore it, as I felt it was some kind of a cheap trick, which this very clever and manipulative child used to coerce people into serving his needs. I recall once finding a theater poster from the nineteenth century with the opening date on it, including the day. I asked Peter what day January 15, 1875, fell on, sure that this would show the child up to me and dispel my discomfort. The child, noticeably surprised and disappointed that I too was getting involved in his date maneuver, calmly told me "Thursday." And Thursday it was. The poster said so. That cured me. Never again did I ask him for a day, but never again did I doubt this ability of his.

I realized once again that I would never understand a great part of Peter. Precisely because I lacked his gifts, there was a part of his world I would never be able to enter. But I realized too that the logical (if unknown) process he used to solve the equation of the year, month, and day, he must also use in his complexly set up world. And as the one was a mystery to most of us, so probably would the other be.

After that I understood that it was not Peter's gifts I resented, but the way the child used them. He was able to coerce people through them into giving him the "information" he needed at his "price"; to have contact with people on his terms. The price to Peter himself was high. To feel that powerful when one is really so helpless must be frightening to a child. To have little respect or security in other people's understanding must be hopelessly defeating. To have your "fairy tale" reinforced by the rest of the world is dangerous. To feel gawked at and marveled at even though transparently disliked, no matter how the dislike is camouflaged, must be very painful, even though to Peter it was at the same time reassuring within the scope of his crippled world.

And so after a year and a half of not doing anything about stopping him from his attacks on people, the time seemed to have come to take action.

Our relationship appeared strong enough to withstand many a jolt. Peter was using my strength for himself and my words often became his.

So I decided: No more attacking people in the park,

street, or playground—no matter how much Peter screamed. If he broke my rule, we wouldn't go out, I told him, knowing how important it was for him to go outside on the chance of meeting "his cats."

After a great deal of testing me, Peter accepted the new situation. In the school, however, I let him go on with the attacks for another year, for when I did try to stop him, he got so terrified that I felt somehow I had no right to do it yet.

Of course the meaning of what he did was still a complete mystery to me. Whenever the thought came to me that he attacked because he wanted to be close to people, to get love and reassurance, it did not ring true, since in this act of his something else was present that was designed to push people away as well as bring them close. The urgency and desperation with which he "needed to know" spelled a terror of, a hatred toward, and a pain for the person, as well as a need to possess that person and a terrible dependency on him.

Then one day Peter "forgot" to attack someone at the school in his usual way. It was the first time since I had known him that such a thing had happened. I took the clue and set up a rule: I'd let him "ask" five people and not the sixth. Later we could "ask" four and skip the second; then he'd "ask" three and we'd skip three. The screams accompanying my new rules were beyond belief. But when they didn't help, Peter became "rational" and pleaded with me.

"But Peter must know," he said.

"Why?"

"Because he must."

"Why? I don't 'ask,' neither does anyone else."

"It makes him feel better," he'd say and then, "It soothes him; it calms his nerves." He'd weep bitterly, holding on to both my arms as if they had the power to change things for him.

But my "why" wasn't answered. So in spite of his pressure, I persisted with the new rule and with my repetitions of "why" to his "Peter must." It was nerve-racking to both of us, but after a year of it, one day Peter suddenly answered. To my "why," he said, "Because they are strangers." When I continued to press, he added, "Peter is afraid of them." And then a few days later, to my relentless "why,"—it came. "These people have some of Peter's parts," he said. Suddenly the clouds broke.

"If you know who they are, and where they live, do they still have your parts?" I asked. "Yes," Peter answered. "But then Peter knows where to find them."

Some of it had become clearer—why Peter "needed to know" so desperately. For some reason or other, this poor little being needed to dismember himself and to hide or give away his parts. Everyone he ever came in contact with had some of his scattered, missing parts. And to keep track of his parts, Peter had to know where all these people were at any given time.

He had no friends and no acquaintances, but he remembered everyone who ever crossed his path. Not as a friend but as an enemy, as a keeper of his parts. This sort of loneliness was terrifying. He asked people for the information he wanted—name, address, telephone number, date, etc.—not to get close to them, to get to know them, but as a defense against them.

After that whenever a stranger came into the room, I would anticipate Peter's questions with—"He doesn't have your parts. He has his own and you have yours." Sometimes it worked, more often it did not. It only worked when he already knew the name, address, and so on, of the visitor from before. But if he did not, I'd let him "ask" the visitor. As time went on, Peter began to centralize the parts. Instead of "parts," it became "part," and to me it seemed that it was because he was getting more integrated.

Now whenever a stranger came into the room, Peter would run to the toilet. One day a man named Dick arrived. Peter immediately proceeded to "noodge" him for information about his name, address, etc.

When I tried to reassure the child that he and Dick each had his own parts, Peter definitely told me, "No." So I asked, "Which part do you think Dick has of yours?" The child answered, "The leg." I suggested that he touch his own and Dick's legs to see the difference. He did and then said, "No, not the leg." Then he quickly and fearfully ran to the door and yelled, "Peter must go to the toilet." To my, "What for?" his curt, "He must," was the only thing I got. "Do you by any chance think he has your penis?" I asked. And Peter jumped up with glee and excitedly yelled out, relieved, "Yes!" So I suggested he go and check. When he came back from the toilet, he announced, "Peter has his own."

His coordination became better; he dared to swing on swings, run faster, walk straighter, climb the monkey bars. He even dared to taste new foods. And so it looked like Peter was being put together more and more. He talked more clearly and controlled himself better.

For a long time he would still ask people for names, addresses, and so on. However, the urgency and desperation in the questions were gone, as the reasons for his doing it changed. Now he did it as a way of establishing contact with others—as a topic of conversation. As he put it, "So what should Peter talk about to people? Peter doesn't know what interests them." And, too, he did it to see if I would stop him from doing it, to reassure himself that I cared enough to stop him—especially when things went wrong between the two of us. He did it to "reestablish" the relationship between us, to get me "reinvolved" with him.

Then one day, after about two years of our working together, a strange thing happened.

I was lying on the floor on my stomach putting together a puzzle with another child in the group. Peter was at the easel painting his cats. Suddenly, I felt a head on my backside. I continued with the puzzle without turning, not wanting to disturb the child who was trying to find comfort in me, when I realized it was Peter. He seemed very still but was making little noises. Before I could ask what was wrong, Peter wiggled his head down my legs to the floor, stood up, and looked up at me with a curious expression on his face—an expression that seemed to have in it remnants of effort and concentration and a beginning of peace. "Peter came out," he said. I stared at him not comprehending, and he, sensing my bewilderment, said, "Peter came out of Mira." Then he added, "Like from Mommy. Got born," he explained, as if to remove all doubts, and went back to his paints.

After that, Peter became more cooperative and almost imperceptibly more independent. As before, he let me tell him what to do and lead him as though he were blind, helpless, and dependent; and he still substituted my will for his, my strength for his; but now he called that strength his own. And I sensed a trust now for me rather than just the desperate need to hide in me that had existed before. The desperation of the drowning man who tries to drag his saviour with him into the depths was gone. Even this was a frightening experience to me. I did not savor that much faith and that much responsibility. It is all right for me to turn chaos into order. It is also all right to turn order into chaos. But order into chaos into order is a responsibility I do not like to bear.

The absorption with "no exit," "dead end," "traffic lights," "wrong turns," and so on, was as strong as ever, but seemed to me more and more connected with Peter's preoccupation with "cemeteries." Here the initiative in understanding what it meant was taken, surprisingly, by the child himself.

Peter seemed obsessed with the question of whether a road was "a one-way road" or a "two-way road." Was a street "dead end"? Did it have "no exit"? Would the "driver make the lights" or not? These concerns seemed to be a cause of constant pain, glee, terror, relief, and, at times, seemingly a matter of life and death. Whenever Peter talked about them or asked the questions, I got the feeling that he wasn't really talking to anyone but was addressing himself; that he was sharing some deliciously terrifying secret with himself.

So one day while we were both swinging on some playground swings, and Peter was having a great time at it, the child suddenly turned to me and said, "No exit." I ignored it as usual, thinking that again he was trying to pull me into his world. Peter continued to swing. "It is a round road," he said. "You go around and around and there is no exit." I looked up, realizing that the child was trying to explain. Peter said with a laugh, "Then you are *mishuga*" (Yiddish for crazy, confused, mixed up). "Ah?" I asked, and the child said, "Sure, you go round and round with no exit, so you just can't get off it—so you get *mishuga*."

What he was saying became clear to me. When you get confused, you go round and round in your head and don't get anywhere. Confusion leads to terror, or terror leads to confusion. Or was it terror of confusion?

Whatever the case, Peter seemed to sense when his confusion was about to set in, although he did not understand what it was that terrified him, so that it drove him to get confused in order not to face it. But he knew quite consciously when the confusion came on, and he gave meaning to his landmark.

"Wrong turn?" I asked. "Is it on the way to the no exit road?" "Yes," he said, trembling. "And you mustn't take it because then you'll be on the 'no exit road.'" His voice got higher and higher in his excitement.

"And a dead end, and the traffic lights?" I continued casually, trying not to scare the child away.

"Then there is just the cemetery," he said.

"What?" I pushed on.

"That's all," Peter said fiercely and got off the swings. "That was all!"

And that was all. He had told me his whole story: That what he was most afraid of was his destruction, his death. At the end of the road for all of us is death, the cemetery. So was it for Peter, but he knew this better than we did, and was constantly more terrified of it and aware of it than the rest of us humans.

After that any time the little boy turned panicky and began to yell, "No exit road," "wrong turn," I would intercept with "Look, Peter, there is an exit. I'll show you. You just get on it and get off that road." And Peter would calm down and "get off" his dangerous road. Whatever the road was. Whether it led to confusion and then to death, or because it might lead directly to death, dangerous it was. And Peter sensed that if for whatever reason the confusion came, he might then forget the magic that kept him from death and go headlong into that death—hence "cemetery."

There was many a road that I took him off. A time came when he was able to come to me and just say calmly, "Peter took the 'wrong turn'; the lights weren't working. Mira must show him the exit." A time came too when the talk about roads disappeared completely, and Peter would say to me, "Remember the time when Peter was afraid of a 'no exit road'?" But that was much later on.

His *counting* lasted and lasted and lasted. It seemed we would never break through it. He could count for an hour, he could count for two, he could count for three. Always starting with one and going up consecutively.

"Peter, what gives?" I'd ask. "Peter, why are you counting?" I'd persist. "Peter, are you happy?" I'd grope. "Peter, are you unhappy?" I would try to understand.

But the monotonous droning continued.

"Peter must" was the nearly inaudible reply, "Because Peter must."

There is a magic in numbers. The kabala.

The rhythm in the counting was frightening and very seductive. Many a time I found myself sitting on my haunches near the child and nodding my head to the beat of the numbers. Many a time I found myself tantalized by it into a strange nothingness—where time and space, as we know them, would disappear and a languid timelessness take their place. Many a time I woke myself out of it only by sheer strength of will power, God only knows after how long.

Peter was counting and I was helpless. The child seemed to sense my defeat and would say appeasingly, "All right, no more counting." And yet as if beyond his control, his lips would move as in opiate addiction to his wondrous chant or prayer, and if I watched them closely I could read 17,101, 17,102 . . .

Two years after I started working with him, Peter

and I and the two other kids in the group were at the beach. The waves were beating loudly against each other and the sand, persistently reaching out to us. As the other two children and I were moving back and laughing at the waves, Peter began to count. We moved further back. Peter counted. We rose to move again. Peter was up to 2,000. He seemed glued to the spot, counting, unable to move at all, so I dragged him along with us. Suddenly shrieking, beside himself, Peter yelled out: "Mira and Peter must go back! The waves are too hungry and noisy. It scares him." And he continued the counting. I asked him whether the counting was to tell me that he was afraid, or to keep the fear away, or to keep the thing that was frightening him away. And Peter said, "It takes the scare away. It puts it away so it won't scare Peter." After this clarification, whenever he began to count, his mother or I would ask him what he was afraid of and usually by explaining things to him would be able to help him stop.

Ever since I can remember, I myself have had a certain feeling about cats. A dog can have rules laid out for his behavior, but not a cat. In my way of feeling, no rules apply, no judgment can be made. A cat is neither right nor wrong; it just is. An enigma. Something beyond my understanding. Magic. (Perhaps the worship of the cat by some early ancestor of mine left traces in me.) A cat.

Here was a child who had a need to know cats, to have cats, to hold cats, to feel cats, to be a cat. From the first time I saw him until about four years later, at least half of Peter's waking and most likely sleeping hours were spent in his search for cats. Cellars, alleys, stairs, roofs, balconies, other people's houses, other people's backyards were invaded by Peter looking for cats. If a cat was within physical reach, he caught it, hugged it, carried it with him. He would see cats where there weren't any and see cats where there were. He'd talk cats, eat cats, sleep cats. They were all shapes and colors. He drew cats, made them out of clay, or cut them out of magazines. He looked for cats in his "hidden place" and was forever searching for his "hidden place," as he knew his "special" cats were there.

When he saw a cat, he'd get terribly excited. His eyes would begin to shine and he'd run after it as if propelled or compelled by something. You could talk to him, yell at him; he didn't hear you. All he saw was the cat. And when he chased it and grabbed it, it was with a strange combination of excitement, terror, delight, and rage. He'd squeeze it hard, as if he was afraid it would run away, as if he'd finally found some long-lost part of it and wanted to make it part of him, or to be one with it. At the same time it was as if he wanted to destroy it and perhaps be destroyed by it, and as if he wanted to be swallowed by it or merge with it.

A picture of cats was enough to evoke in him a similar reaction. If there weren't any cats to talk about, he'd conjure them out of his imagination, produce them from his memory, then insist on people discussing their color with him, how many there were, and their size. "How many cats were at the shoemaker's?" "What color cats were on page seventy-three in that magazine?" "How many cats were on the fence?" And if no correct answer was forthcoming, there would be the distraught intensity, the usual panic, and the screams.

When he got mad with me (or anyone else, for that matter), he'd begin to wail, "Meow, meow, you shall have no fish," as if he the cat were depriving me, the other cat, of my favorite repast.

As Peter began to express his anger more actively, he'd make catlike motions, bare his teeth. His eyes would start shining. His fingers would become clawlike and he'd look ready to stalk and leap. Yet, at the same time, he would become arrested on the spot and unable to do anything. Finally, he would manage to say, "Meow, meow."

As time went on and Peter began to get better, the cats started to get sexual differentiations. There were "cats with tails and these were boys," Peter would tell me, "and pussies with open mouths were girls—any kind of mouths." And he would shudder and obviously be frightening and delighted at the thought of the mouth.

249

It was at that time that he told me he wanted to touch my teeth. I told him it was all right, but he didn't dare and kept on asking, "Will Mira bite? Will Mira say meow?" until he accomplished the feat and said in utter surprise, "Mira doesn't bite. Mira just doesn't bite." And it was at that time that he began to draw cats that he used to give names to: "Mira Cat," "Peter Cat," "Matthew Kitten and Robie Kitten." I was the "Mama cat" and they were "the three little cats." I began to realize, then, that the only "safe" relationship Peter used to have before I entered the picture was with a cat, not only because of its immortality, but because before he even needed this concept—before the cats got hurt—it was the only safe (nonsymbiotic) relationship he had. The cat was his safe mother, his safe intermediary between himself and the world around him—life. (The animal—wolf, etc.—in feral children.)

In order to get test responses out of Peter, I made up a "test" by drawing pictures of cats. Then and only then could we begin to get some animation and some insight into his identification with the cats. I drew cats in different positions and with various expressions that I felt might mean something to Peter. Violent situations, gentle ones, bloody ones, and loving ones; some were in color, some just black and white. Attacking cats, killing cats, living cats, dying cats. Mommy cats, Daddy cats . . .

It was at that time, after looking at one of my pictures, that he told me the blood of a cat had a smell. He liked that smell—it was sweet. I asked his mother about any real happening with a cat. "We had a dog, Tippy," she told me. "He was very gentle but when he saw a cat, he'd become a raging maniac, and Peter saw him kill two cats." When I asked, "What were the cats like?" she said, "Also like raging maniacs." She asked me if I thought Peter identified himself with the cats that Tippy attacked. I thought that perhaps that was so, but perhaps at times he was also Tippy. I asked Peter about his cats. He could give me no answer except that "Cats don't have to die. They have nine lives." Thus they were his ticket to immortality, the elimination of *death.* For if Peter became a cat, he took on the "magic" of the cat—the strength of the cat. Part of the magic was that they had nine lives and did not need to die. To reassure himself of their conquest of death, he searched for them. But to make sure that cats have all those lives, he had to find his two dead cats alive. And it occurred to me then that perhaps what Peter was doing in his search in the cellars and alleys was looking for his own cats. The cats who, even though dead, "didn't die"—as they had all these nine lives. To reassure himself of their conquest of death, Peter searched. And so the search for the "hidden place," in addition to his search for his hidden self, would also be the search for the place where these two cats lived. When Peter finally began to mention his dead brother, Matthew, he'd say that he and the cats were all in "the hidden place." And if I asked if they were all dead, Peter would violently deny it and say that "the cats and Matthew are alive." When I asked him whether part of himself was in the "hidden place," with them, Peter would say, "Yes, but only when Peter was little."

These were the bits and pieces I was able to get out of Peter, and no more. This, therefore, was how it looked to me:

The "hidden place" was where he would find all the dead cats alive, and where he would find his dead brother alive. The hidden place was always searched for at the end of cellars, end of stairs, on roofs—rather isolated and uninhabited places. Perhaps it was synonymous with the grave. Perhaps this too was a way he rejected the reality of the grave, the finality of living.

Because if the grave is no grave—empty—there is no dying.

Peter's brother, Matthew, who was a feebleminded child, died in some accidental way. According to Peter, his mother supposedly pushed him down the stairs. Another version was that Peter did it. Peter was five years old when Matthew died. He saw the body, spent the night with the body. To Peter this death was incomprehensible and yet real. I do not know if this is where the "cemetery" symbol came into being for him, but I am sure that witnessing or being a party to violence made his fear of death more specific and reinforced it immensely.

Even though Peter had buried his self long before his brother's death, as the world wasn't safe for him, I think he also identified with his brother's death and felt that he himself was "buried" along with his brother (perhaps within his brother). Thus his hidden self was in the "hidden place," the self in the shell, the self which he protected against the world, the self he put away to rest, away from the world. Whenever he searched for the "hidden place," it was as if he was pulled by a magnet he had to search for, as if he had to *find* the "hidden place," and had to find his self, his brother, the cats, life itself, within it.

Sometime later, when he was much better, Peter told me a story about his dog.

"*I* had a dog and his name was Tippy. Tippy chased after a cat. Tippy liked to hurt cats. Tippy slept in my room. Then one day Mommy sent Tippy to be put away—dead. And then *you* didn't have a dog but *you* slept in Mommy's room. And the cats. Mommy had them put away too."

It is interesting to see that Peter starts the story here with "I." When he had a dog, Peter dared to use his identity. When the dog was put away, Peter somehow became "you." He started to address himself in the second person and his identity became scattered—more scattered, anyhow.

As it was not safe to be either a boy or a dog (both die), Peter would become a cat. Cats do not die—you can put them away. You can destroy them, but as they have all these lives, they really do not die.

Mommy killed the dog and the two cats and took Peter into her room, which meant Peter could get killed by her too. There was no safety. And "I" became "you."

After about two years of our working together, I began to limit Peter's talk of cats.

It was also then that he allowed himself to have a

brace put on his teeth. And simultaneously with the brace, as if for protection against his devouring quality and his cat fangs, he began to be able to get angry physically, more like a boy than a cat.

After two and a half years Peter came to tell me that "Peter decided not to talk about cats any more." It was more a wish than an actuality.

After three years of our working together, his relationship to the cats changed. He did not need them so desperately anymore; nor did he seem to fear them so and love and hate them so strongly. He wanted them around, but he would pick them up differently. The glee was not there any longer, nor the excitement. But there definitely was a relationship between him and the cats, almost an unspoken understanding—as always before.

During that period a picture stands out in my mind.

Peter was at camp and I came to visit him there. The rain had just stopped. The smell of mushrooms and bathed pine was in the air. A little boy was winding his way toward me among the trees. He wore a yellow raincoat and a yellow rain hat and black boots. Around his neck he had a black fur collar, which he fingered constantly. The beauty and the incongruity struck me as funny. A slicker with a fur piece in the middle of the summer.

The boy came closer and I bent down to kiss him. Suddenly the fur piece moved from its complacency and struck out at the intrusion that was me.

It was a cat around Peter's neck.

I remember Peter's Bar Mitzvah.

He was his parents' only surviving son. Crazy, disjointed, pathetic. But he was going through the rites of manhood for them. For the illusion that they had a son like anybody else's. And he would be a man.

The synagogue was large, full of people. The rabbi was old and wise. And Peter with his phenomenal memory had learned all there was to say. I was scared for Peter. For the pathos of the parents. For myself.

Peter, in a new suit and terrified face, looked worse than I'd seen him in a long time. I got all dressed up,

253

with hat, high heels, new dress, and proceeded to hide in the last row.

Peter went up to the altar, put on his shawl and yarmulke, opened the prayer book and began to read. Suddenly, he turned to the rabbi, put his arms around the old man's neck in a viselike fashion, boring his eyes into the rabbi's with a demonic strength, and began to wail: "How many cats are on the fence of the synagogue? Peter must know, Peter must." The poor old man, trying to disengage himself from Peter's embrace, started to shout for help. The synagogue went into a panic and I went clacking on my heels the length of the aisle. I retrieved the child, freed the rabbi, and took Peter outside to look for the "how many cats were . . ."

And Peter, later, told me that "the cats came." He had to know about the cats because all those many people looking at him frightened him.

"Only the cats made Peter comfortable." And "Mira was too far away."

I also remember, during a walk in Brooklyn Heights, Peter telling me that he knew how to find a wife. "Peter will go in a cat house," he told me, yelling at the top of his lungs—"and there are a lot of pussies in the cat house. He will pick one out and marry her." When I seemed surprised at the idea, he told me, "Daddy's friend told Peter so," and, "He is a friend so he must know."

When a baby is born, it has no relationship with the world at all except through its mother. If the baby is left alone without the intermediary—the mother—it has a completely chaotic relationship to the world, with disastrous results for the baby. For some reason or other, Peter's mother herself had a chaotic relationship to the world—she could not act as his intermediary. She could not bring Peter comfort ("adequacy" is the word a colleague, Kurt Goldstein,* used), and the result was complete and utter chaos and terror for Peter.

---

* Kurt Goldstein, a neuropsychiatrist, was of invaluable help to me with Peter. See his notes in the Appendix.

The only intermediary between him and the world was the cat. Instead of "mother adequacy," for him it became "cat adequacy." But then when his mother killed the cats (and took over Peter), Peter's intermediaries—the cats—were gone and he needed them to make him immortal. So he constantly searched for them.

The first drawing of cats: never in parts

In his drawings at his worst time, when everything and everyone was scattered, the only whole thing he drew was the cat. The cat was never scattered. Later on, when I became an intermediary, the cat lost some of its powers.

However, for a long time after he seemingly gave up the strangeness in his relationship to cats, he became very interested in dogs. No matter what their size, he'd try to get himself bitten by them. With tremendous excitement, he'd put his hand into a dog's mouth and sometimes even try to get his head into it.

Until February 1956, Peter was all alone at the school. He was a solitary animal. No friends. No acquaintances. No relationships with other children. Just a complete dependency on me. Then a boy named Matthew joined the group. Peter began to take an interest in him. Slowly, a friendship was formed. At the start, it only amounted to Peter's asking, "Where is Matthew?" but as time went on they began to hold hands in the street, share the seesaw together, eventually cuddle and wrestle. It was strange to see Peter waiting

255

at the entrance door of the school for Matthew. When the child arrived, they'd take each other by the hand and walk into the room together. Whenever Peter talked to Matthew, he was completely in reality. He used no symbols and hardly ever talked of streets and numbers. It was amazing to see those two strange, solitary beings suddenly take to each other. Matthew always on the attack, Peter emerging from the world of scattered and shattered parts. Together they reached out long enough to build a house of blocks.

For a long time the relationship held. After a while, they called each other on the phone, visited each others' homes, and eventually even went to the movies together. But the very interesting thing about it was that both Peter and Matthew, so uncertain as to their identities, so unknowing about their boundaries, were always separate from each other. Whenever they were together, Matthew, who needed to be every child but himself, was himself with Peter. And Peter, with his need to climb in and merge with everyone and everything, who was threatened by everyone's identity, kept his own in relationship to Matthew. When Peter sometimes demanded, "Say streets," to Matthew, the child would ask, "What'd you say, Peter? I don't understand" —in all earnestness. And Peter would answer, "Peter just wants to cuddle with Matthew on the mat."

I often think that it was no coincidence that Peter's first and only friendship with another child was formed with a boy whose name and age was the same as that of Peter's dead brother.

At the beginning of our relationship, Peter showed very little anger, except that every now and then he'd remove the thing that annoyed him, as he had removed Robie off the rocks into the water. However, he'd take no responsibility for an act of anger in any conscious way. When our relationship began to form, if Peter got mad with me, he would become a cat and yell, "Meow, meow. You shall have no fish" (making me into the other cat).

As his attachment to me increased, he became braver

and was better able to get verbally angry, more as a boy than a cat. "Peter wants Mira to swallow a razor. Peter wants Mira to swallow a rusty razor."

"Why rusty?" I asked.

"So she'll get infected and die for sure."

Later he added, "Peter wants to put Mira in a garbage can."

But you just couldn't get Peter to hit out or hit back. Not only did he not hit, he did not know how to cuddle, as if this kind of physical expression though positive was a dangerous expression. So at first we learned how to cuddle, and then I began to teach him how to hit and kick. It was rough going, and Peter was terrified to learn. But finally he mastered it—on my shins.

Along with his greater feeling of self came greater coordination of body. He could concentrate all of himself long enough to kick, push, even hit. After a while, Peter began to express anger and aggression and his freed energy in a rather violent hugging of me, pushing me, shoving me, and hitting me. (It was especially true after the brace was put on his teeth.) I still remember my sudden realization of and fear of his strength when he announced he'd push me down the stairs, and then did it. When I complained to Dr. Goldstein that I'd built a Frankenstein his reply was: "You've unleashed it, and you'll find a way to help him handle his energy." (If I live long enough, I thought.)

With this newly found energy Peter began to skate rather well, ride a bicycle, wrestle with his father. What was interesting was that he did not learn to skate, ride a bike, and so on, the way other children do, but did each well instantaneously—on the first try. After a while I tried to channel this energy into his monotonous way of talking and into his reading, for his vitality seemed to me to be the very juice of life that we were both handling. For weeks on end I'd correct his talking and ask him to put energy into his voice, "To be alive when you talk," as I put it.

I felt that I didn't get the point across, so I tried the same technique with his reading. "Come on, Peter," I'd say, "read the story as if you really mean it. Don't just mumble the words; read it alive."

Something in those words must have registered. I got a swift kick in the shin. I caught his leg and, to illustrate my point, told him: "That strength, that energy you used in kicking me, put it into your reading, into your voice." Finally, in utter exasperation, Peter began to read as he kicked—with energy, with vitality.

One day he was reading a story to me with more energy and animation than I'd ever heard before. "That's wonderful," I exclaimed, "that's just what I mean." Suddenly, Peter looked up at me in utter terror and caught himself by the mouth. Completely taken aback by the expression on his face, I stammered out, "What's the matter, Peter?" and Peter just yelled out, "Because after that is the cemetery!" "After what?" I asked. And all he said was, "After you're okay. Then there is a dead end and a cemetery." It occurred to me that perhaps what he meant was that it is after you come to life you have to die. And I said so to the child. He began to tremble and there was sweat above his lip. He then ran to the window, became flabby again, folded up as if wilted, and began to count—something he hadn't done for a long long time. Needless to say, his speech and reading once more took on their lifeless, monotonous quality.

After this reading experience, Peter tried to avoid me. He'd tell his mother that he "didn't want her to talk to me," and when asked why, he'd say, "Mira will tell Mommy and then Peter can't bother Mommy any more." He would say to me, "Peter doesn't want you to come with him to Dr. Goldstein's." When asked why, he'd only say, "Because Mira will tell Dr. Goldstein." To my "Tell what?" his reply was invariably either "Because Mira knows," or "The truth."

After the reading episode we could not get as close to each other as we had been. It set us back in this area for about half a year.

Still, as time went on and I was getting more and more through to the Peter behind his defenses, and he was finding many more avenues out of his maze, I felt it was safe to resume the "academic work" which he longed for: his reading, spelling, and arithmetic.

And so back to work we went. His handwriting, while more legible, still looked fractured, like twisted twigs broken and put together into letters, the words running into each other. His spelling, of course, was way beyond his age. His arithmetic beyond anybody's, and his reading perfect. The child who at the age of seven did the crossword puzzles in *The New York Times* would hardly need my help.

However, the ritual of "academic work" was a help in getting to his psychological problems. I did not let him use it in place of human relationships, or to control relationships with others by seducing them with his genius, but to get him to use this whole self—to be alive —at least in his reading.

And, slowly, I began to understand more and more.

As Peter's consciousness of himself, of his problems, of his conflicts and his manipulations increased, it became clearer that the outer shell was made out of panics, defenses, and rituals. Those were all just symptoms of his fears, just as red spots are symptoms of measles. Peter "broke out" with them when he was frightened, but he was very seldom fully conscious of what frightened him. And we who knew him were mostly conscious of and often fascinated by the symptoms, for he used them magnificently.

Peter's was a system in which, I had the very definite feeling, lay a conglomeration of fears either based on past realities or on misinterpretations of realities, which he converted into or covered up with or opposed by fantasies or "fairy tales" of his own making. It constantly amazed me how tightly organized his system of defenses was, and how well he used it; how much energy and brilliance went into it. To those who could see behind the defenses, they were his signs, his big neon signs, which told us he was afraid. To those who were frightened of them, stopped by them, bewildered by them, they were just a means to push them away and hold them at a distance great enough so that their danger would not be too overwhelming.

When my awe of and fascination with Peter's symptoms diminished, I began to search for the real fear behind them. Peter had been changing, there was no doubt about it. But how deep was the change? I began to search for the answers in his relationship to me, in his relationship to the world, in his relationship to himself.

First I began to examine his relationship to me and mine to him. At the start, I was Peter's strength, Peter's health, his contact with reality, his maker, and his saviour. I allowed him and forbade him. I took fear and pain away, and protected and guarded him against his evils. He was completely and utterly dependent on me, not because he knew it was right, but because it was the only thing he knew how to do. He constantly tried to climb inside of my boundaries. I would provide him with the strength, let him depend on me, and let his strength feed on mine. I would set limits, whether for his panics or his rituals, or for the nonacceptance of his rituals. I would pick up his scattered parts and put them together for him. I would get him off the "no exit" road and lead him to the exit, get him out of the "dead ends." I would support, support, support, limit, and permit.

My job was to get him off the "no exit road," to stop him from talking about cats, to tell him the numbers and colors of his imaginary cats, to tell him to look, to eat, to move his bowels, to not be afraid. To live. "How many cats on the windowsill?" "I don't know." "Mira must tell Peter. No matter what number, give a number." Peter wanted no responsibility for taking part in his life other than in his fantasy. When I pushed him to make choices, his answer would be, "What does Mira prefer?" Mira had to "prefer" whether Peter was sick or well; whether "the bus got stuck or not"; whether Peter drew or painted or, or, or . . .

Peter could not even take responsibility for his pain. He would scream and cry, and you had to be a first-class detective to find out where he ached. He never told you. You had to find out whether he was crying because he was scared, because he couldn't get the cat, because someone wouldn't answer his questions, because he got frustrated, or because he had a bellyache. As Peter could take no responsibility for his physical pain, so he couldn't localize it either. If rain canceled out a scheduled trip to the beach, "Mira had to make the sun come out." No explanations meant anything to Peter. "Mira had to." If the sun shone and the weather forecast said it would rain, Mira had to make it rain "because that is what it said." And "that was the rule." And so on.

During this first period it was tough, really, truly tough being his strength while not understanding his symbols, and at the same time trying to get a frame around him so that whenever he spilled he wouldn't spill all over the world but within the frame I set out for him. At the same time I could not let him invade me.

Our relationship changed after he told me that he had come out of me, as I felt then that it was time to begin to shift more of the responsibility for his actions onto Peter. For after one is born, even symbolically, one does take on new responsibilities. Peter didn't like it. He'd say, "I want to push into Mira; I want to go back into Mira"; but I explained to him that once you come out, you can't go back. "You can't go back into Mira just like you can't go back into Mommy, because you came out of there, and that is it." Peter wasn't happy with the explanation. He would dutifully repeat my words, but he would not accept them. Eventually, however, he began to take more and more of the responsibility upon himself. Instead of "How many crayons were in the box? Peter must know," it was now "Peter thinks there are seventeen crayons. Does Mira think so too?" I still had to confirm the number because Peter still wasn't sure of reality. He had to compare his reality with mine. And, too, Peter was afraid to lose contact with me. Especially his control.

Slowly Peter was becoming a separate human being, beginning to evolve his own identity. No longer did one hear the constant "Mira must make up Peter's mind for him. It'll soothe him. It'll make him more comfortable." More and more it was "I want to," "I will stop myself," "I did it because I was scared." After a while it was noticeable that Peter was beginning openly to hate his dependency on me and try to shake it. Until finally (in 1962) he was able to say to me, "I want to see you just for a little while, but not all the time." And thus the symbiosis was being broken.

As opposed to his need to be with me physically and emotionally at all times, he was able to go away from his mother for half a summer in 1957. Then for half a summer in 1958; then for a whole summer in 1959 and 1960; and finally to a year-round school out of town. I still recall our trepidation before the first prolonged separation. And Peter's clear insight into his own and his mother's conflicts about it when he told me, "Peter is taking Mommy to see Dr. Goldstein." When I asked, "What for?" he replied, "So Dr. Goldstein can help make up the mind to go to camp." "Your mind?" I asked, and the child answered, "No, Peter made up his mind. He wants to go, but Mommy doesn't and he'll help Mommy." Or to my "Do you want to go?" Peter's "Yes"; and to my response, "But what about Mommy?" his reply: "Peter wants Mommy to come with him, but better he wants Mommy to stay home with Daddy."

Then came the reading incident already described, and it led to the break between us. After about three years of working together, we withdrew from each other. I told him that I felt he was making believe he was dead because perhaps he was really afraid that if he came to life he might die. Peter pulled away from me then and would often try to hurt me physically since "Mira knows the truth." I became somehow frightened of his anger toward me and, I think, of mine toward him, and withdrew too. Peter returned to his cats; however, all of his other achievements he kept up. (Even though I felt terribly guilty about my withdrawal and tried desperately to reach Peter, my attempts were mainly intellectual, had no heart in them, and thus were of no success. So I tried to convince everyone concerned,

262

especially Dr. Goldstein, to find someone else to work with the child. But no one would listen.)

Then one day after about a half year of emotional coldness, I took "my" three children to the museum to hear the "Songs of the Auvergne." I did not let Peter sit next to me, but surrounded myself with the other two. Somehow, in the middle of the concert, peace came over me and I became unafraid. I reached my hand out to Peter and the child simultaneously reached his hand out to me. With my fear of him and myself gone, some of Peter's fear, too, seemed to have vanished. We resumed our relationship. Peter immediately gave up the cats and we proceeded from where we had left off. But he allowed himself to live more intently.

The more I saw Peter, the more I thought about him, the more I got the feeling that he scattered himself or never really put himself together for a very definite and specific reason. Whether he was ever completely one being with real boundaries, I do not know, but in some part of him, on some level, he was. Peter, I feel clearly, built defenses for self-protection. I think that he was terrified of death, of this one finality that he witnessed and in a sense was part of—whether in relation to the cats or to the dog, or in relation to the little brother who had died in an inexplicable fashion when Peter was about four or five, or in relation to himself. To avoid ever facing death, he scattered himself all over the place, all over the world. That way all of himself would never die. But at the same time, as each part of him was some place else for safe-keeping, he was in constant search for his scattered parts. Parts of him could be taken away by people—as a matter of fact, he would *give* parts of himself away—but he would know where to find the recipients. He'd have their addresses and phone numbers. At the same time, if he placed different parts of himself with different people, how could he possibly die, all of himself? Who could find these parts except Peter himself? If death found one of his parts, it certainly could not find all of them.

As terrifying as his scattering felt to him, it still was safer than the ultimate disintegration—death.

Peter, I think, had no sense of time in spite of his skill with dates, his preoccupation with time, his endless watching of the clock. I think he somehow eliminated the concept of the passing of time, and so all the yesterdays, todays, and tomorrows were in essence one to him. And in this there lay the security of no beginning and no end—and thus no dying.

It was for this reason that he needed to know dates, to remember selectively what happened on each one of these dates, so that he could own it, control it, eliminate it (if it denied his concept of life or death), edit it—this life of his. His memory of life was a horizontal one, not a vertical one, with no beginning and no end, one event as important as the other. Life to him was a canvas, I think, which he himself had painstakingly and selectively embroidered, each detail of which he had gone over. The embroidery had no beginning, no end. The canvas was constructed of an endless, ghostlike series of events, to avoid that one terrible event—destruction, disintegration, death. All the details had to be in their places, arranged by Peter, and that was the reason for Peter's desperate search for and repetition of all the details of his "life." The rearranging (or scattering) of any of it might have meant a real sequence, and thus real life, and therefore death.

Peter told me cats didn't really die "because cats have nine lives." It was safe to be a cat. "If there are fourteen crayons in a box, that means," Peter said, "there are fourteen lives." So if a crayon were broken, it upset him and he wept bitterly, since "There is one less life, one broken life." Numbers had magic. They kept fear and death away: "Peter likes to be a cat because then he has nine lives." Yet at the same time, every now and then, he knew that the cats were killed only once and are still dead. He never found them in the "hidden place." He would tell me, "Peter has three cats—the one he's got now and the two cats that had nine lives." Yet in the same breath he'd say, "You have

264

one cat, because Mommy sent the others to be put away."

When he talked about Tippy, the dog that was destroyed, he would say, "*I* had a dog. He slept in my room. And then Mommy had him killed. Because he killed cats. And then *you* [meaning himself] didn't have a dog and *you* slept in Mommy's room." In the face of death it was safer not to have an identity. And "I" became "you."

The streets and addresses—as well as the birthdays, the numbers, and the cats—were all for protection, an attempt at timelessness and immortality. There he would scatter, there he would hide his parts. On the other hand, streets were his landmarks, as places to find his scattered parts, locations for each part he dared to uncover. And thus, these landmarks put some sort of limits on his vast, limitless fear, and perhaps eliminated it momentarily.

Peter became a cat when he got mad, terribly mad, and this too was part of his whole fairy tale, part of the whole picture. A cat can scratch, claw, and hurt, and still have all those lives. But then Tippy killed a cat. And sometimes Peter would go "Bow-wow," though not for long. "A dog has only one life," he said.

Peter's absorption with numbers, especially the counting when he was afraid, was also a kind of reassurance. Numbers are the only thing that never ends. There is no last number, there is only infinity. But as there is no last number, so there is no end, no death.

What was most remarkable to me was that, in spite of all this, this terribly frightened and lonely little boy eventually dared to rearrange some of his patterns, dared to give up some of his protection, dared to dare.

By 1962, he traveled alone to his school for disturbed children by subway and bus, went shopping with his mother for clothes, shopped for things in the house, did dishes, ate alone in a restaurant, skated, rode a bicycle, swam, played ball, hardly ever talked of his cats, began to learn to type, seldom looked for his parts,

265

counted very seldom, seldom talked roads, and asked birthdays and addresses more as a conversational device than as an actual need to find his parts.

When Peter was fifteen, he went alone as far as Connecticut, where he attended a residential school for children with emotional problems. The talk and drive after the cats had stopped completely. So had the search for the "hidden place." So had the search for his parts. He never threw up any more and seldom walked on tiptoe. His coordination was much better, was graceful more often than not. (Anyhow, he was making a conscious effort at it.) He was much calmer, much happier, and had a real ability to love and show his feelings. He was very clear about what he wanted, when he wanted it. He insisted on making his own rules and setting his own limits. He was very definite about it.

The child was evolving an identity and was quite separate from others most of the time. However, every now and then, he still became one with his mother, and then he had an uncanny way of knowing what his mother's real wants were, no matter how unconscious.

He wanted relationships, but didn't know how to go about getting them. When he was trying to establish a relationship he still "noodged," usually by the repetitive asking of irrelevant questions in a tone so nagging that it drove people away. When I pointed this out to him, he'd say, in utter desperation, "How should one make conversation? What should I say? I want to have friends." His other way of getting people involved with himself was by suddenly becoming passive and trying to trap them into making up his mind for him. "Should I do this puzzle now or the other?" However, whenever he spotted anyone who really knew him, especially me, he would cut it out immediately. Peter often made this plea: "I don't want to 'noodge' any more. I want to give up the 'noodging.' Please, Mira, stop Peter from 'noodging' so he can have friends." It was when it came to the "noodging" that I still seemed to have his lifeline in my hands.

Peter was very much aware of what he wanted, or

what he needed. Once when I was in a hospital, he sent me a letter, airmail, asking me to get well very fast because he had to see me, for I had to help him stop the "noodging." He was very aware of the fact that what we called the "noodging" was something that needed to be stopped; but somehow he still could not take the full responsibility for change.

He was still a very strange boy. He looked at times quite graceful, at times still fractured. Under great pressure, he could be made to be in reality. But he still tried to get away with as much as possible when it came to strangers. He still wanted to put a great deal of responsibility on them. His memory was still fantastic. His ability with numbers was still remarkable, but he was beginning to forget dates, confuse addresses; and the telephone numbers, at this point, he often just made up. The extreme energy that had been put into his mathematical system was now being pulled out a little bit at a time and used in all the other areas of living. Still, most of the energy remained in this mathematical orbit of his, this memory orbit of his, and therefore the child still appeared or almost was psychologically fractured, as if in parts. Frequently it seemed that there was no connection between some of the very different things that the child understood. At times he was extremely concrete, while at other times extremely abstract, and it was the connection and transition between these two areas that appeared most difficult for him.

He once told me what mitosis and amitosis were—he had learned in his science class. Correctly, he said, "Mitosis is an equal division of cells and amitosis is unequal division of cells." But when I asked him what the cells were, he said, "Of course, rooms in a jail with bars on them."

Another time, after seeing the show *The Music Man,* he came to tell me about it. He remembered all the words and all the music of the show, but when I insisted on the story, he would not tell me. Finally, disturbed and disgusted with my pressuring him, he said: "It's just a lot of people acting, making believe that they are somebody else and getting paid for it." He could give a most abstract definition of a word and knew the synonym for it. He could play any word game. He could describe himself, his way of feeling or state of psychological being, in a most abstract way and yet at other times could be only concrete. The same held true with his symbols. "A no exit is *mishuga* and *mishuga* is around and around with no way to get off," he once told me; and yet his mathematical formulas, whatever they were, seemed to be very abstract and mostly incomprehensible to the rest of us mortals.

Under great pressure, when he was aware of the fact that he would not be allowed to get away with his defenses, Peter would combine all his faculties and make them into one. Then his understanding was quite good —and then his being in reality was quite good.

It was interesting to see people's attitudes toward him change. He was warm and loving so often that he no longer evoked revulsion and fascination but real interest, liking, and often admiration. In spite of the fact that he still was rather friendless, friends of mine spontaneously began to befriend him and often work with him, friends who through their own interest were able to give him the feeling of not being "so alone" and of their being his "friends"—even though, as he said, "They are really older friends, but still friends."

The tremendous energy and strength that had been used for his panics, for the setting up of the rules for his illness, he now used to set controls on his illness and to set up his rules for getting better. He decided, "No cat talk." He decided when and how not to panic. He decided on separation from me, mother, and home.

And so the dance goes on. The symmetry of motion is undisturbed. Until suddenly, the dancer wavers and falls off the rope. Nothing happens. Quite amazedly, the dancer gets on the rope again. A compilation of his movements, picked up, goes on. But then, often, the dancer willfully, deliberately, consciously, breaks through the rhythmic need and gets off the rope. He does not die; but still he does not trust enough, so onto the rope he goes again.

This wondrously strange child, half genius, half idiot, so alone in his brilliance, so alone in his confusion, alone by the very nature of his brilliance, was just as alone by the very nature of his confusion. The frightening brilliance I left alone, since I could never enter his world of genius. His confusion I tried to understand and let the little boy lead me there.

I saw Peter yesterday, December 17, 1976. He is twenty-eight years old. He lives in a young adult center which houses sixteen young people of both sexes. He gets along well with the others living there, has friends and a girlfriend, he tells me.

During the day he has a job as a messenger. In the evenings and weekends he leads a relatively normal social life. He goes to movies, theaters, and concerts with some of the other young people from the center. He goes to Chinatown, he tells me, goes dancing, to restaurants, and on other trips. He watches TV, plays Scrabble, and so on. And he is working on his high school equivalency. He seems well liked by the other young people.

But, unfortunately, in this world we are not ready for the Peters—the genius that is also the idiot. We can neither keep up with nor understand his logic, his way of doing things, his shortcircuiting, his compressing, his telescoping.

Thus we remain living in two different worlds on two different planets: "The Peters" and "us." And all we have is a narrow, narrow bridge between us—much more a tightrope than a bridge—upon which we walk toward each other slowly, haltingly, dangerously, slightly touching each other's selves but never fully embracing, never fully understanding.

When I talked to the people at the center about his spelling, they said, "Yes, he beats everyone in Scrabble. Always. Yesterday he beat some professor by 250 points, for example, and he does it so fast."

Peter looks at me and smiles—we both understand.

"And he does all the puzzles in the *Times* and every

place else," they said with amazement, adding, "and so fast." And Peter smiles again and we both understand.

When I ask him if he is still interested in cats, he says, "No, not at all, but they are friendly creatures."

The other people asked, "Why cats? We don't even have one at the center." We both smile again, but Peter only slightly.

Then he asked me how I got to the center, and when I told him, he assured me that I had taken the wrong route, and told me of "another much simpler one, and a quicker one." He explained the direction of the traffic on the streets with all the old landmarks, such as "dead ends," "one-way streets," and so on, but quite devoid of the emotional involvement they once had; he was only interested in the facts and in getting me to my destination quicker. I took his route back. He was right —he saved me fifteen minutes. His memory is still as phenomenal as ever.

I mentioned Dr. Goldstein and asked Peter if he remembered when we first met him. He gave me the date— the day, month, year—and what day of the week it was.

Then I asked him when Dr. Goldstein died. He gave me the same accurate information. Whatever facts I asked him about from our common past, he told them to me, again with total recall, down to the time of day any incident occurred. He even remembered the color of the clothes I wore that day. But none of this information was volunteered by him, and all was said with factual detachment and some pleasure for remembrance of things past.

When I asked him when my birthday was, what day it fell on this year, he told me immediately. When I asked him what day it fell on twenty years ago, he told me, again without hesitation.

When I asked him about his math, if he could still do it and if he were doing it, he said very casually, "Of course I can, but there is no need to; nobody asks me to, nobody needs it."

And in that lies the whole tragedy: the waste of

270

Peter. "He's a human computer," someone said, "but we don't need human computers; we have machines."

How Peter is being wasted!

Everything about him seems to be telescoped. He is young and yet he looks very, very old, as if the span of his physical life is also telescoped. I think he will die soon. As that too is part of his way of being.

What is Peter? *Why* is Peter? Is he a biological link with the past or with the future? Is he a regression in our evolution or a progression? Is he a link between the past and present or the future and present? Is this what he is all about?

APPENDIXES

APPENDIX A

A Note on Blueberry Treatment Centers

Blueberry Treatment Centers, as it is now called, was set up in 1958 by Zev Spanier (who returned to Israel a few years later), Tev Goldsman, and myself.

We started it as a camp for schizophrenic and autistic children, which then grew in response to the children's needs. We added a day treatment center, then a residence where the children who cannot be contained at home live, then a village for adolescent children who are well enough to function in a protective society but not in our city streets.

M.R.

APPENDIX B

Notes on Chaim

by

Joost A.M. Meerloo, M.D.

The scientific observer should not be defeated by this gradual downfall of a schizophrenic child. Mira Rothenberg describes so well with her penetrating report how year-long extreme efforts were undertaken to reach to the core of the boy's conflicts.

What conclusions can we distill out of our failures? In the first place we see here what we have seen with many children of concentration camp inmates. Hitler's persecutions go over into the next generations. Though former inmates of the camps get married, the shadow of the camps always lives with them. The trauma of the holocaust, the systematic intentional extermination, lock death and dying up in their characters. What we call the concentration camp syndrome is a definite change in personality in which the nightmare of inhumanity remains alive day to day. Chaim's mother had no screen memories any more from the time before the camp. Her life starts with the Armageddon.

The children are continually accompanied by the dreams and nightmares of their parents. These are not stories systematically told to them, but the children, in their struggle to break through the parents' continual preoccupations, grasp and break through, as it were, the surface of their parents' involvements and become part of their fears and nightmares.

As we saw, Chaim felt nearly telepathically while away from his mother that she again was in a psychotic state.

Symbolically, we can see that already very early in his life he was able to see into his mother. There must have been great turmoil in the initial eye-language between mother and child. He sees himself in the mirror of her glances as the distorted being she fears herself to be. He fights against her hexing evil eye, and maybe he makes the same antihexing sign his mother used as magic defense in the camp. The incestuous involvement between this mutually symbiotic and parasitic mother-son pair reminds me of a case in which the mother acted out with her oldest son the way she used her sexuality in the camp to appease the camp guards.

Chaim acted out many visions (or stories) from his parents. Burning the doll in the toy oven was one of them; refusing any verbal contact, another. Nonetheless, the year-long attempt to break through his communication defenses proved impossible. Impossible? I have seen catatonics in institutions who have stood for thirty years in their corner suddenly finding someone they could get in contact with, because they experienced the mutuality of exchange.

One indication that such new contact is possible is proved in Chaim's case by operation "survival." All during World War II we could observe that in extreme emergencies schizophrenics behaved like normal people. Some catatonic patients helped to extinguish fires in their bombed institutions and were thus brought to react adequately to the emergency. With Chaim we saw the same: when he was not protected, he adjusted well to operation survival. He made the fire to cook the food, he spoke, he rode a bicycle, had conversations, could stand long walks without getting tired—until with his parents who came to fetch him the nightmares and

278

panics entered his life and he almost immediately regressed.

I treated two such cases myself. I succeeded in separating the symbiotic mothers from their overdependent children permanently until they were twelve years of age. When they met each other afterwards, the mother was never recognized as "Mom," but a peculiar ritual developed in which both children tried to dominate their natural mothers completely; they had built up enough ego defenses to keep mental distance from their mothers' domination. The mothers had been in treatment in the meantime and were prepared for the children's aloofness or to become their slaves.

Yet, in the case of Chaim, we can see how penetrating the unconscious communication between mother and child was. It went far beyond normal space, and we don't know what the means of communication were. We speak here of telepathy to give this communication-from-afar a name. Future science will better define what those channels of communication really are.

What about Chaim's prognosis? This depends on the institution; whether it can handle his tremendous suicidal and violent behavior. Most of the institutions will not have the personnel to manage such horror. Drugs will be given endlessly. I have one suggestion to make, arising out of my own experience. A tremendous suicidal and violent catatonic was given insulin shock treatment, which initially had no effect until we started to give hypnotic treatment during the phase when the patient slowly awoke out of his coma. That made the right contact and transference. The shock was experienced by the patient as a command to "die and revive." After revival, he found his guide ready to reenact with him his ancient terrors. From insulin coma we went gradually into a phase of hypnocatharsis only, and after three months he could be dismissed as a well-adjusted introvert.

We hope Chaim will find such an institutional milieu.

APPENDIX C

Notes on Sara

by
Joost A.M. Meerloo, M.D.

Some Remarks About the Primal Scene

What we call the primal scene does not mean exactly that the child is eyewitness to the sexual intercourse of the parents. It can be a kind of overhearing of rhythms during the night, an awakening because the parents are awake, a nightly waiting for the orgiastic moment. Because that is the clue that the sexual rhythm is ready in everybody, ready to co-oscillate with the same rhythm perceived in others. It may happen in another room; maybe telepathy plays a role; but it means being taken up in the orgiastic world of others, with all the fears of unripe experiences. There is fear of people attacking and devouring each other. There is double identification with the suffering mother and the attacking father. While experiencing the primal scene, the child is the passive sufferer and the dominant aggressor at the same time. Children who precociously see sexual movies often enter the same twilight state of not knowing to what role they belong.

The sexual rhythm lives from birth on in them; it is the same to-and-fro rhythm as develops between the baby and the maternal nipple, hence there must be tremendous envy because in the sexual interplay something is taken away from the baby. The feeling of oral deprivation and endless yearning can be the result of witnessing parental loveplay.

APPENDIX D

Notes on Peter

Dr. Kurt Goldstein's Involvement

After a year or so of working with Peter, I was invited to come with him to Kurt Goldstein, the famous scientist who—along with his other interests—was fascinated by the problem of the "idiot-savant." From that point on until his death, Dr. Goldstein was deeply involved in my relationship with Peter; in the fact that I was able to get the child better, and in the question of "how" I was doing it.

He was interested both in the philosophical overview and in my day-to-day work with the child. For it was clear that, in spite of the prevalent conviction (his and others') at the time that one could not help the child, Peter was getting better. Dr. Goldstein was deeply involved in the study of, not only the development and true nature of the "idiot-savant," but also in the actual working of the genius part, and in the connection between genius and psychological problems and the retarded part of Peter.

Even though we had differences of opinion as to

"condition Peter," he was full of respect and admiration for my work with the child and studied it closely. He published papers on "condition Peter" and on the condition of "Mira and Peter." He was greatly interested in the development and growth of my own relationship with Peter. He read my manuscript on Peter and commented throughout—painstakingly, carefully, and lovingly.

I saw Dr. Goldstein with Peter on the average a few times a year. I saw him myself more often, as he was so interested in my explanations of my work with Peter.

He shared his vast wisdom in many areas with me generously. And I shared my limited one with him lovingly.

What follows are some of his observations on my manuscript.

Dr. Kurt Goldstein's Comments on Peter

Pages 233–238
RE: chaos, control

Mira produced a participation in outer world by Peter—"An adequacy."

The baby searches for adequacy; it achieves it through its relationship with mother.

When mother is not afraid of child, she gives him this feeling. Peter achieved an adequacy with Mira. This relationship with outer world resulted from this adequacy with Mira.

Chaos—some adequacy—adequacy.

Peter learned a relationship to other things. Example: Bus. Could not bring together the moving and the parts. The parts are part of a whole. Mira brought more and more Peter by insistence into the situation. Now he began to participate—not simply confronted with chaos—but participate with the world.

Pages 241–243

There was a real transference relationship between these two people [Peter and Mira]—and so he learns.

284

The idea of the parts is very interesting. And the fact that Mira didn't know the theoretical behind it but did it all intuitively is very remarkable and interesting.

Peter tries to come to a world where he can come in contact. Interesting points in this paper—how the individual learns to handle wholes.

How Mira taught him and helped him to develop step by step. Adequacy—different relationship—separateness.

Page 244

RE: *"So what should Peter talk about to people? Peter doesn't know what interests them."*

It was a compulsive act which he did not need any more; because he has acquired contact need with you, so his anxiety has reduced.

Page 246

RE: *"Confusion leads to terror, or terror leads to confusion. Or was it terror of confusion?"*

Yes! First terror.

I do not think so, the disorder is the terror. Does not precede terror!

terror —) confusion

Confusion itself then becomes terror again.

Page 247

RE: *Peter's counting and my reaction to it*

This behavior evokes something unbearable (that) was in Peter as in you. You could stop it; Peter only with your help. "He must."

Page 248

RE: *counting and the waves*

Such examples very frequent in sudden produced anxiety with patients.

Page 248

RE: *cat—enigma*

Not an enigma but an explanation by pathology.

Page 249
RE: swallowed
   Who can prove that swallowing is destroying?

Page 249
RE: combination of excitement, terror ...
   Together? First terror. Then looking (for cats), then delight?

Page 249
RE: my favorite repast
   As before, he was trusting *you* as help against anxiety which he experiences as alleviation from fear.

Page 250
RE: "Mira cat," "Peter cat," etc.
   Was better protection if he gave "concrete" character personal name, etc.

   Constantly throughout the manuscript KG questions: "Why did he learn to read, do arithmetic, puzzles, etc." and how?

Page 264
RE: Peter, I think, had no sense of time
   As all these children—because his knowledge has nothing to do with real things.
   (He has) no visual memory.

RE: time concept and canvas
   Because he cannot select, has no time.

Page 267
RE: abstract
   Stereotyped, not abstract.

Page 268
RE: could give a most abstract definition of. . . . He could play any word game.
   Is not abstract, because not concrete either.

286

Page 268
RE: "abstract way"
 Stereotyped, not abstract.

Pages 267-268
 KG inserted a number of question marks on these pages. Apparently he doesn't totally agree with my definition of abstraction, of the difference between abstract and concrete. He seems to feel that Peter's expressions are more stereotyped than abstract and does not agree that Peter has reached the ability of abstraction yet.

Some Other General Comments from KG about Peter and Me:

RE: drawings of people, bus, etc.
 Whatever Peter drew at the start was in parts, as Mira observed, except for one thing, as she noticed—the cat. It is so, as she says, the only thing he was in relation with, safe with, at ease with, with whom his relationship produced a pleasant feeling—an adequate feeling—so that it seemed complete, fulfilled to him (adequate), was the cat. Later on Mira.

 Mira was the other cat. Since the only adequacy he [knew] heretofore was with the cat. In this sense Mira was whole to him like the cat.

KG—agrees with Mira
 It seems that when a baby is tiny, it has no relationship with the world at all except through the mother. The baby left alone in the world, without the intermediary, the mother, has a completely chaotic relationship to the world—or perhaps none at all. Thus chaos and destruction results for the baby.

A Paraphrase of KG's Explanation to Me of What I've Done for Peter

Adequacy

In any kind of decent psychological survival ("survives in a way that he feels well"), the baby will search for a comfort or ease, or to use KG's terms, an "adequacy," which only the right relationship with the mother will produce. (Baby, adult, any living thing probably.)

As this comfort, "well being with," or "well being" or easy flow, or fluidity—adequacy—goes on between baby and mother, or whatever mother does for baby, the baby reaches out into the world for this adequacy. So out of no adequacy with the world at all, the baby through adequacy with the mother (cat adequacy with Peter) goes on to some adequacy with the world at large, and eventually to a full adequacy in his relationship with the world—thus maturity.

Peter had a difficulty, as his relationship with his mother, for whatever reason, was inadequate and therefore he could not grow. But as he found an adequacy in his relationship with me, I then became the intermediary between him and the world. "And by bringing him more and more by Mira's insistence into various situations in which he had to do, he found his adequacy in the world.

"He was beginning to find some adequacy with other things than just with you, and thus you [Mira] produced in him the participation in the outer world, where he managed to find some adequacy."

(But it was not constant. Sometimes there was an adequacy—at the beginning. It went back and forth.) "And thus started on his own to participate, not simply confronted with chaos, but participated with the world."

MR's Explanation of KG's Adequacy Concept

It seems to me that in any kind of treatment, or psychological growth, this concept first and foremost

288

has to be found—between the person being helped to grow and the person who helps him to grow. As it is this fulfillment or well-being or adequacy which is the climate and the nature—the soil—in which growth is possible. For some reason, Peter found adequacy in his relationship with me.

KG

Mira was right in stopping the arithmetic and spelling after a while. He did not perform with his gifts because he wanted to show off—he wasn't aware of the excellence of his performance but used it as a means to overcome his fears, in relation to his fears of scattering, so as to have contact—not to be alone.